The first millennium AD in Europe and the Mediterranean

THE
FIRST MILLENNIUM AD
IN EUROPE AND
THE MEDITERRANEAN

AN ARCHAEOLOGICAL ESSAY

KLAVS RANDSBORG

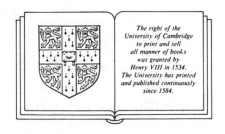

*The right of the
University of Cambridge
to print and sell
all manner of books
was granted by
Henry VIII in 1534.
The University has printed
and published continuously
since 1584.*

CAMBRIDGE UNIVERSITY PRESS

Cambridge
New York   Port Chester
Melbourne   Sydney

Published by the Press Syndicate of the University of Cambridge
The Pitt Building, Trumpington Street, Cambridge CB2 1RP
40 West 20th Street, New York, NY 10011, USA
10 Stamford Road, Oakleigh, Melbourne 3166, Australia

First published 1991

Printed in Great Britain at the University Press, Cambridge

British Library cataloguing in publication data

Randsborg, Klavs
    The first millennium AD in Europe and the
    Mediterranean : an archaeological essay.
    1. Europe. Human settlements. Archaeological investigation
    I. Title
    940.1

Library of Congress cataloguing in publication data

Randsborg. Klavs.
    The first millennium AD in Europe and the Mediterranean : an
    archaeological essay / by Klavs Randsborg.
        p.   cm.
    Includes bibliographical references.
    ISBN 0 521 38401 X. – ISBN 0 521 38787 6 (pbk.)
    1. Europe – Antiquities.   2. Mediterranean Region.
    3. Rome – Antiquities.   I. Title.
    CC 165.R36   1990
    930 – dc20   89-22310   CIP

ISBN 0 521 38401 X hard covers
ISBN 0 521 38787 6 paperback

To Mari

CONTENTS

ILLUSTRATIONS

TABLES

PREFACE

Limit time to the present
Marcus Aurelius (AD 121–180)

This book has given me the opportunity to draw on much archaeological and personal experience – from my early student days, extensive travel and study abroad, library research, and meetings with colleagues – and the scientific view of the world that this experience has instilled in me. Central to the book's approach is my view of the material archaeological sources as testimony not only to techniques and economy but also to interpersonal relationships ranging from the exchange of products to the communication of norms and ideas. Behind their physical reality, it seems to me, breathe invisible forces – desire for self-expression through movement, language, and symbols, social competition, and the various processes that govern society. The humanities and the social sciences seem inclined to let abstract phenomena produce the physical world, and this view certainly underlines many of the ideas I deal with in this book. Nevertheless, we must also allow the physical world a measure of autonomy: we see, we choose, and we take action. These processes are determined not only by a logical universe, a Newtonian sociology, but also by chance and, in the final analysis, perhaps by man's ability to act independently.

My own inclinations have carried me far from my original starting point and continually led me into new worlds. Thus, chance discoveries have often proved to lead to problems on which – sometimes despairing – I have had to spend much time in order to come to a better understanding. My work has chiefly been carried out at the Archaeological Institute of the University of Copenhagen, an establishment that I have the pleasure of administering. In addition, I have held posts as visiting professor at Washington University in St Louis and at the University of Amsterdam. Some years ago American contacts revived an interest in archaeology and society, first aroused by travel, for example, in the Mediterranean area, and by fieldwork in the Sudan. My time in the Netherlands also gave me the opportunity to build upon earlier experience, while knowledge of modern provincial Roman archaeology acquired through contacts with foreign colleagues inspired me to turn my own Northern European perspective upside down. In the same period I was able to pursue some of the studies to which my interest in the emergence of states had led me and to develop a general archaeological methodology acquired through studies focused on the Stone, Bronze, and Iron Ages.

In acknowledging my debts, besides my students and university colleagues, mention must be made of the archaeologists in the admirable museum circles of Denmark and especially the National Museum, whose library, archives, and collections are invaluable for a study such as this one. To a great extent I have relied on surveys – sometimes virtual commando raids – of the museums and libraries of many institutions in several countries. Two periods of study in the friendly atmosphere of the Accademia di Danimarca in Rome led, through collaboration with this institute, to an international symposium on the subject of this book held in 1987 and supported by the British and Swedish institutes in Rome. All this bears witness to the debt I owe to colleagues both in the Nordic area and elsewhere in Europe, where I particularly appreciate the hard-working and imaginative British archaeologists. I must acknowledge too my relationship with the broad-based, sober work and results of German archaeology. My confrontation with classical archaeology has also been of special significance.

Mention must also be made of the many colleagues and others who have shared their knowledge with me. I am grateful for all the support that I have received on innumerable journeys to almost all of the countries of Europe and the Mediterranean and to a multitude of museums, libraries, and other institutions, particularly those in Rome. I am also indebted to Poul Christensen, whose professional skill has helped me with the illustrations, to Jennifer Paris for translation, to Siri Louekari and especially to Dr Barbara Metzger for further linguistic and other assistance, to Deborah Hodges for the index, and to Richard Hodges, director of the British School at Rome, for friendly advice and support. Finally, I am grateful to the Danish Research Council for the Humanities, to the Carlsberg Foundation, and to Copenhagen University for financial support for the translation of this book, for a number of travel grants, and for the production of the figures.

The book is dedicated to my little daughter: she may well have more pleasure in seeing it today than she will when she is able to read it in some ten years' time. By then it will probably betray its origins as a product of the mid-eighties; but by then, too, we may hope to have moved with the times and gained new inspiration and pleasure from identifying and attempting to interpret the patterns and structures in the archaeological record.

Copenhagen, August 1987

ACKNOWLEDGEMENTS

The author and publisher gratefully acknowledge the permission of the following to reproduce their illustrations in this book: Akademie-Verlag, Berlin (East): figs. 16 and 36; Geuthner, Paris: figs. 22, 24 and 57; drawing by Howard Mason in M. G. Jarret and S. Wrathmell, *Whitton: An Iron Age and Roman Farmstead in South Glamorgan*, University of Wales Press, Cardiff: fig. 31; Joachim Werner and Eugen Ewig, *Von der Spätantike zum frühen Mittelalter*, vol. 25 in the series 'Vorträge und Vorschungen', Jan Thorbecke Verlag, Sigmaringen 1979, p. 152: fig. 34; after K. Weidemann, in *Ausgrabungen in Deutschland*, Köln, Monographien des Römisch-Germanischen Zentralmuseums 1/2, 1975, p. 439: fig. 39; Paul Elek Ltd, London: fig. 41; Vandenhoeck & Ruprecht Verlag, Göttingen: fig. 47; Konrad Theiss, Stuttgart: fig. 68.

1

INTRODUCTION

This work attempts to consider a remote world through the material traces that it has left us. The world is that of the first millennium A D, in which Europe and the Mediterranean passed from Antiquity into the Middle Ages, barbarian Europe came under the influence of powerful social and economic forces, and the door was opened to the development of the Western world.

The first millennium presents a number of scholarly challenges. One of these is the interaction between the archaeological material and written sources – the latter, though essential, limited in number, the former increasing at an exponential rate and providing new information every day. The appeal of archaeology lies in its potential for new discoveries and for illumination of circumstances that written sources seldom or never touch upon – obscure aspects of life and geographical areas in which written sources are inadequate or non-existent. Furthermore, it is just as powerful a tool where there are written sources. It is a truism that one gets a very different impression from seeing a place than from simply reading about it, and the same applies to the material world revealed through archaeological surveys and excavations. It should also be taken into account that archaeology has an exciting interdisciplinary side, manifested in collaboration with the biological, natural, and social sciences and the other humanities, especially history. Finally, theory and method in archaeology have developed rapidly in the last few decades, in particular in the area of social history. The question increasingly being asked is what archaeology can tell us about past society – its economy, social systems, and mental attitudes.

The first millennium was the first period in which the various societies of the Old World, whether of northern Scandinavia, eastern Africa, or Japan, exercised direct influence on one another. The preceding millennium had witnessed the emergence of the Greco-Roman world, which periodically has had immeasurable influence on the development and self-comprehension of society, particularly in Western Europe. The decline and fall of especially the Western Roman Empire has fascinated scholars since long before the time of Gibbon (1776–88) (fig. 1).

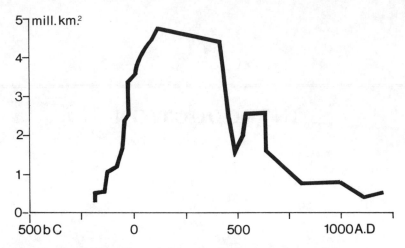

Fig. 1. The 'Roman Empire', from the third-century-BC confederate state in Italy through the Late Republican expanding territorial empire in the Mediterranean and in Gaul, the Early and Late Roman Empires proper, and the Eastern Empire to the Byzantine Empire of the beginning of the second millennium

The roots of Western European society lie at the end of the first millennium BC, but the idea of collapse has nevertheless dogged – at times virtually haunted – the West at least since the fifth century. It is odd, then, that we are not more surprised or pleased at the stability of Western Europe, which has already lasted for a millennium. One reason for this is probably that the world is still deeply absorbed by the problems of nation-states and less concerned with the fate of economic systems. It is in fact characteristic of Europe at the end of the second millennium that its economic systems function without the political framework established and maintained by the old empires and also once provided by nation-states. This is not, of course, to say that national ideologies and feelings of identity are irrelevant to social development. Just as in the time of the Roman Empire, they have a great influence on the pattern of events.

Western Europe, which today forms an integrated economic whole in competition with the countries beyond the dividing line of the bisected Germany, was under the Roman Empire divided into two apparently incompatible areas, one within the empire, one beyond its frontiers. With the fall of the Western Empire, barbarian princes who were able to provide the necessary military security came to dominate the old imperial provinces. This particular development was, however, hardly inevitable and could just as well have taken place under Roman petty emperors, kings, or warlords. Western Europe remained, moreover, even under the Germanic peoples, divided ethno-geographically. A new cohesion nevertheless came into being as formerly barbaric regions were incorporated into the mainstream through political alliances, trade, and exchange. Thus broad areas of Europe came to share a number of institutions ranging from a common symbolic language, the Christian religion, regional and relatively weak princely powers, 'private' rights to resources, etc., to agrarian techniques and technical knowledge. Special significance must be ascribed to the development of the Islamic realm, politically and militarily first of all, for the remnants of the Eastern Roman Empire – Byzantium – but economically also for Western Europe, to which it provided resources and knowledge until the voyages of discovery around AD 1500. In comparison, the north-eastern countries of Europe played only a marginal role, although it must be conceded that archaeological work may some day alter this perception somewhat.

For linguistic, professional, and socio-historical reasons, this work concentrates on the geographical belt running north-west to south-east from Britain to the Levant, bounded on the west by Spain and on the north by southern Scandinavia. Archaeological material is the main focus, but information derived from written sources, especially those illuminating the economic and hence the associated social circumstances, is also taken into account. The reason for this is that archaeological method offers insight primarily into the economic aspects of the material sources, and the intention here is to provide a more broadly based socio-historical synthesis that includes culture and mental attitudes as well. The reader will search unsuccessfully, however, for any detailed treatment of many of the aspects of, for example, classical Roman culture that are normally found in a work of this general nature. Although this book is designed to require only limited background knowledge, it assumes that certain facts are generally known. I hope it will nevertheless arouse interest for the point of view it expresses and its treatment of the archaeological material and, particularly, that it will serve to build a bridge between disciplines.

Primarily, we shall be dealing with evidence of settlement and the information on subsistence economy, exchange, etc., that can be derived from it. Towns play a smaller part in the account than might be expected. The picture is, however, fleshed out with discussions of physical conditions and man's effect upon them, the cultivation of plants and livestock raising, the character of settlement in the various regions, the varying sizes, types, functions, and distribution patterns of towns, Roman forts, craft production (for instance, the production and distribution of pottery), developments in water transport, the changing character of minting, etc. In addition, there is discussion of Roman inscriptions, mosaics, and churches and of graves. The contents of graves illuminate the relationships between the sexes and between social strata and offer insight into cultural standards and patterns of 'private' behaviour that allows consideration of mental attitudes, art, and communication.

Because one of the central themes running through this account is an interest in historical and particularly socio-historical and economic processes, emphasis is placed on the development, where possible, of culture-historical sequences, especially those apparent in quantitative data. A typical example (fig. 2) builds on the excavations at the important and well-defined administrative, economic, and

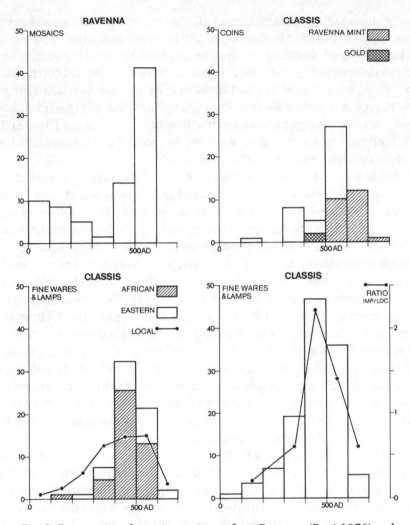

Fig. 2. Frequencies of mosaic pavements from Ravenna (Berti 1976) and
changing numbers of (mainly base-metal) coins, fine ceramic wares, and
lamps from an excavation at Classis, its port (*Source*: Montanari 1983)

cultural centre of Ravenna (Berti 1976, 1983; Coscarella 1983; Curima 1983;
Maioli 1983; cf. Montanari 1983). The first graph of the figure shows the
number of floor mosaics found at Ravenna that date from between the birth of
Christ and AD 700, most of them falling between AD 400 and 600. The next
three graphs relate to an important excavation in Ravenna's port, Classis, where
the majority of buildings date from this same period. In the graph dealing with
the coin material, it is notable that those dating from after AD 600 were all struck
locally, probably reflecting the increasing regionalization of the market economy. In the third graph, relating to the finer pottery, it is apparent that imported
'African' (Tunisian) table-ware was important in the period AD 400–600. The

last graph indicates very active trade in the fifth century, even though it was then that the Western Empire collapsed. Thus the archaeological material from Ravenna provides us with a correction to the common perception that there is a positive correlation between political stability and trade. In addition, the evidence of the mosaic floors points to the sixth century as the period of most building activity. It was then, for example, that San Vitale, with its wall mosaics of the emperor Justinian and empress Theodora, was erected (Krautheimer 1965). At the same time, the pottery from the excavation indicates that finer wares of local origin were more important and wares imported from the East, the surviving area of the empire, more in evidence than before. The finds from Classis, though relatively few, correspond to those from other contexts.

Sequences such as this can thus serve as historical 'weather stations', and they demonstrate the great potential of archaeology for the identification and analysis of conditions within a chronological and spatial framework. Written sources help us to identify the content and character of the social development for which archaeology has established the framework; in other words, they elucidate the past structures observed in the archaeological material. Archaeological method can often be applied to the study of the written sources as well, giving them a topographical dimension often neglected in works of pure history and even in many archaeological ones.

In evaluating archaeological material it is important to understand that, roughly speaking, we are operating with two different kinds of source, one 'unconscious', consisting, for instance, of the remains of buildings, rubbish dumps, etc., the other 'conscious', comprising burials, cultic areas, etc. Assuming the necessary insight into the character, quality, and amount of the material in question, the unconscious type can be made to yield systematic testimony to past population development, economy, social structure, etc. It must, of course, be assumed that the character of the material does not vary within the area of interest. The conscious type, in contrast, must be treated with caution, because a 'cultic' filter has been inserted between the everyday life of the past and the archaeological material. This means that identical phenomena – for example, burials – may from an archaeological viewpoint be highly visible or almost invisible, depending on cultic norms. The number of graves recorded for periods or areas in which burial with rich grave goods was the custom will be greater than for situations in which graves are 'poor', without any necessary connection with population statistics or social structure.

For example, there is a considerable amount of material, both settlement traces and graves, from the first millennium in a small area of Lower Saxony near Lüchow (Harck 1977) (fig. 3). The settlements predominantly date from around the birth of Christ, the graves predominantly from the middle to end of the millennium. Part of the explanation for this disjunction lies in the fact that the settlements dating from the early part of the period are relatively easily recognized by their numerous rubbish pits, a phenomenon rare on the later sites. As is

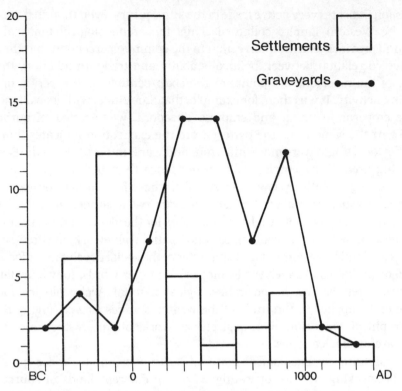

Fig. 3. Changing numbers of settlements and cemeteries from the late first millennium BC to the beginning of the second millennium AD in an area near Lüchow in Lower Saxony (*Source*: Harck 1977)

typical of barbarian areas in Central and Northern Europe, buildings were of timber in all of the settlements and this makes them far more difficult to recognize that Roman sites comprising the remains of stone buildings. Further, in the earlier period the quantity of grave goods was modest.

Another example may be found in a number of hoards, each containing several silver spoons, often decorated with Christian symbols, that have been found in the Mediterranean area and in other Roman or formerly Roman provinces (Milojčíc 1968). The distribution of these hoards probably indicates the areas of manufacture and primary use of the spoons. The overwhelming majority of finds fall, however, along the Rhine–Danube line, where such spoons, almost always just a single one at a time, are fairly frequently found in barbarian graves dating from the post-Roman period. The Germanic and other peoples near the old imperial frontiers seem to have considered these spoons valuable exotics and included them in their rich grave goods, whereas in the 'civilized' regions they were not deposited in graves.

The crucial role that archaeology may play in reconstructing the first millennium is apparent from close examination of the *Anglo-Saxon Chronicle*, one of the main documents on the early history of Britain (Douglas and Greenaway 1953;

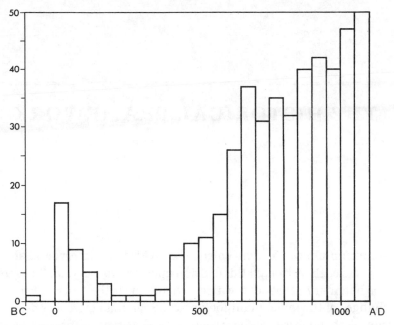

Fig. 4. Changing numbers of years for which there is information in the *Anglo-Saxon Chronicle* per fifty-year period of the first millennium (*Source*: Douglas & Greenaway 1953; Whitelock 1955)

Whitelock 1955) (fig. 4). Most of the information that this document provides on the first millennium is political, military, or religious in character and concentrated in the later centuries. Information for each individual calendar year is given beginning only in the latter half of the eleventh century; there is very little information relating to the time before AD 600 and especially before AD 400, where only archaeology can 'write' the local history of Britain. (The Early Roman period – before AD 200 – constitutes an excepton but the information relating to this period is derived from later copies of classical works surviving elsewhere.)

As time passes and archaeological source material increases in quantity and quality, we can expect the history of the first millennium to be modified in a number of respects. Our understanding of historical processes may well eventually be based chiefly on the material sources, with the written sources serving more to fill in the gaps, for example, in studies of past cultural milieus and mental attitudes and of matters requiring detailed chronological information and in the elaboration of new methods for studying the material data. This essay may be seen as an attempt to show what can be done by taking the material data as a point of departure, even when the period in question is well known to written history, and thus to demonstrate the great potential of the archaeological sources for providing systematic information about the past. It is, however, important to remember that archaeology primarily compares and interprets patterns that it has itself identified and does not necessarily tell us whether these patterns apply in other contexts or, indeed, correspond to past reality.

2

THE HISTORICAL FRAMEWORK

The first millennium can for convenience be divided into intervals of about two hundred years each. Although this division appears arbitrary, it allows us to set our period boundaries at about the times when some of the crucial historical and social changes of the millennium took place. Regional differences do not seem significant, probably because the trends of development in the various regions were for the most part linked. This is not, however, to say that these trends were congruent: progress can perfectly well be made in one area at the same time as there is crisis or regression in another. Thus we find five main periods: AD 0–200, the Early Roman or Early Empire period; 200–400, the Late Roman or Late Empire period; 400–600, Late Antiquity and the beginnings of the Germanic successor states; 600–800, the Early Byzantine, Early Islamic, and, for the eighth century, Early Carolingian period; 800–1000, the Middle Byzantine and Islamic periods and, for the tenth century, the initial phases of the Western European state societies. (For later Western Europe alone, one might have operated with the periods AD 500–700, 700–900, and 900–1100.) The following brief description of each of these periods draws in part on the written sources (which, as noted above, particularly concern political and military affairs) and in part on the archaeological evidence – chiefly architecture, settlement, and trade and exchange – to be considered in detail in the chapters that follow.

To provide a sense of direction in this vast and complex material, another – again apparently arbitrary – approach is suggested. Throughout the first millennium every other century is characterized by profound social change and associated economic or other disruption. The intervening centuries are just as clearly marked by relatively stable social conditions. Centuries with odd numbers are unstable, centuries with even ones stable. The first, third, fifth, seventh, and ninth centuries are therefore centuries of change; the second, fourth, sixth, eighth, and tenth centuries of consolidation. In the first century the Roman Empire came into being, and at the same time profound changes occurred both in the conquered societies and in the unconquered ones beyond the imperial frontiers. The third century was a time of crisis and structural reorganization in the empire. In the fifth century, the time of great migrations, the Western Roman Empire collapsed. In the seventh century the Eastern or Byzantine realm was reduced and restructured as a result of Islamic expansion. In the ninth century a number of new social collapses and transformations took place, ranging from that of the Carolingian realm in the west to that of the Abbasid dynasty in Mesopotamia in the east. In addition, there were new 'migrations' and raids, for instance those of the Vikings. In contrast, the second century was the golden age of the Roman Empire while the fourth saw the reconstruction of the Constantinian empire, the sixth the reconstitution of the Justinian empire, the eighth the birth of the Carolingian realm, early Abbasid Islam, etc., and the tenth the emergence of state societies in Western Europe and elsewhere.

This scheme of course is subject to the criticism that hundred-year periods are no divinely instituted scale for the categorization of historical events. It is, however, possible that one to two centuries was the maximum life-span of a highly developed society in early Europe and the Mediterranean, perhaps because of degradation of the core lands of the early states and empires. In any case, these divisions can serve as a heuristic device. The following survey, which is brief and supported for the moment by no argument or documentation (but see appendix 1), should be considered only an *aide-mémoire*.

AD 0–200

The Early Roman period begins with the founding of the Roman Empire and covers its final military expansion, including the conquest of Britain and later of Dacia (fig. 5). During this period the infrastructure of the northern provinces was extended by means of roads, forts, towns (for example, veterans' colonies), and, in the agricultural sector, villas, a process often known as 'Romanization'. The first phase of this development was accompanied by unrest and frontier skirmishes. Nevertheless, particularly in societies that were already highly organized and stratified, it was possible for Romanization to take place relatively painlessly. The Roman secret was to engage the local élites in the development process, thus making them the underpinnings of the structure. Romanization did not, however, proceed without profound social and economic changes, and it cannot be overlooked that in many areas Roman occupation was accompanied by economic regression in a number of sectors. The empire itself, however, did not invest very large sums in the military or in administration, and the Roman élite was certainly able to profit greatly from the development. The early Roman Empire was organized around autonomous town and tribal territories, a form of organization typical in both the ancient and the Northern Alpine world. In addition to cultural norms, the Romans had also acquired much technical and economic knowledge from earlier Mediterranean, particularly Greek and Hellenistic, traditions. A large part of the workforce in the central and western regions

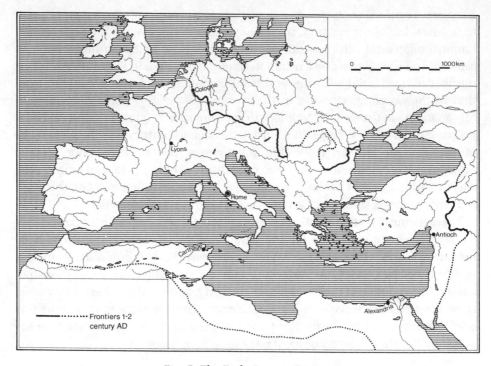

Fig. 5. The Early Roman Empire

of the empire – its heartland and development area – was made up of slaves, often the spoils of wars under the late republic and the very early empire. The slave economy was less pronounced in the last part of this period, although slaves continued to be numerous throughout the millennium.

North of the empire this period was marked by the efforts of societies to adapt to new circumstances. Traditional, thousand-year-old relations with the southern tribes had been severed by the Roman expansion and replaced by new but strictly regulated connections with the empire itself. One of the consequences of the Roman conquest was the disappearance of the most advanced communities to the north and east of the Alps, in particular the Celtic and Dacian *oppida*. East of the Rhine, in contrast, many Germanic Iron Age societies persisted, characterized by simple village settlements with farmsteads, the core of each of which was a longhouse that sheltered both the family and its livestock. To the south-east, the Roman Empire faced the Persian or Parthian kingdom, but in the Early Roman period this posed no very great military or political problem. At the end of the period, in AD 166–180, the battles known as the Marcomannic wars were fought along the Danubian frontier. These hostilities revealed a number of weaknesses in the Roman armies and occurred, furthermore, at a time when the internal economy of the empire was already ailing.

AD 200–400

In the Late Roman period the empire underwent structural changes necessitated by numerous general signs of unrest. Italy, the heartland of the empire, had ceased to export products to other provinces as early as the second century as Rome became dependent on imports of foodstuffs and other commodities. At first this development was offset by economic expansion in the provinces, but the Italian agricultural recession, marked in particular by a sharp reduction in the number of medium-sized and smaller villas, was followed by a corresponding recession in the north-western provinces. Both there and in Italy the decline was accompanied by a change in the structure of towns; monument building, for example, virtually came to an end. One reason for this was the reduction in the market and the decline of towns and their territories as autonomous administrative units. To the east (and south) – for instance, in the Balkans, in 'Africa', and in the Levant – there is, however, no sign of reduction in the number of agrarian units; on the contrary. The removal of the imperial capital eastward to Byzantium, rechristened 'Constantinopolis', in AD 330 can thus be viewed as a consequence of agricultural trends in the empire and the associated shift of economic emphasis south and east. In the third century the Roman Empire suffered, moreover, from problems along its lengthy frontiers. Trouble arose both with the barbarian tribes in the north and with the Persian kingdom, the latter having found new strength under the Sassanids. At the end of the century a double empire came into being under the emperor Diocletian, with both emperors, western and eastern, being provided with deputies, in an attempt to solve some of the leadership difficulties revealed by the century's military and political crises (fig. 6).

The military, administrative, and economic problems called for greater military strength and better administration to collect revenues, a task previously performed by the organization based on town territories. In several areas during the course of the troubled third century there seems to have been a concentration of land into large, extensively cultivated units, the owners of which did not necessarily reside on them. These estates, somewhat diffuse in character, can be seen as contrasting with the capital-intensive villas of the Early Empire period, whose products were intended especially for the broader market. Large land-owners often held high administrative posts and therefore shared the state's interest in stable conditions that would ensure production and the collection of revenues and land rents. Medium-sized farms, whose owners were closely associated with the local political and economic environment, declined or even vanished. With the towns' loss of independence and the recession in the private economy, local interest in and ability to invest in monumental architecture waned, and an important aspect of the urban culture and cultural tradition of Antiquity came to an end.

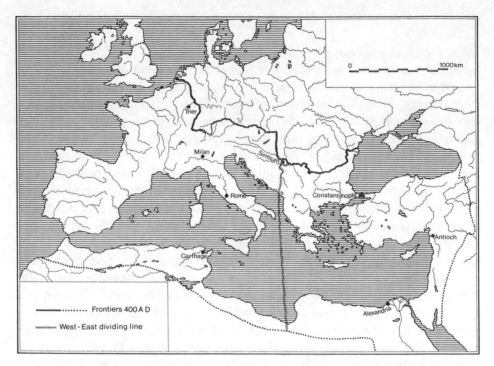

Fig. 6. The divided Roman Empire at AD 400, with the regional capitals of
Trier, Milan, Sirmium, Constantinople (also supreme capital), and Antioch

North of the empire the Late Roman period was notable for a number of
changes in the dominant Germanic communities, which had hitherto organized
themselves into larger groups only during the battles against the advancing
Roman legions. From the third and especially the fourth century, this area
contained stable communities characterized by village settlements with large
farmsteads of considerable economic potential. These communities were linked
in tribal confederations, and their development was accompanied by the establishment of centres containing, for example, facilities for the offloading of ships,
craft production, and trading. From these centres efforts were made to control the
interregional exchange of exotica, etc. with continual battles in their train. This
development led to the establishment of centre–periphery relationships different
from those of earlier times, when all that had mattered was distance from the
empire. The position of the Roman Empire in the face of these processes was
weak. In spite of improvements in the fourth century, the imperial armies were
faced with massive and, in the case of the Germanic tribes, recurrent problems in
protecting the northern provinces from outside attack. Another problem was
frequent factional hostilities, almost civil wars, between emperors and
pretenders.

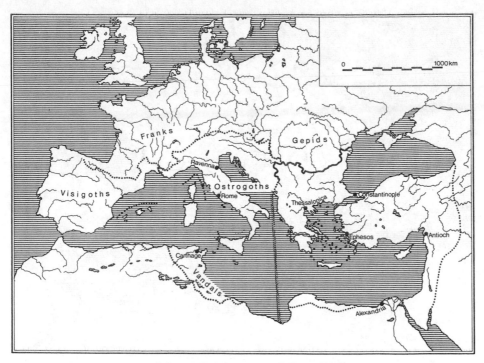

Fig. 7. Europe and the Mediterranean, including the major Germanic
realms and the Eastern Roman Empire, at about AD 500

AD 400–600

By AD 400 it had become impossible for the Roman army to defend the empire's
extensive north-western frontier (fig. 7), even with the introduction of 'defence-
in-depth' techniques employing mobile first-class units as tactical reserves. The
battle against the Visigoths at Adrianople (in present-day Bulgaria) in AD 378
was of crucial significance in that much of the Roman field army was destroyed.
This meant, among other things, that there were groups of Gothic warriors in
various places in the northern empire until, in AD 418, having plundered Rome
in 410, they were settled in Aquitania in south-western Gaul. By this time other
Germanic tribes had crossed the Rhine: of these the Swabians settled in north-
western Spain, while an agreement was not reached with the Vandals until AD
435, when parts of western North Africa were actually handed over to them.
Such agreements were to become common during the fifth century; ten years
later the Vandals also dominated the rich regions of 'Africa', partly because the
empire at the time was occupied in countering threats from the Huns (who,
however, were beaten in Gaul in AD 451). Nevertheless, twenty-five years later
the imperial military and political apparatus was in disarray throughout the

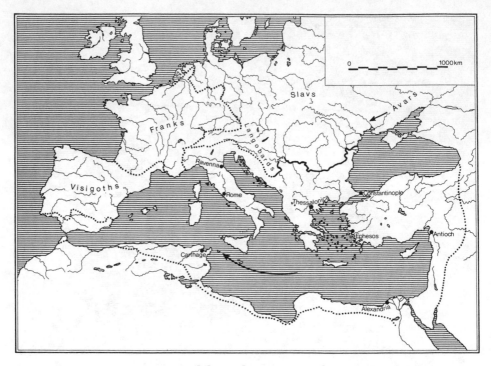

Fig. 8. Europe and the Mediterranean at about AD 550

Western Roman Empire, and Germanic kings and princes took over the emperor's rights, assisted by those sectors of the bureaucracy that were still
functioning, as in Italy. About AD 500 the situation stabilized both politically and
militarily under the Franks in northern Gaul and, until they too came under
Frankish, or Merovingian, domination, the Burgundians along the Rhône in
eastern Gaul. Spain was subjected to the Visigoths (the majority of Visigothic
southern Gaul was surrendered to the Franks in AD 507), while the Ostrogoths
held Italy and Dalmatia.

The Eastern Roman emperor, Justinian, began in the AD 530s to reconquer
'Africa', southern Spain, Italy, Dalmatia, etc., the central parts of the old Western
Roman Empire (fig. 8). Italy was conquered in the AD 550s, but more than fifteen
years of hostilities failed to yield stable conditions. In AD 566 Italy was reinvaded,
this time by Langobardian warriors who, like the Ostrogoths, entered the
country from Pannonia (western Hungary). Byzantium maintained control of
large parts of southern Italy, however. Justinian was also forced to wage war
against the Persians under the emperor Chosroes I. For almost a hundred years,
until the Islamic expansion, Eastern Rome and the Persians exhausted themselves in a series of conflicts.

Military and political conditions during the years AD 400–600 were compli-
cated but crucial for Europe's further development. This period is one of the

'hinges' of history, its most critical phase being the six or seven decades between the invasion of Italy by the Langobardians and the Islamic subjugation of the Levant in the AD 630s. The continuity in this development should not, however, be overlooked. As early as the fourth century officers from Germanic tribes, particularly Franks and Alamanni (both from the eastern bank of the Rhine), were common in regiments of Roman guards, some even holding senior rank. There was also a very large number of German auxiliaries in the Roman armies, as invaders in many cases were incorporated into the army or settled as 'federates' in different regions. Among other things, this was done to ensure that the economic system could enjoy a measure of peace that widespread unrest, including uprisings of the agrarian population, rarely allowed it. Gifts of land or perhaps a transfer of rights to taxes could be a small price to pay for avoiding total collapse, and it is certainly not insignificant that the Roman senate, along with the bureaucracy, seems to have collaborated reasonably well with the new Germanic lords.

Rural settlement in the region around Rome was marked by further decline. More remarkable, in the north of the empire there was a general reorganization of settlement, which became dominated by fortified or easily defensible sites – many doubtless estate centres, others more like villages. In addition there were numbers of settlements in open country, for example near Rome, many grouped around churches. Although some older buildings were reused or continued in use during this period, villas like those of the Early and Late Roman periods were no longer built; the main dwelling structures of estates, when recognizable, have an entirely different, compact or 'medieval' character. The same settlement picture appears, for instance, in the southern Balkans, but an impression of recession or decay is first notable here only after AD 600. The settlements of Late Antiquity in the Balkans had often been founded in the Late Roman period as fortified sites.

In northern Syria, very rich settlements appear in the fifth and sixth centuries; some of these were large complexes such as monasteries, some ordinary but independent and quite compact farmsteads. Often called 'villas', these are far from the distinctive classical villas of the Western Empire, which were sited on large, open tracts of land. With the exception of the monasteries, there are few examples of aristocratic country residences, and society's leaders must probably be sought in the booming late Eastern Roman towns. Taken as a whole, this 'Migration period' was a phase not of general decline in the agrarian economy but primarily of reorganization. With the fall of the Western Empire, the Mediterranean market economy was reduced in both volume and geographical extent. Gradually the broader trade in foodstuffs and craft products became confined to the eastern Mediterranean.

There were political and economic changes along the old northern frontier of the empire as well. In Britain, Anglo-Saxon supremacy was established in the eastern parts of the old Roman province. On the continent, both banks of the

Rhine came under Frankish control, and during the sixth century the Franks also subjugated the Germanic tribal confederations on the Upper Danube (for example, the Alamanni). Farther east, on the Middle Danube, along with a number of minor 'peoples', we find the Ostrogoths, followed by the Langobardians, and the Gepids (east of Pannonia) during the fifth century. Both the Langobardians and the Gepids were replaced in the sixth century by the Turkish-speaking Avars. In this wide area none of the Roman economic system as a rule survived, except for some technical knowledge. A possible exception is the Rhine area, which, as part of the Frankish realm, had contacts with the south, for instance through the ecclesiastical institutions. Written sources characterize the period as one of estate building. Typical of the archaeological material from this area are the many richly equipped individual graves, a phenomenon that usually distinguishes open societies with a high degree of competition among their members. Settlements almost exclusively comprise wooden buildings, including pit houses, in farm complexes, often grouped. It is characteristic of these settlements, at any rate of the best-known ones in the Rhineland, that they were not built on the same sites as the Roman ones. Considerable growth of forest cover, often in areas inhabited during imperial times, is also part of this picture.

North of this zone along the Rhine and the Danube there were societies and areas that only indirectly felt the fall of the Western Empire and the emergence of the Eastern as the economic and political centre of gravity in the Mediterranean. In Scandinavia, for example, we see an orientation towards the new Germanic kingdoms or associations of kingdoms, primarily those of the North Sea basin. Developments differed in the area east of the Elbe (and north of the Carpathians), which during the sixth century became dominated by Slavs. These early northern Slavic communities apparently did not build large estates or share their neighbours' interest in or opportunities for exchange of exotic luxuries. In the seventh century the Slavs settled south of the Carpathians as well, even reaching Greece. North and east of the Germanic–Slavic area there were, of course, other societies of less interest to us in the present context. Their resources – for example, furs – began to play a role in international trade by the middle of the first millennium and were exploited by both Late Antique Eastern Empire and the contemporary Persian kingdom.

AD 600–800

In the Early Byzantine/Islamic/Carolingian period several dramatic changes took place in Mediterranean societies. One of the most remarkable was the conquest by Muslim armies of the southern Mediterranean basin and the rest of the Near East – the Levant and Mesopotamia in the AD 630s, Egypt and most of the Persian highlands in the 640s, and 'Africa' in the latter half of the seventh century. At the beginning of the eighth century Spain was taken from the

Visigoths, and the last Byzantine enclaves in the western Mediterranean were also conquered. With some difficulty the Eastern Roman or Byzantine Empire managed to retain control only of the Anatolian plateau, the Greek coastlands, and parts of southern Italy, which were all organized as self-sufficient military districts. During the final war against the Persians (who at the start of the seventh century briefly controlled both the Levant and Egypt), Byzantium was ejected first from the Middle Danube by the Avars and then from the southern Balkans by the Bulgars, a second Turkic-speaking warrior group which, however, rapidly became Slavicized. In this period building in Byzantium virtually came to an end: in only a few places, such as behind the strong fortifications of Constantinople, are there traces of a market and money economy and of the political and religious life that was formerly enjoyed. The considerable trade in foodstuffs and craft products that distinguished the Mediterranean both in the Roman era and in Late Antiquity was much curtailed and only rarely involved more distant regions. The destruction of religious images of the seventh and early eighth centuries is a well-known expression of the climate of opinion in embattled Byzantium at the time, though it was also connected with strife over the church's institutions and funds.

In many ways early Islam considered itself heir to the Eastern Roman Empire, and until the middle of the eighth century its capital was Damascus in Syria. The architectural idiom expressed, for example, in the main mosque at Damascus is clearly founded on the norms of Late Antiquity. In AD 763, however, under the Abbasid dynasty, Baghdad was established as a new capital, and thus there was a 'Persianization' of Islamic culture and economy. Just as important in the long run were contemporary developments in distant Western Europe, where the last relics of Roman forms of taxation and administration had vanished by the end of the Merovingian dynasty if not as early as in the sixth century. In the eighth century there was an expansion of the Frankish kingdom, whose income now in the main came from plunder and conquest, trade, and, not least, extensive estates. This Frankish federation of states, stretching in the time of Charlemagne (about AD 800) from the Elbe to the Pyrenees and central Italy and from the Atlantic to the Middle Danube, invested much of its wealth in prestige activities (including a colossal church-building programme), craft production, and exchange, particularly with neighbouring peoples. Thus, although conscious of its Roman heritage, Western Europe was for the first time making an independent attempt at establishing a lasting 'civilization' that affected even Italy, the original heartland of the Roman Empire.

The Carolingian realm had a profound effect on its barbarian neighbours in the north through exchange, especially in the many new Carolingian and other emporia. Trade contacts with Mediterranean regions were probably still limited. The chief partners of the Carolingians in northern Europe were the Christian Anglo-Saxon kingdoms, the Nordic area, and the north-western Slavic societies. In addition there were the Frisians and the Saxons, who, however, were very soon incorporated into the Frankish kingdom and forced to convert to Christianity.

Northern Carolingian society was not as different from, for instance, Germanic Denmark as the Roman Empire had been, and thus the Carolingians and in particular their successors came to serve as models for social development.

For the north-western Slavs the years AD 600–800 constituted a first organizational and economic climax. Fortress complexes associated with 'open' settlements functioned as residences for the leaders, as cult centres, etc., but are on the whole more characteristic of later periods. Similar fortresses are known in the previous period in the Nordic area, particularly in Sweden, and there too they served a local need for defence. Such complexes are, however, virtually unknown in Denmark and south-eastern Britain, both highly organized areas, in which the inhabitants apparently sought security through regional arrangements. This seems indicated also by boundary earthworks separating areas or 'kingdoms'. Village fortresses thus seem to be situated chiefly in areas with relatively weak and defence-oriented political and military organization. To the south and east small wooden huts were typical everywhere for both Slavic and non-Slavic people; in addition, there were a few fortified sites.

AD 800–1000

In the last main period, the ninth century witnessed a general collapse, of both interregional contacts and societies (fig. 9). The decades around AD 800 had, however, constituted a zenith, making the following changes the more dramatic. In Mesopotamia, the heartland of the Abbasid dynasty, there was, to judge by the archaeological sources, an almost total collapse of settlement. At the same time, Islam's international contacts were dramatically reduced, trade with China, for instance, virtually coming to a standstill. One consequence of this reduction was greater political and economic independence for the Islamic provinces: they had always, however, had greater local resources at their disposal than the Roman provinces. In the west, the Carolingian realm fell into a decline expressed politically by dynastic strife followed by a division of the realm into Italian, Western Frankish (French), and Eastern Frankish (German) parts. This was accompanied by abandonment of large areas of agrarian settlement, followed by stable growth in the tenth century and probably an intensification of agriculture. This reorganization proved to have been the last before the establishment of the high-medieval settlement pattern distinguished by permanent villages. In the final analysis the crisis in the Carolingian realm – which was followed by political fragmentation but, as noted, also by the development of local resources – must be viewed as the beginning of major changes in Western Europe. Societies chiefly concerned with wars and with status, busy procuring fortunes in chattels and land, were turning into medieval state-societies. In Scandinavia, the decline in international trade (with the Islamic world through Russia and with Western Europe) resulted in plundering expeditions, for example to Britain, followed by

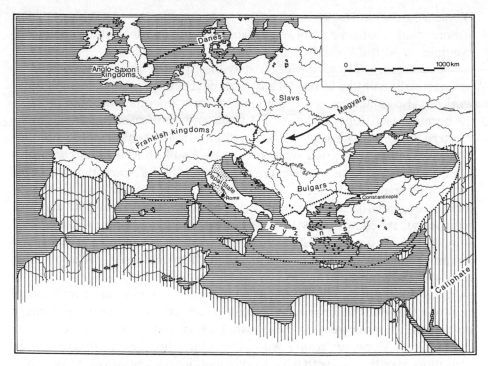

Fig. 9. Europe and the Mediterranean in the ninth century

settlement. The Islamic areas in the Mediterranean took the opportunity of making new conquests, including Sardinia, Sicily, and Crete, in addition to gaining footholds elsewhere, for instance in Italy.

At the end of the ninth century, Hungarian peoples penetrated into Central Europe, and this led, among other things, to the collapse of the Slavic Great Moravian realm, which, like the Bulgarian empire to the south, was similar in some respects to the extensive but still weak Carolingian confederation. After this the Hungarians wholly dominated the Middle Danube. The Moravian realm was, incidentally, somewhat tenuously included in the Byzantine sphere of interest, concentrated on the Lower Danube and southern Russia. In Russia at the end of the ninth century, steps were taken towards the establishment of a territorial realm in the Kiev–Novgorod region: this, too, was to be of lasting significance. In the tenth century the Bulgarian empire was subjugated by Byzantium, which also recovered parts of south-eastern Anatolia from Islam. These latter developments constituted a restoration of the Eastern Roman Empire, though it was entirely different in character from Justinian's. In AD 800–1000 coins became common again in the whole of Byzantium as towns began to be reconstructed. In the tenth century, too, state societies emerged in Northern Europe, for instance in western Denmark (there modelled on examples in

Western Europe) and in Britain after the expulsion of the Danish Vikings. Finally, a more stable political system was established among the northern Slavs, for example, in central Poland.

The emergence of states meant not only the establishment of lasting political arrangements within a territorial although not necessarily unchanging framework but also stable economic conditions, primarily a permanent organization of the agrarian landscape and its use. From the tenth century on, agrarian sites in Western Europe are characterized by stability and reflect considerable continuity in social relations. In certain areas, such as the Frankish Rhineland, continuity can be traced even farther back in time, but only with the reservation that there was widespread abandonment of older settlements in the disturbed ninth century. In the Nordic area, the north-western continent, and Britain the picture is of spacious village complexes with large farmsteads built of timber. Houses with stone-built walls appear chiefly in the Mediterranean, for instance in the typical Italian mountain- or hill-top settlements, with their densely packed, almost town-like communities.

In the Slavic areas in Central Europe the more irregular, open settlements continued, as did the fortress complexes, which primarily served as princely residences. The latter were associated with various crafts and now sometimes, as in the Great Moravian realm, with stone-built churches. Here there is no continuity of settlement with later periods apart from a few fortress towns, such as Prague, that survived in the towns of the High Middle Ages. The Bulgarian empire had princely residences with palaces that were comparable to those of the Carolingians and even at times surpassed them. In addition, as in the northern Slavic area, there were ordinary settlements containing small houses, often pit houses. In Byzantium too there seems to be settlement continuity from the tenth century on. In addition, there was considerable expansion at the beginning of the second millennium.

Towns constitute another characteristic feature of the tenth-century Western European landscape. New ones appeared, and there was expansion of old centres that had almost vanished in the post-Roman era. The Carolingian world had consisted more of monasteries, royal centres, and emporia than of towns. From the tenth century on, towns became so numerous and so close together in many regions that, as in Roman times, they could serve as regular market centres for the region or locality concerned and thus regain an important economic function. Towns also served as centres for royal and aristocratic powers and for ecclesiastical institutions and thus became important areas of investment by competing social élites. This is illustrated, for instance, in the widespread building of churches. The élites were, however, not as tied to the towns in Central and Northern Europe as they were, for instance, in Italy, where there are several early examples of secular buildings in the town centres.

In the society of medieval Western Europe, primary producers were independent and often prosperous. This is underlined by the high degree of continuity, in

Northern Europe between the pre-state, late Iron Age communities and the medieval ones. The underlying element in both types of society is clearly the lineage, in whose hands rested the basic means of production. The fact that there were rich and less rich families and more or less prominent members of each – apart from slaves and other subordinated persons – does not affect the basic structure, which seems to have been the same from the Nordic area to the Mediterranean. Thus the early-medieval Western European state levied taxes only in the form of services, for example military services, and tolls. Generally speaking, the state could be described as weak in relation to the widespread system of land owning, ranked lineages, but the new economies, including widespread production and market systems, certainly were not.

In Eastern Europe distinguished families seem to have wielded economic and political influence mainly by virtue of their rank, wealth, and control of the production of valuables and certain craft products. Control of the agrarian means of production might be said to have been in the hands of the primary producers, but they hardly owned them. In Byzantium there is evidence in the written sources of the important part played by peasants in the Early Byzantine period, while in the so-called tax-collecting state there is at the same time a remnant of Antiquity. The later 'feudal' Byzantine state, and particularly its powerful civilian and military élites, however, prevented the primary producers from maintaining or achieving greater control of the means of production. The Islamic states had at this time a widespread system of taxation and a kind of tribute arrangement for the individual provinces. They also had a differentiated and productive agrarian system with extensive arrangements for irrigation, but this system was not in the hands of the primary producers either, who were generally slaves. This constituted a potential hindrance to development in spite of Islam's vast technical knowledge and considerable economic potential. A special facet of Muslim society was, moreover, the considerable internal and external trade and associated activities, primarily craft production, concentrated in towns. Although Western Europe was 'born' at the end of the first millennium, Islam was clearly its superior in the majority of crafts, in trade, and in organization. Where Western Europe differed from these eastern areas was in the control of the agrarian and hence the primary resources, which rested with the landowning lineages and remained unchallenged by political élites or powerful states.

3

THE PHYSICAL SETTING

The physical conditions in Europe and the Mediterranean basin during the first millennium are little known. Thus, whereas in general the natural world at the birth of Christ probably did not differ entirely from that of today, it may not have been quite as similar as we are often induced to believe. Two problems therefore confront us: elucidating the differences – and changes over time – in climate, plants and animals, and agricultural practices in the various regions, and understanding the relationship between the physical and the cultural circumstances – between changes in climate and the methods of cultivation and living conditions of past societies. The first problem is difficult enough; as for the second, it is, despite declarations to the contrary, still impossible to determine the ecological situation. Emphasis will be placed here on climatic changes and on the natural conditions in the various regions in connection with a discussion of cultivated plants and domestic animals and a brief survey of the various production systems. The presentation does not pretend to be exhaustive; the basic idea is to provide a framework for the social developments, relying especially on the results of recent research. It is appropriate to begin with a few very general aspects of the physical conditions in Europe and the Mediterranean that are of special relevance to social history.

General physical conditions

Winter temperatures, which are of some importance for the length of the growing season, are mild in the Mediterranean, moderate in Western Europe, and low in Northern and Eastern Europe. Summer temperatures are of course highest in the Mediterranean basin and in south-eastern Europe but relatively moderate or low to the north. Precipitation is low – and therefore critical – in the south-eastern Mediterranean and adjacent areas, abundant elsewhere. Eastern Central Europe and southern Russia, for example, are relatively arid, but the comparatively modest amounts of rain here do fall in the growing season, while rainfall in the Mediterranean generally occurs in winter. Irrigation mitigates the water shortage to some extent but was not particularly common until the days of Islam.

Soil conditions in the area are in general suitable for both arable and livestock farming. Forests were common, particularly north of the Alps; to the west these were deciduous, to the east and north mixed deciduous/coniferous. Outside the Mediterranean basin, particularly good soil is found in southern Russia, along the Danube, and in the Central and Western European loess areas, concentrated on the major river systems. In the Mediterranean basin the soil is generally suitable for olives and grapes, for grain, particularly wheat, and for vegetables and fruit. North of the Alps conditions are especially suitable for grain. In addition, this area provided good grazing for cattle (and horses), while pigs competed with cattle for the forest resources and sheep made use of the more marginal, open areas. Sheep have traditionally been very numerous in the vast arid, treeless stretches of the Mediterranean basin. Cattle and even pigs found favourable conditions on the river floodplains and in the forests. Cultivated plants and domestic animals of distinctively Near Eastern type – for example, date palms and dromedaries – flourished in the arid south-eastern Mediterranean. In addition to these foods and other resources there was an abundance of fish and game. Finally, the area was well provided with minerals, although iron and many other metals were more frequent north of the Alps (and in the Balkans).

The picture emerges of a region in which the basic resources were relatively evenly distributed and there were ample opportunities for adaptation. Nevertheless, if special needs arose, for instance, in connection with rapid social development, then deficiencies either of foodstuffs or of materials and minerals might occur. Moreover, climatic changes – for example, reduced precipitation – would potentially have affected the ecological system, particularly in marginal areas. Finally, we must reckon with a number of changes in physical conditions brought about by man himself – for example, erosion associated with intensive cultivation and climatic changes connected with a reduction in forest cover. Furthermore, cultivation patterns and other forms of exploitation, determined partly by the physical setting and resources and partly by social development, may have a crucial effect on the landscape.

Climatic changes

If climatic indicators are to be used in historical study, the data must be unambiguous, susceptible to comparison, and, above all, collected in a systematic way. Many climatic indicators offer no precise knowledge of the phenomena they reflect. For example, a temperature reduction may be general or apply to winter or summer only. For the social historian it is important to know whether the temperature was reduced during the summer, when this would have affected plant growth. These uncertainties make it difficult to compare statements about

climatic change and to distinguish between general and local tendencies. There
are special problems concerning dating, which is often imprecise, and sequences
that are so brief that it is difficult to draw comparisons. In what follows emphasis
is placed on long, well-dated sequences and sequences that are directly comparable with archaeological data (Harding 1982; Lamb 1977 and 1982; Williams
and Wigley 1983).

The information on climate that appears in written sources for the first
millennium is in general rather unreliable. As a rule, these sources contain only
complaints about the weather or remarks on extreme conditions. It is, however,
of interest to trace the percentages of different types of complaint over time. For
convenience I shall use an older collection of data (Hennig 1904), whose quality
does not always meet current standards for historical research. The information
from the earlier centuries is, of course, most abundant for the Mediterranean
area. For temperate Europe, ample material is first found in the second half of the
first millennium and particularly in the second. In the interest of reliability, we
are, moreover, forced to study relatively lengthy periods at a time (fig. 10).

To judge from the complaints, the centuries before Christ in the Mediterranean
had relatively ample precipitation that should probably be interpreted as providing favourable conditions for agriculture. In contrast, the first centuries after
Christ were relatively dry, even though the period is marked by complaints of
river flooding. The floods in question were probably the result of erosion conse-
quent upon overexploitation of the land. (Most of the information for this period
comes from Italy.) A new period of floods during the first few centuries after AD
500 corresponds, however, with renewed complaints about rain. Thus we may
conclude that again in this period there was abundant precipitation. The transitional period around AD 400 seems, moreover, to have been marked by storm
surges, probably reflecting high sea level. If so, this must have been caused by
prolonged thawing of the polar ice, again a result of a preceding period of
warmth. Here it is worth noting that the time around AD 400 is also marked by
complaints about heat and drought. In temperate Europe at the middle and at the
end of the first millennium we find the same trends with respect to precipitation
as noted in the Mediterranean. Periods of abundant precipitation such as the first
centuries after AD 500 also show only a few very cold winters and thus a more
Atlantic climate. In general, but most clearly in the Mediterranean, a connection
can also be seen between the percentage of complaints about heat (in the
summer) and cold (in the winter) – the well-known continental-climate syn-
drome. However deficient this picture of the climate of the time, it is still far more
detailed than that provided by most scientific investigations.

Studies of the annual layers of the Greenland icecap potentially meet the
strictest requirements for chronology, but the main results, although probably
generally applicable to the northern hemisphere, are not as valuable for our
purposes as local observations in Europe and the Mediterranean (Hammer,
Clausen, and Dansgaard 1980). Furthermore, there are dating problems that

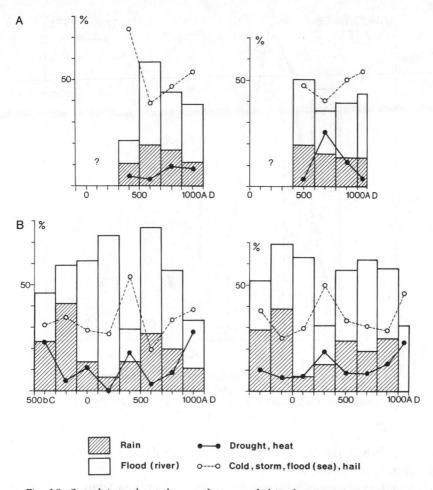

Fig. 10. Complaints about the weather recorded in the written sources, as measured in percentages of (1) rain, (2) river flooding, (3) drought/heat, and (4) cold, storm, sea flooding, and hail, for (A) temperate Europe; (B) the Mediterranean (*Source*: Hennig 1904)

affect the sequences from the highly interesting first half of the first millennium. More useful are studies of the varying thickness of the annual growth-rings of trees in temperature-sensitive areas such as the White Mountains of California, which have provided several very long 'climatic' sequences (LaMarche 1974; Williams and Wigley 1983). Among the features common to these studies are a cold period in the latter half of the first millennium, a period of hot summers at the beginning of the second, and a cold period, the so-called Little Ice Age, in the second half of that millennium. These results are confirmed by other observations in North America that in addition point to a period of hot summers around the middle of the first millennium. There are corresponding observations

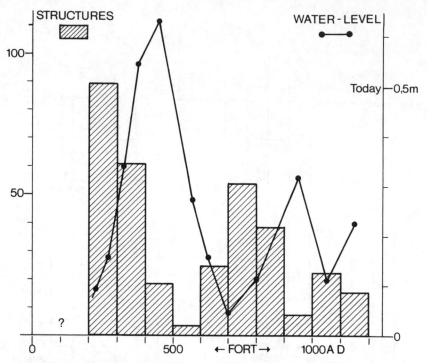

Fig. 11. Changing numbers of structures and fluctuations of the water table at Tornow, showing the negative correlation between the two. The life-span of the fortress component of the site is indicated (*Source*: Herrmann 1973)

for Europe from a number of sources, but considerable uncertainty relating to the first millennium remains.

Information of a more local nature comes, for instance, from studies of coastal dunes in the Netherlands, which reflect alternating drier and wetter periods through time (Jelgersma and van Regteren Altena 1969; Kooijmans 1980). The wet periods have proved to correspond to transgressions of the North Sea in the centuries just before the birth of Christ, around AD 500, and, in a double phase, around AD 1000. These phases correspond exactly to general rises in sea level, which again depend on the volume of water released from the polar ice through thawing. Thus we must conclude that the transgression phases recorded in the Netherlands, on a world scale, were warm and wet, at least in north-western Europe.

In a well-studied archaeological context, the settlement at Tornow in the German Democratic Republic, the two precipitation phases reappear, in the middle of the first millennium and at its end (Herrmann 1973, 1985: 153–4). They can be recognized partly in fluctuations in the water table (fig.11) and partly in the pollen curve of the damp-loving alders. A similar pattern has been revealed by analyses of pollen from Draved Bog, in Jutland, where a wet phase

GLACIATION

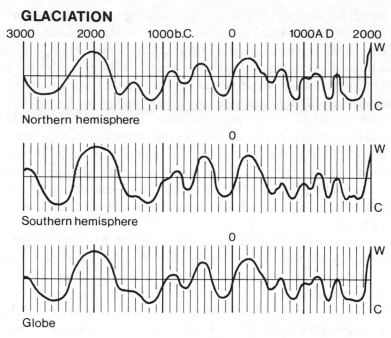

Fig. 12. Glacial advances and retreats, reflecting, respectively, cold (C) and warm (W) periods of world climate (*Source*: Röthlisberger 1986)

has been observed in the period immediately before the birth of Christ, another around the middle of the first millennium, and a third at the end of the millennium (Aaby and Tauber 1975). In these cases the areas under study are, relatively speaking, so close to one another that we may be permitted to believe that the observations reflect the same general phenomena. In other cases it can be more difficult to find any connection between the different sets of climatic information. It does seem possible, however, to relate the North European investigations to the southerly Swiss Alps, where, according to a number of reliable new dates, the glaciers have been found to retreat parallel to the transgression phases noted above (Schneebeli and Röthlisberger 1976; cf. Röthlisberger 1986). The Alpine information has even proved to correspond closely to information from studies of glacial movements in other parts of the world (Röthlisberger 1986) (fig. 12). The results of these investigations do not, however, quite agree with those of earlier studies dealing with the Alps, particularly those employing botanical samples (Frenzel 1977; Eckstein, Wrobel, and Aniol 1983). Such contradictions are in fact often encountered, particularly when the measures differ (precipitation, for instance, contrasting with summer temperature). Climatic data must therefore be used with extreme caution. Nevertheless, even information from the remote Crimea may correspond with the results just reported. Studies on the thickness of deposits in Lake Saki have provided an index of differences in amount of precipitation over a very long period (Lamb 1977). Several phases with abundant precipitation seem to correspond to the above-mentioned increases in sea level, but the link is incomplete.

Modern climatic research operates to a great extent with models, and this leads to knowledge of associations and trends unknown to earlier work. We can therefore expect revisions of current information on the historical development of climate. The relationship between temperature changes and precipitation has, for instance, proved to be very complex and often surprising. According to recent studies, an increase in temperature produces an immediate increase in precipitation in the dry, sensitive eastern Mediterranean but a decrease in the central and western Mediterranean (Wigley, Jones, and Kelly 1980). Whether this tendency is sustained over long periods of time remains to be demonstrated, but it may be significant for economic growth in the eastern Mediterranean in the mid-first millennium.

Other climatic models integrate the scattered data of often limited studies into a common framework. One of these models, depicting the historical development of global temperature as a series of sine curves, is of special interest (B. Denness, personal communication; cf. Burns and Denness 1985) (fig. 13). It includes a very sharp increase in global temperature in the last half of the first millennium BC, with first peak around the birth of Christ, another at just before AD 500, and a third around AD 1000. In spite of the surprising – and perhaps hardly credible – jump in average temperature of at least two degrees Centigrade in the last part of the first millennium BC, this picture corresponds fairly well to the observations discussed above. The transgression phases again appear as periods of warmth, and there is good agreement too with the recent results from the Alps, although the glaciers may respond belatedly to warming trends. Only time will tell whether this model can withstand the incorporation of further data and various chronological corrections, but the results so far are exciting.

With this latest knowledge of climatic conditions, we can consider briefly some possible links between climatic and agrarian systems. It must be emphasized that we are dealing with hypotheses that require more development than can be given here. We have seen that the eastern Mediterranean seems to enjoy increased precipitation at times of increased temperature. It is, of course, doubtful whether this relationship applies under all circumstances, but the consequences seem to be that Early Classical Greece and the Eastern Roman and Early Islamic realms came into being in periods of plentiful precipitation. North of the Alps, where precipitation is generally abundant, the temperature increases would have been of benefit to agriculture. In north-western Europe, for example, there were expansion phases in the pre-Roman period, the Late Roman period, and the tenth century, all periods showing temperature increases. Such periods of warmth may, however, also have had negative effects, particularly in areas of low precipitation, where higher temperatures are associated with drought. Among these regions are south-eastern Russia and adjacent parts of Central

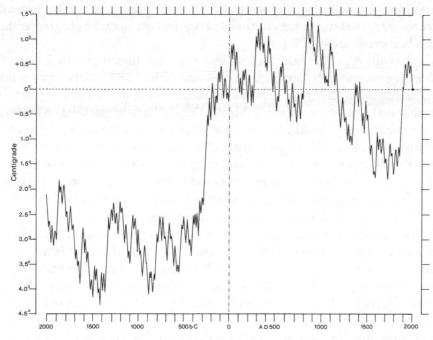

Fig. 13. World temperature changes (data by courtesy of B. Denness)

Asia, where, in the warm Late Roman period, there are signs of general unrest, warlike raiding, and migrations which, via the penetration of the Visigoths and later the Huns into the empire, had profound and lasting influence on military, political, and economic developments in Late Antiquity.

Agriculture and erosion

Agriculture, especially in its intensive form, often has a very strong effect on physical conditions. The felling of forest cover, particularly in relatively arid regions, reduces moisture levels and triggers erosion. Cultivation of the land can have the same effect on the soil, especially when terracing is not carefully maintained, and so can livestock breeding, particularly where numbers of animals are excessive. It is obvious that an increase in rainfall and the flooding associated with erosion will increase the extent of soil movement, which in turn leads to new flooding. It is therefore no surprise that attempts have been made to find climatic causes for the extreme erosion observable in the Mediterranean basin throughout the greater part of the first millennium (Vita-Finzi 1969; cf. Bintliff and van Zeist 1982; van Andel, Runnels, and Pope 1986; van Andel and Runnels 1987). More detailed study makes it appear probable, however, that the main cause was agriculture, with its typical alternation of expansion and decline.

In the Mediterranean, where political and social history is highly dramatic, fluctuations in the level of agricultural activity are correspondingly greater than in the barbarian areas of Europe.

North of the Alps, the study of fossilized wood has meant great advances for archaeological research (Eckstein, Wrobel, and Aniol 1983). In this connection, the tree trunks found in river deposits constitute a well-dated and very valuable contribution to the history of agriculture in Central Europe (Becker 1981, 1982). For the areas along the Rhine, the Upper Danube, and the Main, the years of germination and death of these trees reflect periods of less and more intense cultivation, respectively. The trees ended up in the rivers because of flooding, probably due to soil movement resulting from intense cultivation. In periods of little agricultural activity along these rivers, which run through soils of the highest quality, new forests germinated along their banks.

On the Danube, for instance, the emergence of new forest distinguished the last centuries BC (fig. 14). This growth had ceased by around the birth of Christ at the latest, and new growth did not appear until the fourth century. The Early Roman period and the beginning of the third century, a time in which the Roman frontier provinces were being established and consolidated, saw a large number of tree deaths. A second concentration of deaths lies around AD 600, the Merovingian period, here marking agricultural expansion. In the Main area, outside the empire, we find the same periods of forest germination and death as on the Danube, which implies that the two agrarian systems – the Roman and post-Roman in the frontier provinces and the Germanic in the regions near the Limes – were interconnected. Near the Main the chief Merovingian expansion phase seems, however, to have been a good century later than on the Danube. The Rhine data are fewer but correspond to those from the Danube. River-deposited tree trunks are, moreover, extremely rare after the Merovingian period. The fifth century, which in general is marked by a major reorganization of settlement, growth of new forests, etc., in the old Roman frontier provinces, thus constitutes the last time that forest cover was common along the great river systems of Central Europe.

Cultivated plants

The main species of plants cultivated in Europe and the Mediterranean were largely the same throughout the millennium, with the exception of some important introductions from the Islamic Near East, where there was also a considerable development of irrigation systems (Watson 1983; Garbrecht 1984; Flon 1985). The primary variations lie in the occurrence of, for instance, different grain types at different times and in different places. Differences in emphasis on forest, meadow, and field are apparent in pollen diagrams and also to some extent in livestock numbers (see, e.g., Gringmuth-Dallmer 1972).

The archaeological study of plant cultivation takes as its point of departure the

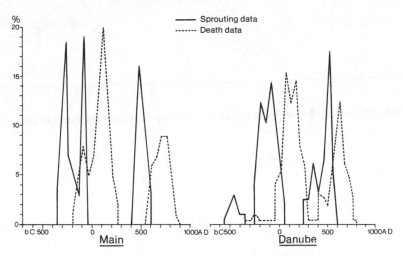

Fig. 14. Germination and death of river-found trees from the Upper Main
and the Upper Danube (*Source*: Becker 1982)

remains of plants and plant impressions in other materials (e.g., Randsborg 1985). These often carbonized botanical remains have, however, frequently been overlooked in excavations, particularly the earlier ones. Until very recently, especially in the Mediterranean area, ecological perspectives have been entirely subservient to cultural ones. One reason for this has undoubtedly been that written sources sometimes give information on plant species, etc., but do not help us to build up a systematic picture of the various areas over time or of production and consumption. In many regions knowledge is still so sketchy that we can ascertain only that conditions did not differ radically from what can be expected on the basis of retrospective conclusions, analogies, or information found in pictorial or written sources.

It is for temperate Europe that we have the most comprehensive material (see Randsborg 1985; cf. Lange 1971). For Central Europe around AD 0–500, settlements in the Roman Rhine–Danube provinces clearly show a higher percentage of rye, which requires thorough soil preparation and, normally, heavy ploughs, than the Germanic settlements across the frontier. The same applies to other sites in non-Roman Central Europe, for example, in Poland. Wheat was the most common species of grain everywhere except in cool north-central Europe, where barley was the dominant grain. Smaller but still signifi-cant quantities of other grains, such as oats and millet, were cultivated. During the period AD 500–1000 the dominance of wheat in Central Europe diminished somewhat in relation to the now generally common rye. Some millet and barley were still cultivated. These observations reflect in part the different habits of cultivation and consumption of Roman and barbarian populations and in part a general trend towards a more central role for the 'bread-grain' species, particu-larly rye. This was accompanied by an important change in cultivation practices

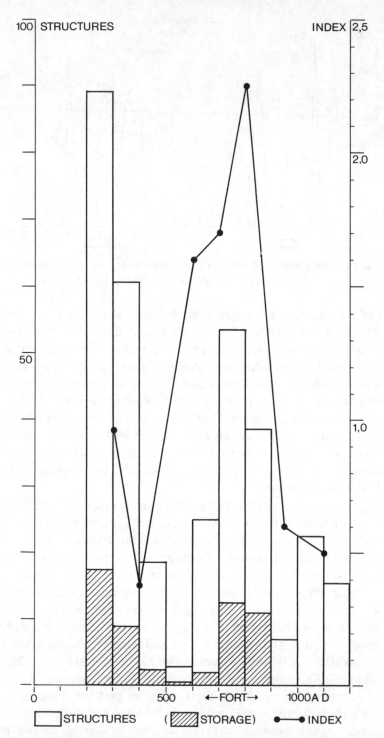

Fig. 15. Changing numbers of structures and fluctuations in the ratio of pollen reflecting cereal cultivation to that reflecting cattle raising (a high index value implies stress on cultivation). Again, as in fig. 11., the life-span of the fortress component of the site is indicated (*Source*: Herrmann 1973)

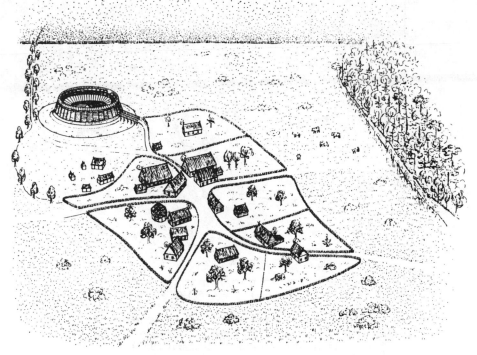

Fig. 16. Reconstruction of the Slavic settlement of Tornow around AD
700 (after Herrmann 1985)

along an axis running basically south–north. In Scandinavia these changes first
occurred at the end of the first millennium, at the same time as settlements
became stabilized in the landscape.

In a very few localities the development of both the physical setting and
agriculture, including plant cultivation, can be followed for a relatively long
period. At Tornow (Herrmann 1973, 1985) (fig. 15), the ordinary Germanic
settlement of the Late Roman period was replaced in the sixth century by a Slavic
settlement that eventually included a small fortress (dating from the seventh to
the ninth centuries). This settlement (fig. 16) came to an end in about AD 1200,
when the present village of Tornow was established. Pollen from plants that are
indicators of cultivation is twice as common in the Germanic as in the Slavic
period, when forest cover must have been more extensive. The pollen from this
early period reveals almost exclusively plants typical of commons, pastures, and
meadows, reflecting widespread cattle raising. In the Slavic period, by contrast,
the pollen of arable plants amounted to as much as 50 per cent of the cultivation-
indicators; the highest percentages of grain are from the earliest periods. It is,
incidentally, characteristic that rye was first introduced to Tornow by the Slavs.
A number of storehouses show, however, that grain was also valued by the

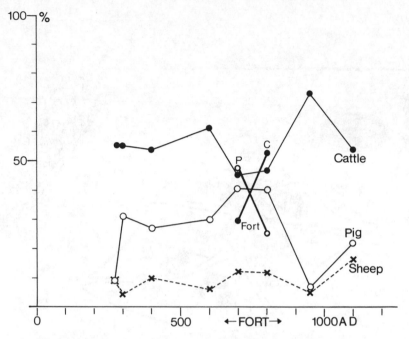

Fig. 17. Changing percentages of cattle, pig, and sheep/goat bone
fragments at Tornow, showing the different percentages for the village
and the fortress (*Source*: Herrmann 1973)

Germanic settlers. Cattle were dominant among livestock, with pigs taking
second place and sheep third (fig. 17). Pigs were most common in phases with
fewer cattle and more widespread cultivation of grain.

In northern England, pollen samples dated to the Roman period show a greater
abundance of pollen from plants typical of commons north of Hadrian's Wall (the
permanent northern frontier of the empire) than south of it (Clack 1982). In
contrast, samples taken from areas within the empire reveal a far greater
abundance of pollen from grain and other plants reflecting arable farming. Here
there are obviously two different systems of agriculture: one related to the
production of foodstuffs for the Roman frontier troops and perhaps also for sale on
the general market, the other emphasizing cattle raising and more like the system
in Free Germany. Tribal peoples with such a subsistence economy might be
imagined to have colonized new areas with relative ease if and when the
opportunity arose.

Domestic animals

Animal bones, generally the remains of butchering and of meals, found on
archaeological sites are among the most important materials for the reconstruction of farming and its natural conditions, the distribution of livestock products,

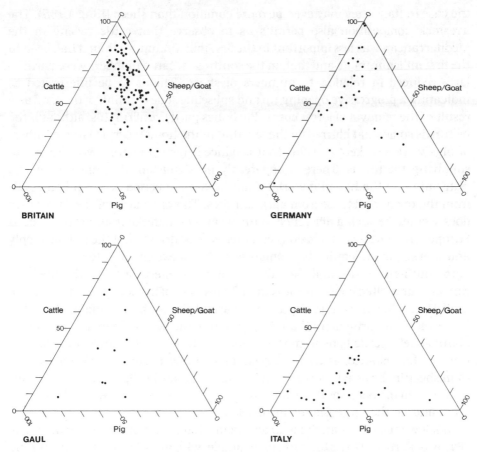

Fig. 18. Percentages of cattle, pig, and sheep/goat bone fragments from
Roman sites in Britain, (Roman) Germany, Gaul, and Italy (*Source*: King
1985)

etc. (Randsborg 1980, 1985). Bone material is examined with a view to calculat-
ing the representation of the various species of animals, the age of the animal at
slaughter, the characteristics of the breed, etc. In the majority of cases, however,
only the numbers of fragments of individual species are reported, and we have to
make do with this information in dealing with a large and representative study
area (appendix 2). This is particularly true in the Mediterranean, where in many
cases animal bones are the only ecologically relevant archaeological material
available.

The knowledge of physical conditions provided by the study of numbers of
bone fragments of different species is relatively simple and normally limited but
none the less important. In the Mediterranean area, for instance, cattle, which
require reasonably good grazing, are rare in the first millennium in the dry
eastern and southern regions, where sheep predominate (fig. 18). Pigs, which
thrive in forested areas, are found mainly in the north and west, where, as is often

the case in Italy, they may even be more common than sheep (King 1985). The livestock composition also permits us to observe that cattle raising in the Mediterranean was less important in the first millennium AD than it had been in the first millennium BC and that, in the south-east, cattle numbers were particularly reduced in relation to numbers of sheep. This is to be interpreted as indicating a progressive opening up and subsequent desiccation of the land as a result of the removal of forest cover. Pig bones partly confirm this, although the picture is somewhat blurred by the fact that in the Roman period large numbers of pigs were also kept in villas that produced them primarily with a view to supplying the towns. There is apparently no significant difference in species distribution in the Italian material from the Roman period between bone finds from the towns and those from agrarian sites. This is remarkable because there does seem to be such a difference in the wealth of material from north-western Europe. The cautious conclusions can therefore be drawn that the Italian supply and marketing system in the Roman period was extremely extensive.

In southern France and the adjacent north-western areas of the Mediterranean, cattle often contribute less than 25 per cent of the bone material on a site (Luff 1982). In contrast, in Central and Eastern Europe and Scandinavia, cattle bones often comprise more than 50 per cent of the bones. There is a particular abundance of cattle bone from the regions north of the Roman Rhine–Danube frontier, for instance, as we have seen, at Tornow. There were also more pigs than sheep in the heavily forested regions of temperate Europe. Exceptions occur, however, in the open south-eastern North Sea coastlands, in the Middle Danube area, and on the large islands in the Baltic.

In a few areas the material is so abundant that trends of development can be clearly discerned. This is the case, for example, with agrarian sites in the Bolzano region of northern Italy (Riedel 1986). The number of cattle bones is high in the first millennium BC and the later first millennium AD and low in Roman times, when pigs are particularly common. Sheep bones are more numerous than those of pigs and usually also than those of cattle. In the region of Venice cattle are common and sheep much rarer than in the southern Alps; in the early medieval centre of Torcello, a small island in the lagoon, which is not a natural environment for pigs, the bones of pigs are so common that they probably represent a choice imported meat.

The material from southern Britain is particularly rich, and some sites even show evidence of several phases (King 1978, 1984; Luff 1982; cf. Cunliffe 1983) (fig. 19). Here sheep were very common in the late pre-Roman Iron Age, when they were often the most frequent of domestic species. During the Roman period there were drastic changes in livestock raising, sheep numbers being much reduced in favour of cattle. This tendency altered again in the last centuries of the millennium, when sheep were once again at least as common as cattle. The tendency towards increasing numbers of cattle in the Late Roman period is thus the opposite of developments in the Mediterranean, where cattle numbers were if

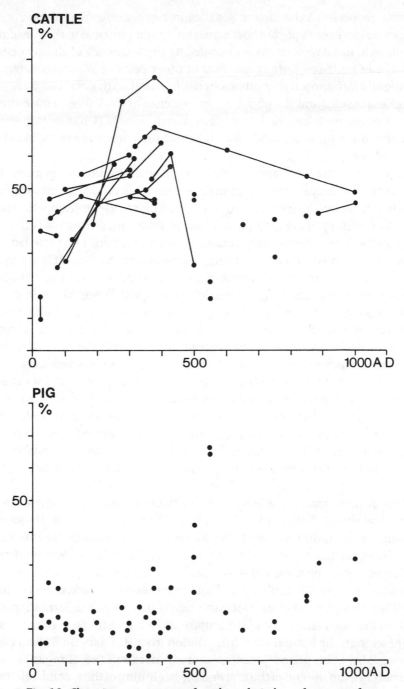

Fig. 19. Changing percentages of cattle and pig bone fragments from Roman and later sites of the first millennium in southern England. The sheep/goat pattern is basically the reverse of that for cattle. Lines connect different phases of the same settlement (*Sources*: King 1978; Rahtz 1979; and others)

anything reduced. In the fifth to sixth centuries there was, moreover, a very remarkable increase in pig numbers, but these soon returned to their traditional third place in these regions. As is indicated by the frequency of sheep bones, the landscape of southern Britain, like that of other parts of Western Europe, was traditionally rather open. Conditions in the fifth and sixth centuries were therefore quite unusual, and the pigs must be evidence of thick forest cover after the abrupt Roman withdrawal. The growth of new forests is something we have noted above in connection with the Rhine–Danube provinces of the same post-Roman phase.

The abundant material from the Roman period in Britain makes it possible to examine the distribution and consumption of livestock products, primarily meat. There is a tendency in the Early Roman period for non-agrarian sites such as towns and military encampments to show a higher percentage of cattle bones than agrarian sites, where sheep bones are more common. The same tendency, only weaker, is noted with respect to pigs. These observations must be interpreted as an expression of the special needs of the towns and forts for supplies of meat derived mainly from the large domestic animals (cattle and pigs). In the Late Roman period the difference between town and country vanishes: with reference to the earlier remarks about Italy, this may mean that marketing systems improve in this phase of important reorganization, with the result that towns now show a more representative selection of the province's products.

Roman towns in the Netherlands also show a higher percentage of cattle and pig bones than agrarian sites, where the bones of sheep and horses are common (Randsborg 1985). This phenomenon appears again in the early Middle Ages, when the famous Carolingian emporium at Dorestad shows a far higher percentage of the bones of large meat animals – here primarily pigs, perhaps also imported from settlements along the Rhine – than the contemporary agrarian sites.

In Hungary the material is less abundant than in Britain, and only a few sites have several phases (Bökönyi 1974; cf. 1984). Here, as in Britain and in southern Germany, cattle raising appears to become more widespread in the Late Roman period, again at the expense of sheep. However, there is no clear evidence of agrarian sites yielding fewer cattle and pig bones than non-agrarian ones. If this observation is correct, it could mean that the Pannonian marketing system, like the Italian, was very effective. Not surprisingly, the so-called Sarmatian settlements on the open lands east of the empire show a greater percentage of sheep and horses than the Roman sites. Information from Hungary on livestock in the following 'Migration period' is scarce, and it is not until the 'Hungarian' settlements dating from the end of the first and the beginning of the second millennium that we again find a reasonable amount of material, which incidentally has a distribution among the different main livestock categories reminiscent of the Roman period and shows the same increase in pig numbers as has been noted in several cases as accompanying the farming of the early Middle Ages.

Finally, if south-eastern Europe is considered as a whole, the inclusion of material from Rumania and Bulgaria gives a slightly more complete picture of the last centuries of the first millennium (Henning 1987:102–3). One of the most interesting things to be noted here is a supposed difference between sites with predecessors in Antiquity and newly established ones. The former show very large numbers of cattle, thus continuing the tendency noted in the Late Roman period. The new sites show fewer but still considerable numbers of cattle, perhaps somewhat larger numbers of sheep, and far greater numbers of pigs. Here again we see the tendency towards increasing pig numbers noted on other sites in the last part of the first millennium.

4

RURAL SETTLEMENT

It may seem impossible to discuss settlement in Europe and the Mediterranean throughout the whole of the first millennium without limiting oneself to commonplaces. Admittedly, much information will have to be ignored but I hope to be able to present a coherent account by emphasizing a few main features that tie the material, or large parts of it, together. Agrarian sites (fig. 20) are the focus of our investigation, but in the first millennium we cannot employ the sharp distinction of later scholarship between rural and urban areas or between, for instance, monastery and fortress. In non-Roman Europe at that time, fortresses were closely associated with the agricultural system, although, of course, they had other functions as well. Correspondingly, the town and its lands constituted a unit. The classification of settlements is ultimately determined by social relations and the organization of work and the economy. Towns are dealt with in the following chapter, as they were often the object of investment by the élite and may therefore contain buildings and monuments that require special treatment. Moreover, considerable craft production, trading in foodstuffs, etc., were associated with urban milieux of this nature. Another reason for postponing the discussion of towns – perhaps rather less valid in this particular connection – is the special function of the centres as market-places, whether for goods produced locally or for exchange on an international level – also a sector much favoured by the élite. Having said this, I should add that throughout the first millennium much exchange took place outside the towns.

As we shall be discussing settlement development over long periods in individual areas, there is less need to take a strictly chronological approach. The dependence of settlement on local social development also supports the idea of taking a more regional line. Apparently arguing against this approach is the existence of the Roman Empire and thus the introduction of foreign cultural and social standards to many areas. Even in this context, however, it is useful to emphasize the local perspective, as physical conditions and resources, methods of

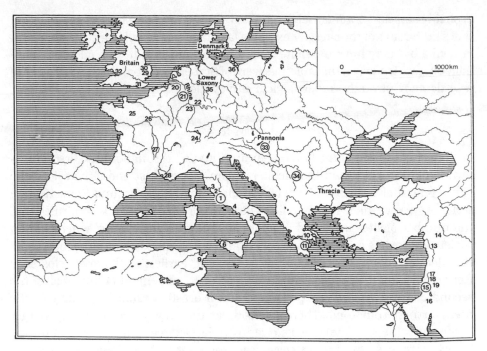

Fig. 20. Regional samples of rural settlement sites. A ring around the
number denotes several surveys (cf. appendix 3)

production, techniques, etc., did not immediately change or, sometimes, change
at all when the Romans conquered a region.

In examining the development of settlement in an area, we confront a number
of archaeological problems, chiefly rooted in the very different visibility of the
material from one area and/or time period to another. Roman villas, for instance,
leave far more material visible on the surface than Danish Iron Age villages,
where all the buildings were of timber and the pottery was more susceptible to
destruction than the harder-fired Mediterranean products. A further problem
may lie in the geological circumstances. The heavy humus layers that develop in
temperate zones make survey work difficult. In the Mediterranean conditions are
generally better, particularly in the arid regions, but here pronounced erosion
may give rise to problems. Finally, both the extent of exploration and research
traditions differ from area to area, making comparisons difficult.

Among other, more technical difficulties is the unequal length of the study
periods. If nothing is said to the contrary, this problem is dealt with by dividing
the number of settlements by the length of the period in question. This device
accentuates another general difficulty, however, namely, that the various settlements do not all persist throughout the period in question. A phase or an area
with very shifting settlement will therefore, from an archaeological viewpoint,

probably appear more densely inhabited than it was. A similar complication
hides in the sizes of the sites; for example, a village is normally larger than a farm
or a villa but may have the same weight in the statistics. It is, in addition, often
difficult, particularly if the buildings were of timber, to recognize the character of
a settlement through archaeological survey alone.

Roman Italy

Both in the last half of the first millennium BC and throughout the first millennium AD, our interest in the Mediterranean focuses first and foremost on the
development of settlement in Italy, especially the region around Rome. Here a
series of surveys made less than fifty kilometres from the city has confirmed that
the number of sites increased dramatically after about 200 BC, when Roman
society entered its most dynamic expansion phase, aimed at absolute mastery of
the Mediterranean. The increase in settlement, earliest in the areas closest to
Rome, was about 300 per cent. The increase in settlement culminated in the
second century AD, whereupon there was a drastic decline, especially in the
areas farthest from Rome. There is considerable survey material relating to Ager
Veientanus (near Rome), Ager Eretanus (relatively close to Rome and on the
Tiber, with easy access to river transport), and Ager Faliscus (north of
Veientanus) (Potter 1979). The expansion and decline in the three areas appear
in table 1. (With respect to the phases of decline, the Ager Faliscus material has
been fine-dated and there is therefore relatively less of it in relation to both its
earlier phases and to the other two areas.) The decline in the Late Roman period is
dramatic but not necessarily unrealistic. There may be ground for some caution,
though, particularly when dealing with Late Antiquity, in that many structures
were then made of timber and therefore difficult to recognize through surveys.
Moreover, the chronology of the local pottery types, especially around the middle
(and the end) of the first millennium, has been revised since the appearance of the
survey data cited.

The majority of the Early Roman sites are villas of various sizes and individual
farms. In the area around Rome, the percentage of large villas increases the closer
one gets to the city. In Ager Veientanus eighty-six large villas and 230 small
villas and individual farms are recorded from 'the second century AD'. Of the
large villas, forty-nine were still inhabited in 'the fourth century AD', whereas
only forty-three of the smaller complexes remained in use. About seventeen large
villas and twenty-eight smaller complexes are recorded in Late Antiquity, the
fifth and sixth centuries – largely the same relationship between the two groups
as in the preceding phase. In Ager Veientanus there was apparently a tendency in
the later periods towards fewer but relatively large agrarian units. A recent study
of Ager Veientanus aimed at elucidating the size of the sites has revealed that
large, medium-sized, and small 'villas' comprised c. 20, 40, and 40 per cent of the
material from the time of the Late Republic to the beginning of the fourth century

Table 1. *Settlement numbers in three areas near Rome,*
500 BC–AD 625

Time period	Ager Veientanus	Ager Eretanus	Ager Faliscus
500–300 BC	64 (127)	? (?)	52 (104)
300–30 BC	90 (242)	20 (53)	53 (142)
30 BC–AD 100	252 (327)	44 (57)	159 (207)
AD 80–320	128 (307)	20 (47)	—
AD 320–450	92 (92)	20 (20)	—
AD 450–625	26 (46)	4 (7)	—

Source: Potter 1979
Note: Numbers calibrated for hundred-year periods; absolute numbers in brackets.
For Ager Faliscus, the absolute numbers are, for AD 100–200, 95; for AD 200–300,
67; for AD 300–400, 31; for AD 400–600, 22

(Dyson 1978). By about AD 400 the ratios were *c.* 35, 40, and 25 per cent, and around the beginning of the sixth century they were 45, 40, and 15 per cent. This grouping also shows that in Ager Veientanus large complexes became more dominant with time.

A survey was also made some distance north of Rome, at ancient Cosa (Dyson 1978). Archaeologically, the area is known in recent times for the excavations of the large villa at Settefinestre, dating from the Early Roman period (Carandini 1985). The survey yielded twenty-five sites per century (a total of sixty-eight) for the period *c.* 300–30 BC, thirty-nine (fifty-one) for the period 30 BC–AD 100 and thirteen (thirty-eight, of which eventually only five survived) for the period AD 100–400. Cosa thus clearly fell into decline earlier than the areas close to Rome. The same result is demonstrated by a survey around Scarlino, still farther north than Cosa (Francovich 1985a). At Cosa, an old veterans' colony, it is furthermore characteristic to find many small farmsteads in the Late Republic.

Whereas it appears that north of Rome villa settlement, at least, showed signs of decline earlier than in the area around Rome, the opposite is the case in southern Italy. In the Liri Valley, north of Naples, smaller sites in particular were common in the Late Roman period, just as they were in the Late Republic (Wightman 1981). Farther south, at Potenza, is San Giovanni, an important complex from the late fifth century, that marks an obvious break architecturally (there is, for instance, a hall with an apse) and in the style of the floor mosaics with the 'villas' of the earlier centuries (Gualtieri, Salvatore, and Small 1983). A general survey around this site gave rise to a number of problems of method but indicated in any case that there was a dense settlement here in the second century that was still vigorous around AD 400 (Small 1985). This tendency is more obvious in Sicily. A survey (albeit relatively modest in scope) made around Monreale, near Palermo, shows no particular signs of regression throughout the period AD 0–600, but both the first centuries after the Roman conquest of Sicily (*c.* 200–0 BC) and the Early Byzantine period (*c.* AD 600–800) were apparently

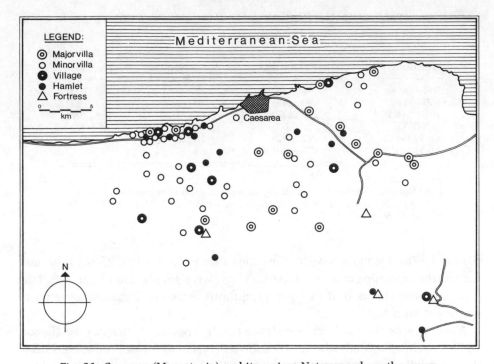

Fig. 21. Caesarea (Mauretania) and its region. Not mapped are the many
very small sites, mainly to the south-west, and villas and villages that
have not been classified according to size. The areas immediately around
Caesarea and the major villas (1,700 square metres or more in size) have
revealed traces of irrigation; olive cultivation was apparently concentrated
in the interior, not uncommonly in villages (one hectare or more in size)
(*Source*: Leveau 1984)

times of crisis (Johns 1985). The Islamic subjugation of the island in the ninth
century involved not the decline that might have been expected but an agrarian
expansion in which settlements doubled in number.

Although our information is modest in amount and none too reliable, it seems
to show that the Italian mainland and Sicily followed dissimilar paths. Settlement
expansion began in central Italy during the Late Republic, while southern Italy
and Sicily had to wait until the Early Empire for such development. Settlement in
central Italy showed signs of regression around AD 200 at the latest, while in
southern Italy and especially in Sicily there was considerable settlement in both
the Late Empire and Late Antiquity.

The Mediterranean in the Roman period

A survey made around ancient Caesarea (Mauretania) on the coast of present-
day Algeria indicates that Roman settlement was widespread in the second to
third century, when it reached its zenith (Leveau 1984; cf. Fentress 1984) (fig.
21). Some reduction occurred from the third century to the Islamic conquest, but

Table 2. *Settlement numbers in Boeotia, 850 BC–AD 1600*

Time period	Number of settlements	
Geometric (850–650 BC)	3	(6)
Archaic (650–480 BC)	14	(23)
Classical (480–330 BC)	68	(101)
Early Hellenistic (330–200 BC)	68	(89)
Late Hellenistic (200–30 BC)	23	(39)
Early Roman (30 BC–AD 250)	23	(55)
Late Roman (AD 250–600)	17	(59)
Early Byzantine (AD 600–900)	0	(1)
Middle Byzantine (AD 900–1200)	4	(13)
Late Byzantine/Frankish (AD 1200–1460)	15	(38)
Early Turkish (AD 1460–1600)	22	(32)

Source: Bintliff and Snodgrass 1985
Note: Numbers calibrated for hundred-year periods; absolute numbers in brackets

this was gradual and without the dramatic changes noted, for instance, in the vicinity of Rome. Incidentally, a survey made around Barcelona shows the same trends (Prevosti i Monclús 1981). The Caesarea investigation clearly demonstrates the range of variation of Roman settlement: a town, villas, a few fortresses, large and small villages, and many small compounds. There is about an equal number of major (more than 1,700 square metres), medium-sized (more than 700 square metres), and minor villas or farmsteads.

East of Caesarea, in fertile 'Africa', the Roman expansion seems to have begun in the Early Empire and continued steadily, perhaps with a temporary standstill in the fourth century, right up to Late Antiquity, when it probably reached its climax (Green in Keller and Rupp 1983; for Segermes, see Ørsted 1984 (E. Poulsen) and Lund and Sørensen 1987). It is also possible that there was roughly the same distribution of large and small properties here throughout the period, but the material on this is still rather unreliable. Thus in 'Africa' a picture emerges that is the opposite of that in Caesarea and shows that this area was an economic centre of gravity for the Mediterranean world. Sicily and, to some extent, southern Italy should certainly be viewed from this regional perspective.

A detailed and methodologically interesting survey made in ancient Boeotia reveals a very large number of settlements in the Classical Greek and Early Hellenistic periods (Bintliff and Snodgrass 1985). The large number of settlements is reached very suddenly and then followed by just as sudden a decrease (table 2), as in the Rome region five hundred years later. These results are obviously open to discussion, but very widespread settlement in Classical times has also been found in several other Greek surveys (e.g., Foley 1988 for Argolis). From the methodological viewpoint it is, moreover, of interest that – judging from the absolute number of sites – the 'Late Roman' period (in the Boeotian survey AD 250–600) saw the culmination of an expansion that according to the surveys began in Late Hellenistic times. Using calibrated numbers, the same period, however, constituted the beginning, although not so pronounced, of the

Table 3. *Settlement numbers by size in*
Argolis, 950 BC–AD 1537

Time period	Number of settlements		
	Large	Medium	Small
950 BC–AD 250	8 (6%)	26 (18%)	109 (76%)
AD 250–600	9 (17%)	12 (23%)	31 (60%)
AD 850–1537	6 (15%)	7 (18%)	27 (68%)

Source: van Andel and Runnels 1987

collapse in settlement that is recorded for Early Byzantine times. As a parallel to this it can be noted that the 'Dionysus' villa on Crete saw a reduction in activity from Early to Late Roman times and came to an end around AD 400 (Hayes 1983). The Late Roman phase in Greece was not, as in Italy, marked by dramatic regression: if anything, there is a parallel with the Sicilian situation. In Boeotia, too, expansion can be traced at the end of the first millennium.

Another Greek survey, from southern Argolis (carried out parallel to important geological studies, some on erosion phenomena), has yielded information on changing settlement sizes through time (van Andel and Runnels 1987). From Geometric to 'Early Roman' times (here ending *c.* AD 250), small settlements comprise about three-quarters of the total; thereafter small producers seem to have lost ground (table 3). The shifts in the figures may not appear large, but as a 'large' (or even a 'medium') settlement possesses far greater potential than a 'small' one there is a strong tendency towards concentrating the agrarian potential in larger units in Late Roman (here AD 250–600) and even in Middle Byzantine/Frankish (AD 850–1537) times. The same tendency towards larger units in periods of settlement decline occurred, as we have seen, at Ager Veientanus. Characteristically, in the medieval period of expansion in Greece there is an increase in the percentage of smaller properties.

There are no Anatolian data at present that correspond in quality and detail to those of the Boeotian investigation, but a survey made near Paphos on Cyprus provides some information on the situation in the eastern Mediterranean (Rupp et al. 1984, 1986). As early as the Late Geometric phase (ninth to eighth century BC) there was a dramatic expansion of settlement here, but this was soon followed by a marked decline in Archaic and again in Classical times – certainly yet another example of the 'Rome effect' seen in Boeotia. At Paphos there was already in the Hellenistic period a very marked increase in the number of settlements. The Roman period saw at first a slight and then a quite considerable decline, in spite of the fact that Paphos was capital of the province. In Late Antiquity there was recovery and even expansion, but this lasted only a relatively short time. Virtually no sites are recorded between *c.* AD 700 and 1100. The countryside seems to have been just as thinly populated as it had been two thousand years earlier. A new, very vigorous expansion occurred around AD

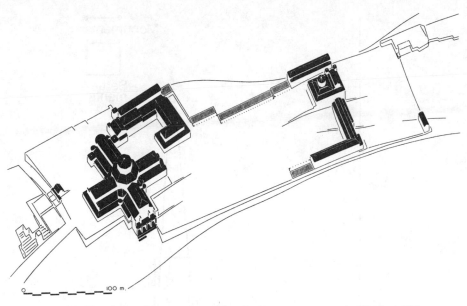

Fig. 22. The Qal'at Si'man, erected by the Roman emperor in the late fifth century around the pillar of the hermit (*inside the octagon*). The stage of the complex illustrated is from the early sixth century (after Tchalenko 1953–58)

1200, contemporary with the establishment of the Crusader kingdom of Cyprus, but this episode was swiftly followed by a decline that has continued to the present. Thus in the Paphos area there are large, perhaps unusually large, fluctuations in the amount of agrarian settlement from period to period. With respect to property size it seems, in contrast to southern Argolis, that there was a steady but slight increase in the number of small properties from the Hellenistic period to recent times, but it should be noted that the material is limited.

The Near East

The Levant has been the object of a considerable number of surveys. Arid regions (in which little humus is created) that have many remains of stone buildings from the past are virtually ideal for regional studies of this kind. Indeed, 'surveys' were made in these areas long before this concept became accepted in archaeological research, with its modern interest in settlement studies and ecology. Such a classic study was, for instance, carried out in the mountainous regions east of ancient Antioch in northern Syria (Tchalenko 1953–58). Particularly in Late Antiquity, this area was marked by very vigorous expansion, the economic basis of which was the intensive cultivation of olives for export. It is renowned for its churches and monasteries, for example the impressive Qal'at Si'man, built around the pillar of Saint Simeon Stylites (d. AD 459) and established by the Eastern Roman emperor himself during the very time span in which the Western Roman Empire collapsed (fig. 22). The number of dated settlements in the area is

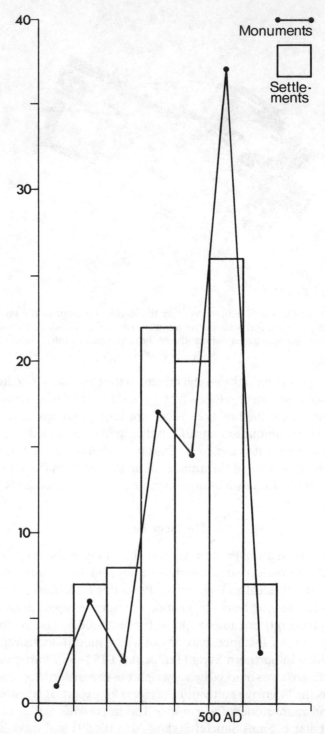

Fig. 23. Frequencies of Roman and Late Antique settlements and
monuments from the Bélus region, east of Antioch in northern Syria
(*Source*: Tchalenko 1953–58)

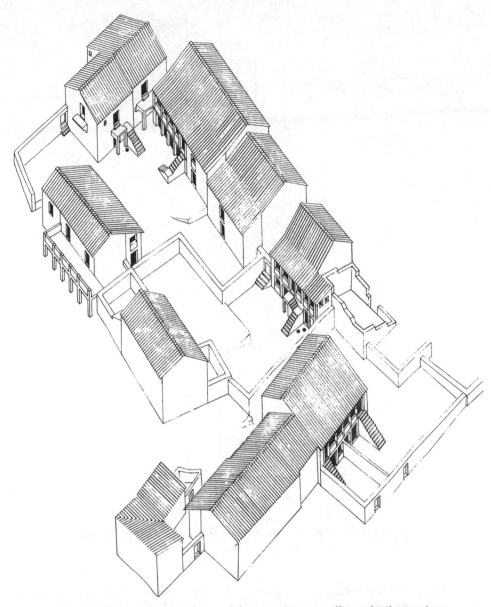

Fig. 24. Reconstruction of part of the Late Antique village of Déhès in the
Bélus region (after Sodini et al. 1980)

modest for the first two centuries (fig. 23), but there is a sharp increase in the
fourth and a peak in the sixth, accompanied by such widespread construction of
monumental edifices that the economic system must have been hard-pressed to
support it (fig. 24). In the seventh century the majority of settlements collapsed
and the area became, as it is today, thinly populated. Apart from the monasteries,
which must be considered landed estates as well as religious institutions, the
general trend in the area seems, as on Cyprus, to be towards smaller holdings.

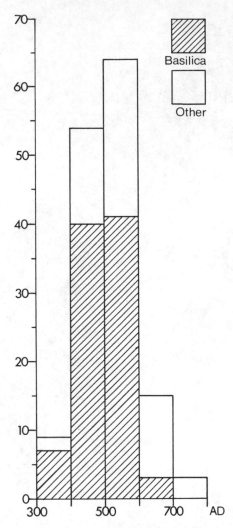

Fig. 25. Late Roman and Late Antique church building in Palestine
(*Source*: Ovadiah 1970)

A survey from the very arid regions of northern Syria near Aleppo suggests considerable settlement in Hellenistic times, followed by a decline in the Early Roman period (Matthers 1981). There are no settlements from the Late Roman period but quite a number from Late Antiquity, around AD 500. The Early Islamic period shows a slight decline, with a recovery at the beginning of the second millennium. On a number of points this survey yields the same results as for the area east of Antioch and the Paphos area of Cyprus. The complete absence of sites dating from Late Roman times might indicate that here, where farming is almost impossible without irrigation, we have an example of the effect of climate (in this case lack of precipitation) on settlement. Other investigations show, as we

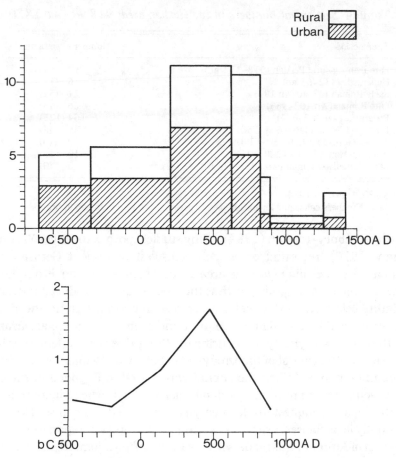

Fig. 26. Changing size of the area of settlement in part of central
Mesopotamia (histograms) (*Source*: Adams 1981) and fluctuating numbers
of settlements in various regions of central Palestine (line) (*Source*:
Patlagean 1977). Figures are calibrated for differing lengths of periods

have seen, that the Hellenistic and the Late Antique to Early Byzantine phases
were wet in the eastern Mediterranean, while the Late Roman phase was
distinctively dry (cf. Sperber 1978).

Other interesting surveys from Israel/Palestine and Jordan also indicate that
climate probably played a role in the development of settlement. It is characteristic of all these surveys that the Hellenistic period is relatively weakly represented and the time around or after AD 500 constitutes the zenith. This is also shown
by the many churches built in Late Antiquity (Ovadiah 1970; Ovadiah and de
Silva 1981, 1982) (fig. 25). Some of the settlement investigations are treated by
Patlagean (1977; cf. Kochavi 1972) with reference to Juda, the Jericho area, the
Jerusalem area and southern Ephraim, and northern Ephraim and part of
Samaria (fig. 26), by Cohen (1981), focusing on the northern Negev (cf. Rosen

Table 4. *Settlement numbers in the Hesbon area, 918 BC–AD 1870*

Time period	Number of settlements	
Late Iron Age and Persian (918–332 BC)	10	(59)
Hellenistic (332–63 BC)	6	(17)
Early Roman (63 BC–AD 193)	21	(54)
Late Roman (AD 193–365)	26	(45)
Byzantine (AD 365–661)	64	(125)
Umayyad (Islamic) (AD 661–750)	36	(32)
Abbasid–Crusader (AD 750–1200)	0	(0)
Abbasid–Mamluk (AD 1200–1456)	19	(49)
Late Mamluk–Ottoman (AD 1456–1870)	0	(0)

Source: LaBianca 1984
Note: Numbers calibrated for hundred-year periods; absolute numbers in brackets

1987), by Hanbury-Tenison (1984), citing studies south of the River Yarmuk, by Mittman (1970), reporting on work north-west of ancient Gerasa, and by LaBianca (1984), dealing with the area around biblical Hesbon. From the point of view of climate it is significant that the Negev survey produced virtually no sites dating before AD 500. It is, however, also important that northern Jordan seems untouched by the Islamic conquest and even shows more agrarian sites under the Umayyad dynasty than during the Byzantine period. Hence it is hardly fortuitous that the capital of the Umayyad caliphs was Damascus, not far from the Jordanian border. When the capital was moved to Baghdad in the eighth century, settlement in northern Jordan underwent a drastic reduction. In other areas the Islamic conquest marks a very pronounced decline in settlement and occasionally its collapse. A survey covering a very long time span from Hesbon, south-west of Amman, was made within a radius of ten kilometres from the town (LaBianca 1984). The results are summarized in table 4.

Information from Mesopotamia confirms the picture in the Levant (fig. 26). Settlement seems to reach its greatest extent under the Sassanids in the mid-first millennium, while the Islamic conquest was accompanied by a slight decline (Adams 1965, 1981). Under the Abbasids Mesopotamia became the catchment area for Baghdad, the capital. The ninth century also saw a number of conspicuous changes, the first being an attempt to establish a gigantic new capital at Samarra (which lies in an area of slightly higher rainfall than Baghdad and north of that city). Samarra was never completed, however, and in the rest of Mesopotamia settlement very rapidly declined. This decline had a pronounced effect on revenue from taxes and was certainly one of the most important factors in the granting to the Islamic provinces of *de facto* independence with respect to the caliphate, at the end of the first millennium. In Mesopotamia matters altered only later in the Middle Ages, when there was a slight increase in settlement, at about the same time as in the Hesbon area of the Levant.

The Susa area in south-western Persia has also been the subject of a survey indicating that the pre-Sassanid or Parthian period (before AD 250) was one of rapid expansion followed by just as dramatic decline (Wenke 1976). Probably this is yet another example of the 'Rome effect', but the area does lie in a climatically sensitive zone, where a temperature increase such as occurred in the Late Roman period and particularly in Late Antiquity does not, as in the Levant, imply an increase in precipitation (Wigley, Jones, and Kelly 1980: fig. 2).

The extent to which the development of early agrarian settlement in the Mediterranean and the Near East correlates with the political and economic situation reported in the written sources is striking. In some cases the archaeological surveys correct or fine-tune the picture, but their most important contribution to the study of history – apart from calling attention to the pronounced dependence of pre-industrial society on agriculture – is in indicating the constant effort of Mediterranean and Near Eastern societies to optimize the exploitation of their resources.

Temperate Western Europe in the Roman period

The Roman expansion, first to the Rhine and then to the Danube, led to profound changes in local societies and thus also in agriculture and settlement. The adaptation to Roman conditions – the so-called Romanization process – occurred more rapidly in the economically central areas than in the more marginal ones. Roman villas are common in Gaul in the first century but not until the second on the Rhine. Production conditions too altered at different rates and to differing degrees. On the site of Rijswijk in the Netherlands, near the northern limit of the empire, the volume of Roman pottery increases steadily through time but only after AD 200 – more than 250 years after Julius Ceasar stood on the banks of the Rhine – surpasses that of the local, hand-made types (Bloemers 1978) (fig. 27). In the nearby Roman forts along the frontier, however, Roman pottery dominates from the time of their establishment.

There are, however, various archaeological problems involved in obtaining a systematic overview of settlement in these distant regions of the Roman Empire. In spite of a long research tradition, particularly in central and north-western Europe, provincial Roman archaeology has only in the last few decades concentrated on general questions of settlement history.

One of the most reliable surveys ever made is Willems's (1986) of the Nijmegen area in the Netherlands; this town was a legionary camp in the Early Roman period. The area is one of the best-known in the world from a geological viewpoint and has been well studied archaeologically. The Nijmegen survey has the further advantage that there are records not only of 'Roman' sites – that is, settlements in which Roman pottery and other objects have been found – but also of 'native' ones, settlements from the first century AD, as yet un-Romanized, that are dated by means of the traditional pottery wares. In addition, there are records covering the Iron Age sites of the area, dating from the centuries before the birth of Christ, and of Frankish sites from the fifth to the beginning of the eighth

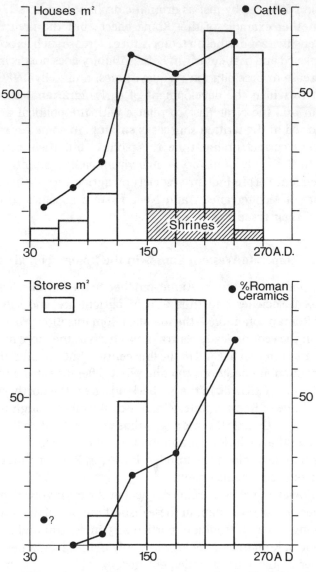

Fig. 27. Changing areas of structures and numbers of byred cattle (top)
and changing areas of stores and percentages of Roman (versus local
hand-made) ceramics (bottom) at Rijswijk (*Source*: Bloemers 1978)

century. Throughout the Iron Age there was a steady increase in the number of
settlements. Around the birth of Christ, and contemporary with the establishment of the first, very large legionary camp, development was explosive. Settlement largely remained at this high level until the last half of the third century,
when there was a dramatic decline. In the fourth and fifth centuries the number
of settlements was only a quarter of what it had been in the Early Roman period.
A new expansion can be noted, however, in the sixth and seventh centuries, the
Merovingian period.

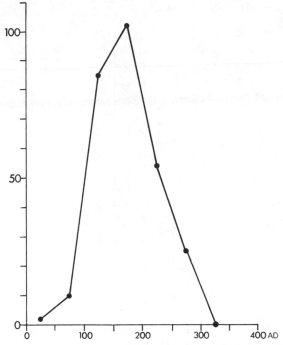

Fig. 28. Changing frequencies of Roman villas east of Mainz (*Source*:
Schell 1964)

In the Cologne area detailed investigations have been made of 'Roman' settlements but not of 'native' ones. This Roman settlement reached its greatest extent in the last half of the second century and at the beginning of the third underwent a reduction that was more dramatic on the poor, more arid soils (Gechter and Kunow 1988). New decline followed at the end of the third century, and around AD 400 settlements of the Roman type vanished altogether – even though the empire retained a certain military presence in the Cologne area for some fifty years longer. The distribution of sites over the main phases, in calibrated figures, is as follows: AD 0–50, 5; 50–100, 61; 100–150, 191; 150–200, 246; 200–275, 124; 275–400, 35; 400–500, 3. The difference between the Nijmegen and the Cologne investigations regarding the period of decline may be due to the fact that the Nijmegen material contains more than twice as many uncertainly dated third-century sites as it does second-century ones. If these are excluded, there is no substantial difference between the two surveys, especially when we recall that the Cologne survey does not include 'native' first-century sites.

From the area round Mainz, also a Roman legionary camp, there is a survey of the agrarian villa sites east of the Rhine, in the northern part of the area between the Upper Rhine and the Upper Danube, which was abandoned in the latter part of the third century (fig. 28). A survey has also been made west of Mainz (fig. 29). In the area east of the Rhine, villa settlement culminated in the middle of the second century, and by the time the area was abandoned settlement had been in

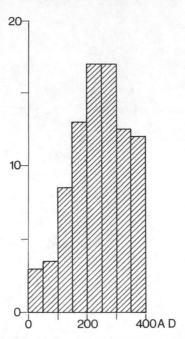

Fig. 29. Changing frequencies of Roman villas west of Mainz (*Source*:
Bayer 1967)

decline for rather more than a hundred years (Schell 1964). In contrast, villa
settlement west of the Rhine seems to have flourished in the relative military and
economic security conferred by the proximity of the legionary camp (Bayer
1967). In any case, the general picture in the Rhine area corresponds fairly well
to the information provided by river-deposited tree-trunks discussed earlier.

In the Alpine valley south of Lake Constance, villa settlements are largely
confined to the second and third centuries: both before and after this period
settlements were generally located on low mountain-tops, a phenomenon very
widespread in Central Europe during the disturbed Late Roman and Late Antiquity periods and often ascribed to military considerations (Overbeck 1982).
Defence was undoubtedly a concern, since many of the sites were fortified, but
these settlements, whether they were complexes built on the Roman model for
individual landowners or whole villages, should be considered mainly as replace-
ments for the villas in the open agrarian landscape. This interpretation gains
support from the finding that such settlements also existed outside the empire, for
example at Urach, south of Stuttgart, in an area abandoned in the last half of the
third century (Milojčíc 1975). Among the examples from the Rhineland are
Wittnauer Horn in Switzerland (Bersu 1945) and a small complex near the
luxurious villa at Echternach, west of Trier, that was incorporated around AD
700 into the monastery founded by Willibrord, the 'apostle of the Frisians' and,
incidentally, first missionary to the Danes (Metzler, Zimmer, and Bakker 1981).

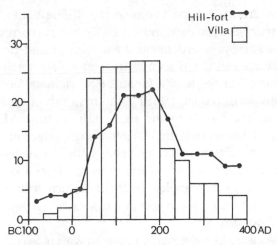

Fig. 30. Changing numbers of Roman villas and hill-top settlements (*oppida*) from the Seguisiavi region, west of Lyons (*Source*: Vallet 1981)

In France, although the volume of material is large, there are few systematic surveys of the development of agrarian settlement. Its extent has recently been confirmed by aerial surveys, for example at Amiens in north-western France (Agache 1975), where the Early Roman landscape appears, as elsewhere in the northern provinces, extremely densely inhabited, with large, indeed often vast villas, small villas, farm complexes, etc. A survey of the Le Mans area, also in north-western France, indicates that the second and third centuries were the great eras of villa settlement, whereas the fourth century saw a clear decline (Lambert and Rioufreyt 1982; cf. Ferdière 1983 for Lion-en-Beauce, near Orléans). In north-eastern France, however, the Late Roman decline may have been less pronounced. A survey of villas from Alsace and Lorraine shows much the same pattern as the area to the west of Mainz mentioned above (Poinsignon 1987). An investigation of an important area in the Upper Loire district, west of Lyons, demonstrates a marked expansion of villa settlement in the first century and a pronounced decline shortly after AD 200 (Vallet 1981) (fig. 30). *Oppida* in the higher-lying areas show similar frequencies except that their decline after AD 200 is less marked and in Late Roman times they are more frequent than villas. In south-eastern France there are also signs of a decline in villa settlement in the Late Roman period (Raynaud 1984).

Villa settlement can also be investigated indirectly by studying mosaic floors; these have been very thoroughly investigated in several areas in Gaul. It should be recalled, however, that the quantity of mosaics – representing an aristocratic investment in the decoration of a dwelling – cannot always be correlated with the number of villas (Stern 1957, 1960, 1967; Stern and Blanchard-Lemée 1975; Daimon and Lavagne 1977; Barral i Altet 1980). Both in northern France and in adjacent areas of Belgium and Western Germany (the province of Belgica), as well as in eastern France around Lyons in the Rhône Valley, the number of mosaics in villas reaches a peak around AD 200, a picture corresponding to that emerging from the surveys of settlements themselves. A tendency for this peak to extend into the fourth century is seen in frequencies for north-central France, and in south-western France – where, for instance, a famous fourth-century villa is found at Montmaurin (Fouet 1969) – the majority of mosaics from villas actually date from the fourth to the early fifth century. This is extremely interesting because it shows that the Visigoths, who arrived in Aquitania at the beginning of the fifth century, were not being settled in an economically marginal area of the empire as might have been supposed. Here, too, development led away from the classical villa complex. In south-eastern France, where mosaics are few in rural settlements, some specimens also date from the Late Roman period and Late Antiquity.

The British villas were likewise richly provided with mosaics; moreover, finds dating from the fourth century are especially numerous (Rainey 1973). Mosaics from this time are unknown on the opposite Channel coast; conditions were evidently too unsettled in north-western Gaul to support investment in permanent decorations for stately homes. There is other, indirect evidence that the Late Roman period was an important era for villas in Britain, many of them, however, relatively small, especially in the east. For example, animal bones are especially numerous from Late Roman villas (Luff 1982). Archaeological investigations also enable us to make a general evaluation of settlement, which in the first century particularly comprised many 'native', that is non-Romanized or only slightly Romanized, settlements or farms. At Whitton in south-eastern Wales, for example, one can follow a 'native' farm complex from the first to the mid-fourth century (fig. 31). To begin with, the farm had traditional round wooden huts, but these were replaced in the second century by square 'Roman' buildings on stone foundations, giving the complex a more villa-like appearance (Jarrett and Wrathmell 1981). To judge by the above-mentioned zoological and, admittedly, indirect studies, agrarian settlement in Britain was most widespread in the first and fourth centuries and least so in the third.

Archaeological survey of southern Cambridgeshire shows largely the same picture, but here attention has been paid only to 'Roman' sites (nevertheless predominantly agrarian) and therefore there are far more sites from the second century than from the first and also from the fourth (Wilkes and Eldrington 1978). In the Fenlands – the very wet, low-lying areas to the south of the Wash, intensively investigated both geologically and archaeologically – Roman settlement reached its zenith in the last half of the second century, whereupon it declined steadily (Phillips 1970; cf. Pryor et al. 1985). The reason for this was probably the rise in sea level known to have begun in the Late Roman period. The Fenlands furthermore show a tendency in this period for settlements to be either very large or, as in the first century, very small. In the middle of the Roman period settlements are typically medium-sized. In south-eastern England villas are

Fig. 31. Reconstruction of the farmstead at Whitton in the early fourth century (after Jarrett and Wrathmell 1981)

numerous in the Late Roman period, but especially near the dangerous Channel coast late-fourth-century specimens are rare (Black 1987) (fig. 32). In the Thames Valley settlement shows no decline from the early to the late fourth century. Finally, an investigation made in southern Wales shows that the number of Roman settlements here was larger in Late than in Early Roman times (Davies 1979).

To sum up the information from Britain, we find a pattern of settlement development that differs from that of the north-western Roman provinces on the continent. Villa settlement almost everywhere on the continent was in steady decline after about AD 200 (an exception is south-western France), while in Britain it often increased in the fourth century. The continental decline set in before the third-century Germanic invasion and must therefore have been the result of an internal crisis in the economic system. In Britain agriculture seems to have been reorganized in Late Roman times, greater emphasis being placed on cattle raising. The character of towns also altered in this period. Both in Britain and on the continent villas came to an end, however, around AD 400, at the same

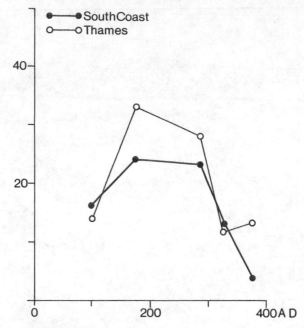

Fig. 32. Changing numbers of Roman villas in south-eastern England,
showing the persistence of villas into the late fourth century in the area
near London (*Source*: Black 1987)

time as the imperial military and political system faltered or collapsed. In Britain,
as in the Netherlands, a strong 'native' or, in the Early Roman period at any rate,
only slightly Romanized element can be noted; perhaps this also existed in the
other western provinces, but it has not been recognized. The distinction of villas
from other types of agrarian settlements is less clear in most provincial Roman
literature on the subject, which further complicates study of the history of the
settlement in Roman times. In Late Roman times, finally, there were also major
agrarian sites that were not villas but either centres of estates or more loosely
organized settlements.

The Danube area in the Roman period

The Roman province of Noricum, most of which lay in (present-day) Austria, is
known for its Roman mining operations and a number of large villas. In Late
Antiquity, particularly on the southern slopes of the Alps, some towns and villas
were replaced by fortified centres, among the best-known of which are Teurnia
and Lavant (the latter a bishop's palace) (Alföldy 1974). One must turn, however, to Pannonia to obtain a systematic overview of settlement development (see
Thomas 1964). The sources for this lie partly in the villas themselves and partly
in a review of settlements from Pannonia to Thrace (present-day Bulgaria) that
have yielded agricultural implements (Henning 1987) (fig. 33). The admittedly

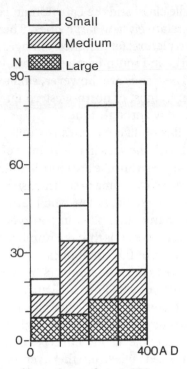

Fig. 33. Frequencies of large (more than 1,700 square metres), medium-sized (more than 600 square metres), and small Roman villas in south-eastern Europe (*Source*: Henning 1987)

indirect method is the more satisfactory, especially in that it offers the opportunity to assess areas of the Balkans that are otherwise very difficult to study. Bulgaria is of special interest both because of its proximity to Constantinople and because it has many settlements covering the entire first millennium.

In this region of Eastern Europe there are villas of various sizes. Large villas are relatively numerous in Bulgaria and south-eastern Yugoslavia, perhaps indicating that this was not particularly well developed in the Roman period in spite of its geographically central position. In general, there were many large and medium-sized villas and few small ones in the first century, from which it is apparent that the 'Romanization' process began at the top of the society. In the second century medium-sized villas were predominant, comprising more than half the material, and large villas fewer than before. In the third to fourth century the number of medium-sized villas fell to slightly more than a tenth of the total; in contrast, the number of small villas increased to two-thirds. The number of large villas was largely unchanged, and, as in other Late Roman villas in these regions, there was widespread use of fortifications. The Early Roman expansion and colonization phase, then, was dominated by relatively large villa complexes. In addition there were some 'native' sites, archaeologically still little-known (see Gabler, Patek, and Vörös 1982). The second century, in contrast, was characterized by a 'middle class' and the Late Roman period by a polarization of many small villas and relatively few large ones. There is a certain degree of regional difference in this picture; for instance, changes from period to period are least apparent in Bulgaria and south-eastern Yugoslavia and most apparent in the rest of Yugoslavia. The trends are, however, similar everywhere. Finally, in contrast to the situation in most of north-western Europe, the number of villa complexes increases steadily through time.

The distribution of villas of different sizes is similar to that in the region of Caesarea, but compared with the sites in the vicinity of Rome the medium-sized and small villas in south-eastern Europe are more like farm complexes. Moreover, the number of villas increases over time in south-eastern Europe while it declines near Rome. Again there are relatively few small farm complexes in the fourth century in Latium and many such sites in south-eastern Europe. A feature common to the two areas, however, is that the number of large complexes shows fewer fluctuations than that of the small ones.

In addition to the increases in cattle numbers in Late Roman times discussed above, south-eastern European villa finds indicate that some Late Roman innovations in agricultural technology, for example the scythe and the vertical coulter (a frontal knife to cut the sod) for the plough, are associated exclusively with large and small villas, while traditional types of implement are found only on the sites of medium-sized villas, on the average relatively early, which underwent a marked decline in number in the Late Roman period. The Late Roman relation between large and small villas may represent the very beginnings of the structure characteristic of Late Antiquity, when centralized, often fortified sites replaced the large villas and it must be assumed that numbers of dependent producers were living either on the site or near it in the countryside. The evidence for crafts, particularly pottery production and metalworking, is common on Roman villa sites in south-eastern Europe, being widespread in Late Roman times in large and medium-sized complexes but rare in the far more numerous small ones. Here again there must have been an economic and social link between the different types of villas.

In south-eastern Europe and elsewhere in the Roman Empire, villa complexes vanished, as indicated, around AD 400 or by the beginning of the fifth century at the latest. Villas, and to a certain extent towns, were replaced by the centralized sites just mentioned, some of them citadels originating in the fourth century. Other agrarian sites have been found in the earlier towns, near churches, and so on, but the lack of a characteristic architecture makes for considerable difficulties in the archaeological search for the settlements of Late Antiquity. The large sites, optimally with fortifications, churches, workshops, and the like, must if anything be described as political and economic centres, possibly of the major landed estates. The writers of Late Antiquity, however, would probably have referred to them as 'fortresses' (*castella, castra*) or 'towns' (*polis*, etc.) – a fact that has confused scholars who study this period primarily through those sources. If a

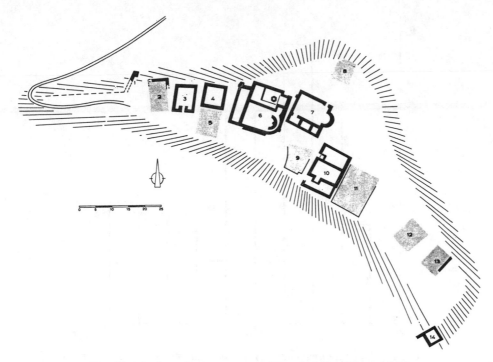

Fig. 34. The Late Antique centre of Vranje (after Ulbert 1979)

state or ecclesiastical system was able to function at all in this chaotic period, it can only have been through these *castra*. Among the best-known sites of this kind in south-eastern Europe is Gamzigrad, south of the Iron Gate, which was a rich, palace-like settlement in the fourth century, and Caricin Grad or Justiania Prima (named for the emperor Justinian), also in eastern Yugoslavia, which was originally almost a town, possessing, for example, an archbishop's palace (Prückner 1982). A more typical Yugoslavian site is the relatively modest Vranje in the north-western part of the country (Ulbert 1979) (fig. 34).

This evidence points to the existence of Late Antique *castra* in a broad zone stretching from the Middle Rhine across the Alps through the regions south of the Danube and on to Bulgaria. Many other *castra* – for instance, in south-western Britain – are of similar character (Alcock 1982). From this perspective it seems that Late Antiquity did not imply decline everywhere; in Bulgaria there are 45 villas dating from the second through the fourth century and 56 sites dating from the fifth through the seventh. For the whole of this south-eastern area of Europe, however, the figures are 198 and 98 sites respectively (Henning 1987). Comparing the fifth through the seventh century with the eighth through the tenth, the number of agrarian sites falls from 98 to 73, in Bulgaria and south-eastern Yugoslavia from 56 to 32. It should be recognized, however, that the late sites, often with wooden buildings only, are difficult to identify archaeologically. If the material from Bulgaria and south-eastern Yugoslavia is distributed over the

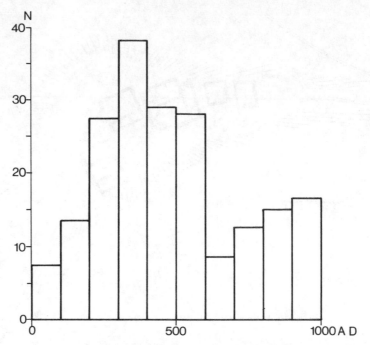

Fig. 35. Changing frequencies of Roman and later settlements in first-millennium Bulgaria (*Source*: Henning 1987)

centuries, there is a marked increase in the number of Romanized agrarian sites throughout the Roman era (fig. 35). In Late Antiquity there is only a slight decline, but in the seventh century, with the Avar invasions and the Slavic settlement of large areas of the inner Balkans and Greece, the pattern does suggest a collapse of agrarian settlement. Slow growth occurs again from the eighth century on.

The Bulgarian and south-eastern Yugoslavian material also allows study of the continuity of agrarian settlement (table 5). None of these sites persists through all three periods, and the proportion of continuing settlements is greater in the last. This suggests that the major break in the continuity of agrarian sites in south-eastern Europe lies between the first and the second period, or between the Roman era and Late Antiquity, rather than in the early Byzantine period, which otherwise implies such great political and other changes for the Eastern Empire.

The question of continuity can also be approached from the point of view of south-eastern Europe in general. Whereas sites dating from the second through the fourth century that continue into Late Antiquity are evenly distributed over the whole area from Hungary to Bulgaria, Roman sites that continue into the sixth century occur only south of the Drava and Danube. A very different geographical picture emerges for the eighth- through the tenth-century sites

Table 5. *Continuity of agrarian settlements in Bulgaria and south-eastern Yugoslavia, second through tenth century*

Duration of settlement	Second through fourth century	Fifth through seventh century	Eighth through tenth century
One period only	29 (69%)	24 (46%)	17 (53%)
Continue into next period	13 (31%)	15 (29%)	—
Continue from preceding period	—	13 (25%)	15 (47%)
Total	42	52	32

Source: Henning 1987

founded in the preceding period. These are found only in Bulgaria and south-eastern Yugoslavia, making this the only area showing continuity from Late Antiquity to Early Byzantine times. Fairly close to Constantinople, this region was less subject to migrations and political upheavals than was the Middle Danube. The character of Bulgarian settlement in this period is more difficult to determine than in the preceding one (von Bülow et al. 1979; etc.) but it does seem certain that, from the end of the first millennium onwards, fortified sites played a lesser role than earlier. It can therefore be assumed that there was greater territorial stability and organization at this time than during the Migration period, which is characterized by changing lords and their followers – the 'peoples' or 'tribes' of the written sources – and an ongoing process of estate formation. On the agrarian sites of the late first millennium there would have been small wooden huts which, as in the rest of Eastern Europe, often seem to have had a sunken floor, a type of building that is relatively easy to recognize. Only future excavations – for example, the uncovering of large surface areas – will demonstrate whether this picture applies to all sites. The political centres apparently had very different architecture derived from Byzantine buildings and known, for instance, from Pliska and Preslav, the early Bulgarian capitals. On these generally little-known sites there are complexes similar in structure to the contemporary Carolingian palaces and Moravian fortress towns but even more impressive (Bojadziev 1970) (fig. 36).

Western Europe in the post-Roman period

In temperate Western Europe, tree trunks found in rivers have revealed the existence of considerable forest cover, reaching its peak around A D 500, followed by renewed expansion of agriculture and settlement. In the Rhine region there is, moreover, much archaeological evidence of agrarian settlement during the whole of the first and the second millennia (Randsborg 1985; Janssen 1977 with alterations) (fig. 37). The material was collected with special reference to 'Germanic' settlements, and therefore purely Roman sites were not included; this

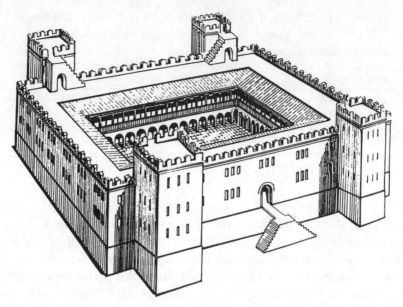

Fig. 36. Reconstruction of the central palace complex of the Bulgarian
capital of Pliska around AD 800, a settlement that covered an area larger
than Constantinople (after Bojadziev 1970)

means that fewer early sites are recorded than in fact existed. From the middle of
the second millennium onwards the number of sites falls markedly because the
archaeological finds become fewer, settlements now rarely being abandoned.
The sample shows an 'expansion phase', here only a technical one, in the first
centuries AD, followed by a real decline until about AD 600; in the seventh to
ninth centuries there is vigorous expansion that is interrupted by a slight decline
in settlement numbers in the tenth century but otherwise continues until about
AD 1200. The period AD 400–700 is notable for the increase in number of sites
established, and the same applies to the expansion phase of the twelfth century.
From AD 700 to 1100, in contrast, the number of sites established declines. The
number of sites abandoned is high in AD 200–600 even though the sample does
not include purely Roman settlements. The explanation can only be that, as the
tree-trunk evidence suggests, the Germanic sites close to the Roman Empire (and
probably also those farther away) depended heavily on the development of the
empire. A last phase in which many agrarian sites were abandoned is the eighth
and ninth centuries. The percentage of sites abandoned is greater than that of
sites established in the third to fifth centuries and in the ninth.

From the founding dates of those settlements in the Rhine region that still
existed in the palmy days of the twelfth century, an impression can be obtained of
the age of the agrarian system that characterized the High Middle Ages in this

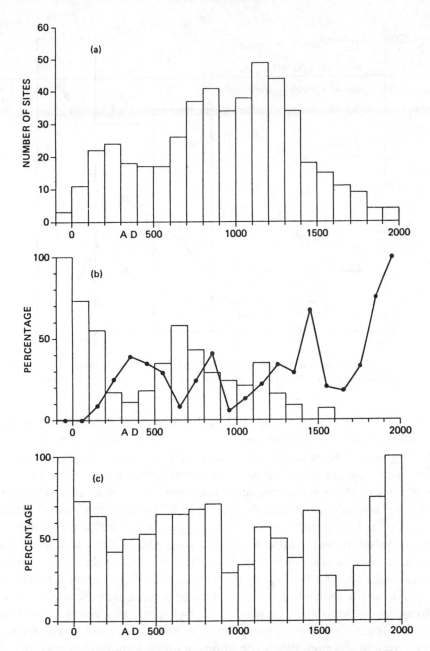

Fig. 37. Changing frequencies of Roman and later settlements from the Rhineland and adjacent regions (after Randsborg 1985; Janssen 1977 with alterations): (a) numbers of settlements per century (Roman sites and settlements of the late second millennium are underrepresented); (b) numbers of foundings (histograms) and abandonments (line) expressed as percentages of the total number of sites from each century; (c) 'instability index', i.e. the sum of the percentages of foundings and abandonments

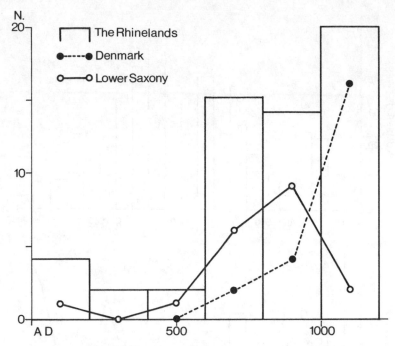

Fig. 38. Founding dates for twelfth-century settlements from the
Rhineland, Lower Saxony, and Denmark (after Randsborg 1988a)

central area of Western Europe (Randsborg 1988a) (fig. 38). Many of these
Rhineland sites were founded around A D 700, the transition between Late
Merovingian and Early Carolingian times, rarely earlier. This means that the
agrarian settlements associated with the Merovingian cemeteries in the Rhineland did not persist into Carolingian or later times. The cemeteries were mainly
established around A D 500 and abandoned by 700 at the latest. Hence a definite
break can be recognized between Merovingian and Carolingian settlement.
Carolingian settlement continued into the High Middle Ages, but, as we have
seen, a number of sites were abandoned in the ninth century. Nevertheless,
because of the continuity of agrarian settlement, the Carolingian period should
be considered the time when a state society, or at least the earliest phase of one
(subsequent to the Roman Empire, of course), came into being in the Rhine
region. It is certainly not insignificant that virtually no rich grave finds are
known from this period. When conditions of estate formation, ownership, etc.
became stabilized, individual families may no longer have felt the need to invest
in grave goods to demonstrate the rank and wealth of their lineages.

Individual Merovingian cemeteries contain the burials of from one to a dozen
nuclear families, on average four to five, over a period covering two to seven
generations or up to 250 years (Steuer 1982: 513–14). This may be taken as an
indication of the relatively small size of the Merovingian settlements, which

might best be considered individual farms, perhaps grouped. Furthermore, it is notable that burial grounds dating from the sixth century contain fewer families than those from the seventh century, indicating that settlements increased in size in Late Merovingian times (Donat and Ullrich 1971). The Carolingian settlements were therefore quite large and rather resembled villages, a fact that must be kept in mind in considering the reasons for the stabilization of many settlements during this period.

In Lower Saxony a different picture emerges (see fig. 38). The majority of the twelfth-century settlements were founded around AD 900, which must be considered the phase in which a state society emerged here. In fact, this was the time when the area was integrated into the Frankish realm (Janssen 1977; Jeppesen 1981; Randsborg 1988a). In Denmark, where a state society first emerged around 1000, the majority of twelfth-century sites date to AD 1100 (Jeppesen 1981). Once again we note the correspondence in time between the introduction of the socio-economically defined state society and the stabilization of the settlement pattern. Both in Lower Saxony and in Denmark, moreover, rich graves were established in the period immediately before the state society came into being or in the transitional period.

In other regions of temperate Western Europe there are few opportunities for systematic studies of the post-Roman periods, although there are a number of individual sites of considerable interest, particularly in Britain (e.g., Longworth and Cherry 1986). In addition, the number of written sources relating to ownership and management increases through time. It is possible to recognize both 'ordinary' villages with individual farm complexes and centres that may range from very large farms with special functions to, for instance, Carolingian royal residences such as Ingelheim, with large stone buildings, including churches (fig. 39). The written sources record, moreover, demesne complexes, both royal ones and those of monasteries and others, of considerable size, as well as cases in which a single distinguished family owned only a modest number of farms (Herrmann 1982). It is still difficult to recognize such socio-economic relationships archaeologically, because archaeology works mainly with the simple qualitative differences between individual settlements. Furthermore, the concepts of settlement archaeology differ from those of history; a 'village', for example, that is perfectly intelligible to the archaeologist may not be mentioned as a social unit or a unit of ownership in the written sources and thus be in danger of being denied existence by the historian.

Several studies conducted in Italy provide insight into the development of the last half of the first millennium. The first concerns Ager Faliscus, where Roman settlement showed a marked decline after about AD 200, the open countryside remaining relatively thinly populated until the latter half of the second millennium (Potter 1976) (fig. 40). In the last quarter of the first millennium there was, however, a marked increase in the number of settlements on hill- or low mountain-tops, fortified sites which make up the well-known medieval villages

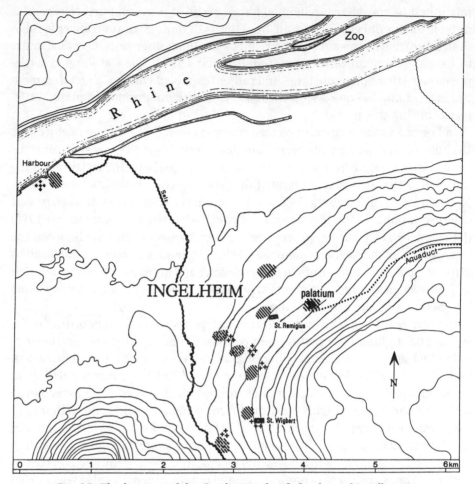

Fig. 39. The location of the Carolingian fortified palace of Ingelheim on
the left bank of the Rhine west of Mainz. A stone-built 'palatium' was
erected by Charlemagne around AD 800 and held a large royal hall of
more than five hundred square metres, richly decorated with frescos of
heathen and Christian Roman emperors, the forefathers of Charles, and
Charlemagne himself, depicted as victor over the Saxons. In addition there
were royal and other living quarters, baths, an eight-kilometre-long
aqueduct, and, from around AD 900 or earlier, a church. A zoo or animal
park was established on an island in the Rhine. The adjacent open
settlements (with cemeteries and a few churches) were mainly founded in
the late Merovingian period. The site of the palatium had a predecessor
(after Weidemann 1975)

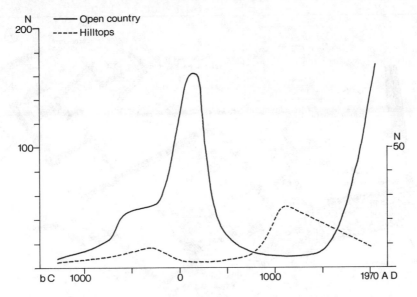

Fig. 40. Changing numbers of hill-top (defended) settlements (right-hand scale) and low-lying sites in the open (left-hand scale) from the period about 1000 BC to AD 2000 in the Ager Faliscus (after Potter 1976)

(and towns) of the Italian landscape. Similar observations have been made in the region around Scarlino in Tuscany (Francovich 1985a).

Such hill-top sites are also common in other parts of the Mediterranean. A good example is found on the outskirts of the town of Tuscania, about eighty kilometres north of Rome (Potter 1979) (fig. 41). On the Colle San Pietro, in addition to some Roman remains, there are traces of early-medieval wooden buildings dating perhaps from the eighth century, following a narrow stretch of former Roman road, stone buildings from the ninth to tenth century, three stone towers from the eleventh century, and larger buildings from the twelfth to the thirteenth centuries. Thereafter, in contrast to most other hill-top sites, this settlement was never densely or continuously inhabited. At the hill-top site of Scarlino, along with Hellenistic buildings we find a sequence beginning with wooden houses probably dating from the late first millennium AD (Francovich 1985a). (Seventh- or eighth-century dates have been established for the site termed 'D 85' in south-central Italy [Hodges et al. 1980].) These wooden buildings were replaced by stone houses and in the tenth century by a citadel. Scarlino is of special interest because of survey data indicating dense settlement in the area around the birth of Christ. As in the Cosa area to the south, this settlement showed a marked decline as early as in the second century that continued up to about AD 600, when a slight increase can be seen. In the tenth century several other hill-top villages were established in the Scarlino area.

There is a large volume of written material originating in Italy and other areas

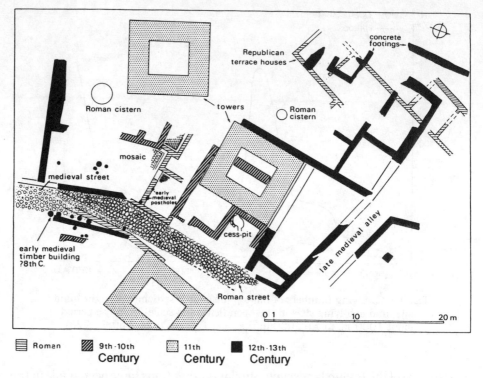

Fig. 41. The multiperiod site of Colle San Pietro (after Potter 1979). Dates
should be accepted with reservations

in the Mediterranean on the development of settlement at the end of the first millennium. The fact that written sources concerning settlement and economic matters are now so abundant strongly implies the emergence of new forms of ownership and relations of production. There is so much material from Italy that it can even be used statistically, although a general problem arises from the facts that it primarily concerns the period after AD 800 and that the amount of material increases with time. Italy also provides us with considerable written material on churches that helps clarify regional development. Here, for instance, series of buildings dating from around AD 600 and especially from around AD 800 are notable (Settia 1984; Dorigo 1983 for the Venice area; Ward-Perkins 1984 for the Lucca area). A third series of churches appeared, according to the written sources, in the tenth century, at the same time as the stone buildings in the hill-top villages.

Northern Europe

Some of the best-known areas with respect to settlement in the first millennium are in Europe north of the Roman Empire. There is an antiquarian tradition of long standing here, and, in addition, there are a number of sites (generally including wooden buildings, etc.) that have been excavated by modern techniques, revealing the ground plans of whole settlements. The results are thus entirely comparable to those of investigations made in regions in which buildings were made of stone. In Scandinavia studies have been made of field systems and other landscape and ecological features. Regional investigations are not unusual in Northern Europe, but the varying state of preservation of the archaeological material seldom permits statistical treatment of any interest to social history.

In many cases there is much more to be gained from the study of pollen diagrams with long sequences. These can reveal, for example, the relative extent of the open landscape, including the cultivated areas, and the character of the agriculture. Thus diagrams from Scandinavia have indicated an expansion of open country at the expense of forest in Roman times, followed by a renewal of forest cover about AD 500 (Berglund 1969; cf. Widgren 1983 for an area in Östergötland, Sweden). A new expansion phase started soon after the middle of the first millennium and came to an end some years into the second. These diagrams are, however, difficult to interpret. For one thing, different plants produced varying quantities of pollen. Rye, for example, is wind-pollinated and produces far more pollen than the other species of grain. Furthermore, given the same number of associated households, an extensive, cattle-dominated type of agriculture often produces a more open landscape than an intensive system typically concentrated on the cultivation of grain. Nevertheless, general patterns must be granted some significance. On the island of Gotland in the Baltic, for instance, the picture just sketched is confirmed by radiocarbon dating of settlements and field systems and by the dominance of sheep over cattle in Late Roman times (Carlsson 1979: 153, 160). In this connection it should be noted, moreover, that forest growth in Scandinavia around the middle of the first millennium does not correspond chronologically to the growth periods indicated by river-deposited tree trunks for Central Europe; here it seems to be of somewhat later date.

There is a large number of well-studied settlements, dating from the whole of the first millennium, along the North Sea from the Netherlands to Jutland. Most of these date from the first part of the period, which is evidently easier to recognize archaeologically in these regions, surface finds being few and the character of the landscape and the distribution of resources seldom revealing the precise positions of sites or their types. Moreover, because these settlements tend to move periodically, even the uncovering of large surface areas does not always capture all phases of a settlement or capture each to the same degree. This implies in turn that, despite the high quality of the material, we must be very cautious in drawing historical conclusions.

One of the earliest investigations in which large areas of a village settlement in the North Sea area were uncovered was at Wijster in the north-eastern Netherlands (van Es 1967). As was common in the period under scrutiny, the village was dominated by large longhouses combining dwelling and livestock areas, and

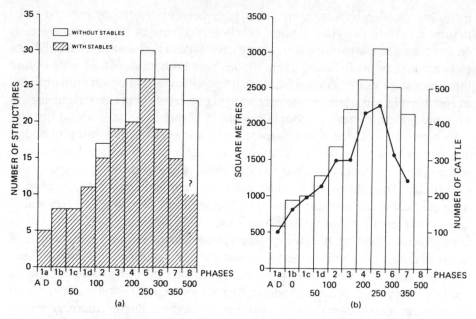

Fig. 42. Development of Feddersen Wierde (after Randsborg 1985): (a)
changing numbers of structures during the life of the settlement; (b) total
size in square metres (histograms) of structures and estimated numbers of
(byred) cattle (line)

longhouse farmsteads were situated, together with smaller buildings, on large,
square, fenced plots. The Wijster village, which expanded steadily, dates from the
Late Roman period and was abandoned shortly after AD 400 – at any rate, as far
as the excavated area is concerned. In any case, we may conclude that, as with so
many other sites in the Netherlands and north-western Germany, the last phase
of settlement came to an end at the same time as the north-western Roman
provinces were being abandoned by the empire. The expansion phases of the
Wijster site seem to coincide exactly with the times that the Roman Empire was
militarily and politically at its weakest (Willems and Brandt 1977; cf. Randsborg
1988a). The explanation for this is not immediately clear, but it is worth noting
that during the same period the Romans were recruiting mercenaries from the
north-western frontier zone. Up to 17 per cent of the Wijster pottery consisted of
imported Roman wares, which must have been transported several hundred
kilometres to the site (van Es 1967: fig. 177).

At Feddersen Wierde on the coastal salt marshes south of the mouth of the
Elbe, considerably farther from the border of the Roman Empire, lies one of the
best-known villages from this period (Haarnagel 1979) (fig. 42). It was founded
before the birth of Christ and, like Wijster, abandoned in the fifth century.
Settlement peaked in the first half of the third century after undergoing expansion in the second, when a large farm was built that housed craft activities and in
which the finds included many Roman imports. This was probably the home of

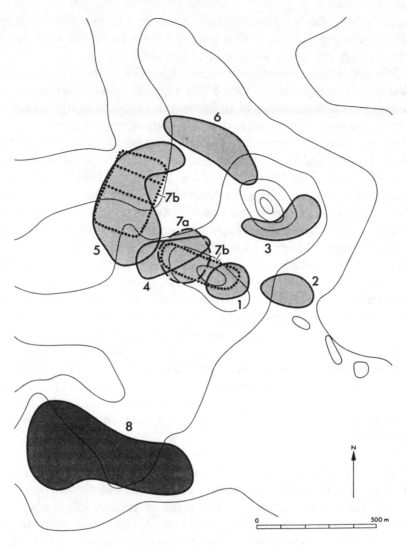

Fig. 43. Successive phases of the village of Vorbasse: (1) first century BC, (2) first century AD, (3) second century, (4) third century, (5) fourth and fifth centuries, (6) sixth and seventh centuries, (7a) eighth through tenth centuries, (7b) eleventh century, (8) late eleventh century and later (after Hvass 1986)

the village's leading family. The Feddersen Vierde inhabitants had to fight against flooding but nevertheless remained in the fertile marshlands for many hundred years. Sites farther inland, for example, Flögeln, show the same pattern – expansion in Early Roman times, decline in Late Roman times, and abandonment in the fifth century (Schmid and Zimmerman 1976; Steuer 1982: 278) – and therefore the abandonment of Feddersen Wierde was not purely a question of floods on the North Sea coast. These Germanic settlements follow the same general rhythm of development as the Roman frontier provinces of the north-western continent. It is likely that their history is bound up with that of the empire, though not in the same way as Wijster's.

A different picture emerges north of the Elbe. One of the best-known sites is Vorbasse in central Jutland (Hvass 1986) (fig. 43), where a settlement can be followed from the first century BC to around AD 1100 and nearly the entire area has been excavated. Settlement in the Early Roman period was relatively modest – a few small farm complexes each primarily consisting of a longhouse contain-ing both dwelling and livestock areas and surrounded by a fence. Jutland has far larger sites dating from the same centuries, for example Hodde, from the end of the first millennium BC, where there were up to twenty-seven farm complexes within a common palisade (Hvass 1985; cf. Kaul 1989). The Vorbasse excava-tions demonstrate that for some thousand years settlement shifted within an area of scarcely a square kilometre a little less than a kilometre north of the present village of Vorbasse, which was established at the very time that the old settlement area was finally abandoned. The third century saw vigorous expansion and reorganization of the settlement, which at that time comprised at least thirteen large farms with longhouses and smaller buildings situated on individual square plots some 2,000 to 3,000 square metres in area. These lay in rows, two farm complexes often sharing a fence. Thus a whole village of the older type, for example Hodde, was no larger than two to three farm plots of a third-century Vorbasse-type village. The same type of settlement continued up to around AD 700. In the fourth century the village reached a provisional climax with, apparently, as many as nineteen farms (fig. 44). In the fifth century the longhouses seem to have been a little smaller, and in the sixth through seventh centuries the village comprised perhaps only seven or eight farms.

From the eighth through the tenth centuries Vorbasse contained seven large farm complexes, basically of the same type as earlier but situated on plots three times the size of the earlier ones. The main longhouse, still containing both dwelling and livestock areas, was now of typical Viking form, with curved long walls. (The Viking Age is the period between the eighth and the eleventh centuries.) Towards AD 1000, however, the seven farm complexes were on crofts as much as 26,000 square metres in area, nearly as large as the whole third-century village (fig. 45). In the midst of these plots there was now a large hall of the same type as the main buildings of the late-tenth-century royal Trelleborg fortresses (Randsborg 1980). Connected to the hall of the largest farm there was a smithy and even a bronze-casting workshop. In this phase too there appeared for the first time large buildings serving exclusively as livestock sheds. Dwellings, workshops, and storehouses, as well as some of the livestock sheds, were lined up along the fences. The largest farm had sufficient stall area to house more than a hundred larger domestic animals, three times as many as the earlier Viking Age farms. It is difficult not to ascribe special significance to the eleventh-century farm that is exactly double the size of the two next-largest ones (as measured by the width of the croft). In the earlier phases of the village there was also one major

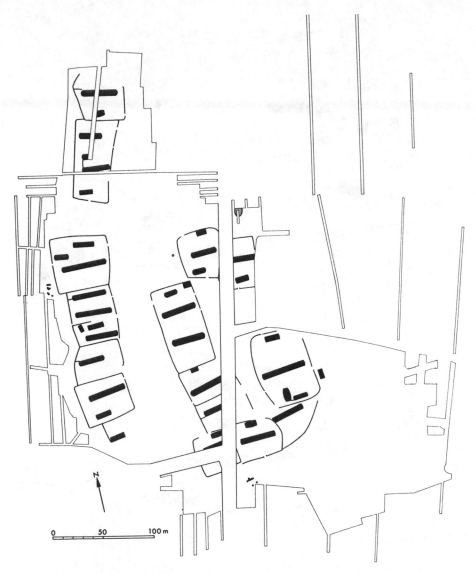

Fig. 44. Vorbasse in the fourth century, showing farmstead longhouses
(with stables) and smaller structures on major fenced 'private' plots,
probably indicating individual family control of the means of production
(after Hvass 1986)

farm, normally only slightly larger than the others, and there was one even at
Hodde around the birth of Christ. In all phases at Vorbasse, however, the
ordinary farms resemble the major farm and control their own means of production. Thus, even in the eleventh century, the largest farm is probably not the
centre of a demesne. The layout of the crofts indicates some general planning,
and it is indeed unlikely that the political and social development in late Viking
Age Denmark was not accompanied by estate formation. Archaeology still faces

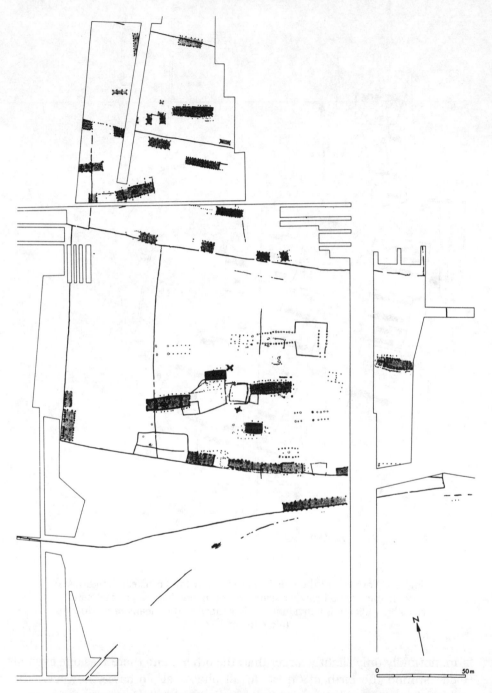

Fig. 45. The western part of Vorbasse in the early eleventh century,
showing three major farmsteads, each situated on a very large fenced
plot. Each complex has a main hall at its centre and other buildings,
including living quarters, workshops, and stables, either next to it or
along the fences (after Hvass 1986)

major difficulties in attempting to outline patterns of ownership and other social relations, but we do see a continuation of the system that was established around AD 200 and made the individual farm rather than the village the basic unit of production and society.

In Late Roman and post-Roman Norway there were large single farm complexes of the same general stamp as those of the third-to-seventh-century Vorbasse (Myhre 1982). The Norwegian farms are often well preserved because of the widespread use of stone in wall construction. In addition, stone boundary walls, some enclosing whole field systems, have been preserved. Similar structures occur in parts of Sweden, for example on the Baltic islands, where there were, as elsewhere in this country, also some fortress complexes. In a few cases, for instance Eketorp on the island of Öland (Näsman and Wegraeus 1976), these have been more or less permanently inhabited. Individual longhouse farmsteads have been found as far away as northern Sweden, for instance the well-investigated Gene in Ångermanland (Ramqvist 1983).

Vorbasse may thus be considered to indicate greater continuity in northern than in southern Germanic societies. Through their closer ties with the Roman Empire the latter were far more profoundly affected by its collapse or transformation and by the events that occurred in its wake. Most marked of these was the Germanic assumption of military and political power in the Western Empire and widespread Germanic settlement within the old frontiers of the empire – with respect to north-western Europe, particularly in the Rhine region, northernmost Gaul, and Britain. Several of these Germanic groups seem to have originated in areas whose settlement, as we have just seen, is characterized by a break at the beginning of the fifth century. We have noted the same process farther south, in the Upper Main area, in connection with river-deposited tree trunks. Finally, a small regional study in Hessen can be interpreted along the same lines as the settlements in north-western Germany that, like Feddersen Wierde, culminated in the second to third century (Mildenberger 1972).

Northern Germanic societies thus were relatively stable but marginal in relation to the Merovingian expansion, even though there is much evidence of contact with areas to the south in the fifth to sixth century. The important fortified settlement at Eketorp not only contained glasses originating in both western and eastern Central Europe but had portcullises, an element of fortification that the builders seem to have borrowed from fortresses of Late Antiquity in south-eastern Europe (Näsman and Wegraeus 1976).

South of the Baltic, in the German Democratic Republic, Poland, and Czechoslovakia, settlement at the beginning of the first millennium is less well known than it is to the west and north, but many of the same features – for example, the Germanic longhouses with dwelling and livestock areas under one roof – reappear here. One example is provided by Tornow, mentioned several times above. Since the Second World War, the Slavic period of the second half of the first millennium has been the subject of much research in Eastern Europe, and in

several areas extensive excavations have yielded a total numerical description of
settlement development. One of these is the Tollensee area in the northern part of
the German Democratic Republic, a relatively isolated region, in many ways
marginal in relation to both western and eastern development (Herrmann 1985:
18–19). Here there was a steady increase in the number of sites from roughly AD
400 to 1100, with the exception of a phase of decline around AD 900. Another
area investigated is Kruszwicka in central Poland, the heartland of the early
Polish state society (Dzieduszycka 1985). Here too there was an increase in the
number of sites in the second half of the first millennium, but the increase around
AD 1000, with the formation of the state-society, was exponential compared
with that of earlier phases. A marked decline in settlement began at the latest
around AD 1100. The figures for settlement calibrated by hundred-year periods
(with absolute figures given in brackets) are as follows: AD 500–600, 6 (6); 600–
800, 8 (15); 800–950, 21 (32); 950–1000, 76 (38); 1000–1050, 90 (45);
1050–1250, 46 (91).

Tornow has been well researched (Herrmann 1973) (fig. 16) and can serve as
a prototype of early Slavic development in regions far from the old imperial
provinces. The site shows three main phases after the cessation of Germanic
settlement around AD 500: an open Slavic settlement, a Slavic settlement a few
hectares in size dating from the seventh to the ninth centuries, to which was
added, in two phases, a small circular fortress, and finally a new open settlement.
The settlement moved to the present village of Tornow after about AD 1200. In
the first phase of the fortress there was only a single building, serving as a
dwelling. In the second phase the fortress contained storerooms as well as several
dwellings, among them one large building taking up half the interior. Immediately outside the fortress were signs of workshop activities, for example pottery
production and the extraction of iron. Somewhat farther off were a number of
dwellings, which in the first fortress phase were spacious, covered an area of up to
a hundred square metres, and belonged to some eight farm complexes. In the
second fortress phase these houses were replaced by lighter wooden structures,
considerably smaller than those of the first. Overall, Slavic Tornow appears to
represent an interesting approach to economic stratification of an extent unknown in contemporary northern Germanic villages. There is no evidence of
livestock areas inside the Tornow houses, but this may have something to do
with the state of preservation of the remains.

Slavic fortress complexes are an interesting problem in social history. On the
one hand, there is evidence of an old tradition of fortresses built for protection in
Central Europe; on the other hand, an example such as Tornow shows that
dominant social groups living in fortresses had already been isolated from the rest
of society by the eighth century at the latest. In later periods, moreover, the
settlements associated with these fortresses were also provided with earthwork
defences (Herrmann 1985: 187–8). At Tornow the rather small fortress part of
the settlement was abandoned in the ninth century, but elsewhere development

continued. In Czechoslovakia there were even very large complexes, for instance Mikulčice in Moravia, which must be described as the central princely seat of the realm (Poulik 1975). This site came into existence in the seventh century and saw very vigorous expansion in the eighth and especially the ninth century. In addition to a fortress enclosing some six hectares of land, there was an outer fortress or 'town' complex covering 200 hectares. Associated with this complex, which was in direct contact regarding political and religious affairs with Byzantium during the ninth century, were at least twelve churches, among them a stone-built basilica covering more than 400 square metres inside the fortress or castle itself. Graves, some richly equipped, have been found in connection with the churches. The ordinary houses at Mikulčice were log cabins, a very common type of building in Slavic settlements, where, however, pit houses were also used to a large extent (Donat 1980). Several structurally similar princely seats with associated townlike 'outer fortresses' were associated with development in Bohemia and with the later Polish state society.

5

TOWNS AND OTHER CENTRES

Traditionally, both history and archaeology have been much concerned with towns. Because they play so large a part in our society, those of the past have been viewed as embryos of future development, and this has led to an overestimation of their importance and a tendency to consider them in isolation from other forms of settlement. Furthermore, when we attempt to define a town we may fail to perceive the pronounced differences in function between towns in different societies. It would be wiser, both analytically and from the viewpoint of social history, to begin by investigating the activities and functions of the different societies, in this way developing a framework within which certain settlements might be singled out as 'towns' within the overall structure. Such an ideal scheme is, however, neither easy to operationalize nor particularly instructive, and therefore we must adopt a rather more traditional approach. It may, for instance, be useful to distinguish sites that differ in size or activities from the usual agrarian settlement. Once we have done this, it may be possible to go on to distinguish, for example, between fortresses and towns. This can be done in the Early Roman period, but in many other cases problems arise. Do the fortified centres of Late Antiquity, with both craft production and agriculture, or the large Slavic fortresses constitute 'towns'? If so, where shall we set the limits for other settlements? When such questions have to be asked, the possibilities offered by traditional methods have been exhausted, and we are forced to employ new definitions. With the traditional methodology there is still one variable – size – that must be assigned special importance, partly because it involves a number of factors relating to supply, thus shedding light on the infrastructure of the society, and partly because it is relatively easy to determine and therefore facilitates comparison of sites.

Thus we shall be dealing to a large extent with the sizes of sites and their geographical distribution and relationships. A thorough functional classification of towns and centres is, however, also necessary to ensure, among other things, their placement in a historical framework. In this connection it is important to determine whether a town or centre served as a marketplace or distribution centre for the surrounding district or for transregional trade and exchange or (usually) both. Political and religious institutions, workshops, and so on, must also be examined. Beyond this, towns and centres were often the object of investment and therefore provided with monuments and inscriptions whose number and character can help us to trace their development. Finally, attention must be given to Roman state factories, almost always situated in towns, and Roman forts.

Classification

Towns and centres typically have hinterlands that provide them with foodstuffs and raw materials. In most cases this area immediately surrounds the town, but certain activities, such as trade, reach beyond it. Where trade and exchange are important, the hinterland may even be of minor importance for its overall economy. In the ancient world there was a close connection between a town and its immediate environs, and no distinction was made between citizens associated with one or the other. A similar structure was found north of the Alps, where the pre-Roman or Celtic fortified sites served as centres for the surrounding territories and tribal groups. The Roman Empire had no effect on this structure. The political, administrative, and military structure of the Early Empire was a kind of umbrella over a system of relatively independent 'city-states' that were, however, politically responsible to and subject to taxation by the central power (see Wickham 1985). In these often well-laid-out and well-regulated towns there was a traditional interest on the part of the leading citizens in investing in monuments, institutions, and popular activities – temples and statues, marketplaces and market buildings, feasts and circus performances, etc. (fig. 46). In Rome, as later in Constantinople, the populace was also fed by the town and the state. This administrative system was very inexpensive for the empire, for, with the exception of military affairs, almost all of the lower-level bureaucracy could be left to the local people.

The Roman towns lost their independence following the crises of the third century. It became difficult, for instance, to find people who would take on the responsibility of collecting taxes, and the 'middle classes', where they still existed, no longer considered the town an object of investment. In terms of art and architecture, ancient culture collapsed. Funds for the military were raised through direct taxation, chiefly on land. Tax collecting was to a great extent in the hands of the state's own bureaucracy – which only increased expenses. Thus there emerged a new dominant class of state bureaucrat-cum-landowners, and while they were also to a certain degree responsible for the erection of buildings (for instance, churches) the ideology clearly differed from that of earlier times. Anonymity was the rule, and ornamental decoration (that also characterizes civic architecture in our own time) was preferred to naturalistic elements.

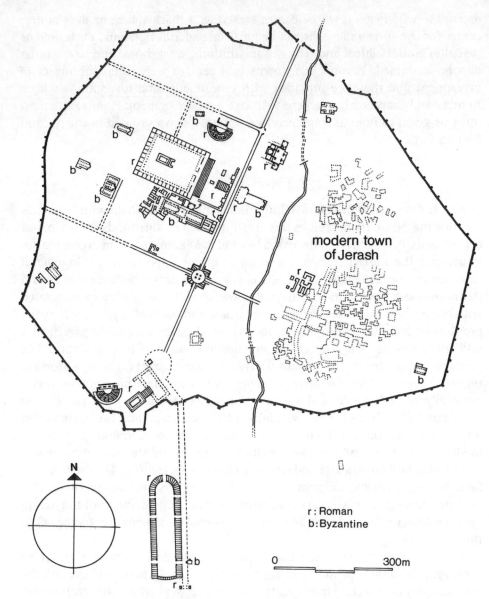

modern town
of Jerash

N

r : Roman
b: Byzantine

0   300m

Fig. 46. The Roman and Late Antique ('Byzantine') town of Gerasa
(Jerash) in Jordan; a smaller Islamic town occupied the eastern half of the
former classical city (after Kraeling 1938)

Table 6. *Public works in Italy during Roman times*

Type of structure	Time period				
	Republican	First century	Second century	Third century	Fourth and fifth centuries
Temples	170	130	65	16	8 (4)
Large constructions (e.g., aqueducts)	59	73	35	14	28 (14)
Utility buildings (e.g., basilicas, baths)	55	52	54	17	38 (19)
Buildings for entertainment (e.g., theatres, amphitheatres)	33	92	38	11	7 (4)
Total	317	347	192	58	81 (41)

Source: Jouffroy 1986
Note: Calibrated figures in brackets. Town walls, commonly erected in Late Roman times and later, are not included

Table 7. *Utility buildings, buildings for entertainment, and triumphal arches in Italy during Roman times*

Type of structure	Time period				
	Republican	First century	Second century	Third century	Fourth and fifth centuries
Basilicas	17	17	5	0	5 (3)
Baths	19	26	35	14	26 (13)
Theatres	24	51	15	9	3 (2)
Amphitheatres	7	40	23	2	2 (1)
Triumphal arches	0	16	6	1	1 (1)

Source: Jouffroy 1986
Note: Calibrated figures in brackets

Although the character of towns changed and in many areas they were much reduced in size, their economic activities, such as serving as market centres for the surrounding area, remained unchanged.

A comparison of important groups of large public buildings and other works in Italy during Roman times gives a good picture of the cultural, social, and economic development of the Roman town (Jouffroy 1986) and underlines a number of these points (table 6). The number of public buildings drops very sharply after about A D 100, but the greatest decline occurs after about 200 in the distribution of various utility buildings, buildings for entertainment, and, not included above, triumphal arches (table 7). It is notable that interest in theatres vanishes relatively early, while interest in baths, as in large construction works, persists to a relatively high degree.

Table 8. *Public works in North Africa during Roman times*

Type of structure	Time period			
	Republican and first century	Second century	Third century	Fourth and fifth centuries
Temples	42	140	112	26 (13)
Large constructions	19	42	51	55 (28)
Utility buildings	13	60	55	76 (38)
Buildings for entertainment	13	30	16	7 (4)
Total	87	272	234	164 (82)

Source: Jouffroy 1986
Note: Calibrated figures in brackets

Table 9. *Utility buildings, buildings for entertainment, and triumphal arches in North Africa during Roman times*

Type of structure	Time period			
	Republican and first century	Second century	Third century	Fourth and fifth centuries
Basilicas	6	27	11	20 (10)
Baths	3	27	35	29 (15)
Theatres	4	17	9	3 (2)
Amphitheatres	7	8	5	3 (2)
Triumphal arches	6	32	36	15 (8)

Source: Jouffroy 1986
Note: Calibrated figures in brackets

Summaries of public works in North Africa (table 8) chiefly reveal that development here occurred later than in Italy and culminated later (Jouffroy 1986). It also appears that there were different cultural standards in North Africa, where, for instance, interest in triumphal arches was marked (table 9).

Towns were further eroded during the new crises of the transitional period leading to Early Byzantine times (AD 600–800). In the majority of cases they were reduced to fairly large fortresses, such as Ephesus, in western Asia Minor, which became the centre of a military district (Foss 1979). These Byzantine fortresses can be compared to the fortified centres that had emerged in the old Rhine–Danube frontier zone in Late Antiquity. Even in the Islamic area towns seemed to decline somewhat relative to the prominent position they had held earlier, particularly in the Persian realm under the Sassanids (Adams 1981). In the old Western European areas towns had already fallen into rapid decline in Late Antiquity, and in the north-west they had simply ceased to exist around or shortly after AD 400. This did not necessarily mean that the sites disappeared entirely. Roads would still have led to at least the larger old towns, and the ecclesiastical institutions located there maintained a minimum of settlement, local markets (often situated just outside the old town), craft production, etc., thus preserving the place-names. At Trier (fig. 47), for example, Merovingian finds are unknown in the centre of the Late Roman town, which cannot have been occupied in this period, and the Merovingian churches, with the exception of the cathedral and Saint Irminen, all lie outside it, no doubt attached to estates and farmsteads. (Saint Irminen had been the site of the Roman granaries, which, having first become a royal Frankish compound, had been granted to the bishop of Trier in the early seventh century and became a nunnery.) Even the Late Antique fortified centres lying between Gaul and Bulgaria, which took over some of the functions of both Roman villas and towns, disappeared in the period AD 600–800. The end of this period saw the emergence of a number of royal centres, monasteries, etc., most of them not sited in or near the old Roman towns, whose size, architecture, and trade gave them a townlike stamp – among them Carolingian Ingelheim, Slavic Mikulčice, and Bulgarian Pliska and Preslav.

In this critical phase between AD 600 and 800 another type of townlike settlement was also making its mark – the emporium or port-of-trade, best known in north-western Europe, where it was an important feature of the economic policy of the Carolingian realm (Hodges 1982, 1988). Good examples are Hamvih, near Southampton, Dorestad on the Rhine in the Netherlands, and Hedeby in Jutland, near the border with Saxony. Small emporia seem to have existed in the Late Roman period among the Germanic societies outside the empire, where they were closely associated with the chiefly centres and had their roots in some of the activities normally associated with the chieftain's dwelling and household – crafts, trade and exchange, etc. (see, e.g., Thrane 1985; Thomsen 1986, 1987; Randsborg 1988c). Such sites, for example Lundeborg (fig. 48), were often on the coast and therefore had connections with communities far and wide. As political territories increased in size and foreign exchange increased in volume, the physical association with the royal residence or residences became less notable and the townlike emporium proper made its appearance.

The Carolingian-period emporia have been divided by Hodges (1982, 1988) into two main types, Type A being a periodic trading place and Type B an urban community in some respects much resembling the archaeological picture of the early provincial town. Hamwih, a Type B emporium of around AD 700, covers almost fifty hectares and has a gridded street plan within a ditched enclosure. The structures lie along the streets, seemingly on crofts without boundary fences; this may indicate that the whole site was considered a royal 'domain'. Dorestad, more than 200 hectares in size, flourished during the eighth century and was also an emporium of Type B. In Dorestad the 'town' was divided into a port and trading area along the bank of the Rhine and another part inland with craft production and even farming. The timber quay facilities at Dorestad are especially impressive.

Hedeby, from around AD 800, also a Type B emporium although only half the size of Hamwih, has a similar layout except that the buildings, mainly work-

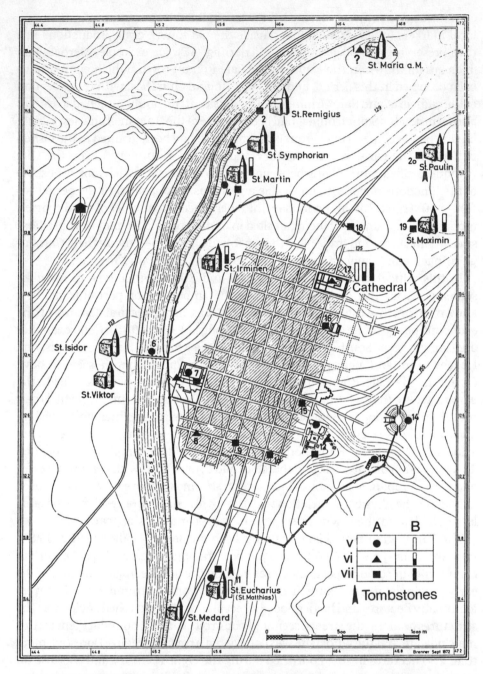

Fig. 47. Late Roman Trier, showing Merovingian churches, surface finds, and graves (4, 11). Sources are indicated as (A) archaeological and (B) written. Roman numerals indicate centuries AD. In the Roman temple area on the outskirts of town (12), scattered Frankish structures and craft activities have been recorded (after Schindler 1973; later finds have confirmed this picture)

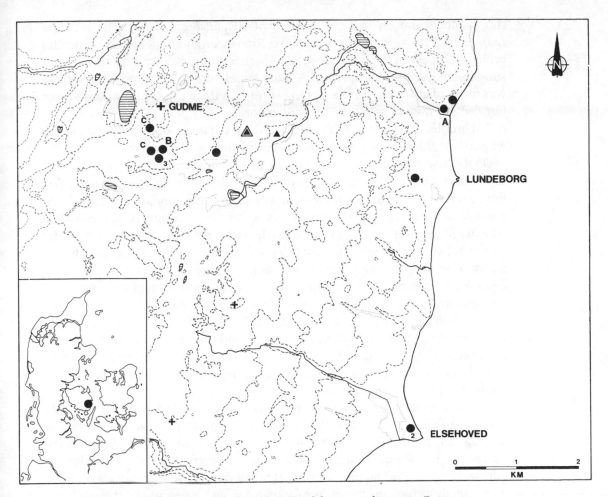

Fig. 48. The chiefly centre at Gudme-Lundeborg, south-eastern Funen,
Denmark (after Randsborg in press), showing (Christian crosses) medieval
stone-built parish churches (early second millennium); (dots) major
hoards of the Migration period (AD 400–600); (triangle) the major pre-
Roman and Roman Iron Age cemetery of Møllegårdsmarken (a
contemporary settlement (framed triangle) was situated 500 metres west
of it); (A) the Late Roman Iron Age harbour, workshop, and seasonal
market site to the north of Lundeborg (third century to shortly after AD
400; the part north of the stream is in general slightly later than the one
to the south); (B) a major concentration in the plough soil of metal
artefacts (revealed by mine detectors) from about AD 200 to 1000 (in
particular AD 400–600/550); (c) excavated Late Roman Iron Age/
Migration period farmsteads (excavations are still under way in the area)

shops, etc., stand on narrow fenced plots (Randsborg 1980). These fences remain, like the street grid, in the same position throughout the history of the site, probably indicating that we are dealing here with a system of registration and subsequent leasing of properties. A more loosely organized Type A emporium was founded at Hedeby in the eighth century. In the tenth century the site was fortified and may have resembled contemporary early provincial towns, the so-called burghs, in England. The Late Roman site of Lundeborg was also a Type A emporium, although it was more ephemeral than early Hedeby.

On the basis of the Danish archaeological data alone we might thus be inclined to attempt a more detailed classification than Hodges's bipartite division. The introduction of Type B emporia was, however, no doubt a major event involving a whole new concept of royal power and economic development and considerable involvement of regional resources (the latter reflected, for instance, in the ceramics found on these settlements). Type B emporia were in some respects the forerunners of provincial towns, in others not. Located on the coast, they were designed for communication with other emporia and interregional and international trade. Provincial towns, in contrast, were primarily located and structured to fulfil a number of regional, in particular market, craft, and ecclesiastical, functions in a state society. Royal power continued to be felt as before, for instance, in the form of a court, a palace, or a mint, but the economy seemed to be less closely controlled than when kings were only local and still held the paramount powers of chieftains.

A few emporia, such as Venice (see Hensel et al. 1966), developed into permanent gateway communities, but in most cases emporia were absorbed by the regional or provincial towns of post-Carolingian times. This development was bound up with the change in political system from one based on tribute and gifts to one based on binding territorial relationships. Development was, however, chiefly dictated by agricultural expansion and especially by the establishment of a dense network of general and local regional markets circulating its products. A multiplicity of craft activities was associated with these markets. At the same time the towns again became the object of investment, for instance by the church and the aristocracy. That many of these towns appear to be continuations of the Roman ones is, of course, attributable to the continuity of the road system and of the ecclesiastical institutions. It is probably significant, further, that the Late Roman market towns and the provincial towns of the High Middle Ages had a broad coincidence of function and therefore their strategic siting in relation to the landscape, resources, and other settlements would often have been the same.

Size and distribution of Roman towns

We have seen that the Early Roman Empire can basically be described as conforming to the ancient city-state principle, individual centres and their territories possessing a large degree of autonomy. Where an administrative area comprised several towns, their links with the 'capital' can be assumed to have been more important and more frequent than those among themselves, and the same must have applied to links between the provincial capitals and Rome. This may explain why, for example, several very large towns might be quite close to each other, as were Lyons and Vienne in the Rhône Valley. If Early Roman society had been entirely dominated by market and transport requirements, the geographical distribution of the large towns would have been different. In fact, it was based mainly on administrative principles with respect not only to political management but also to trade and exchange. This is by no means to say, however, that exchange and market forces were unimportant. It should be recalled, too, that in the Mediterranean basin the empire was exercising its power in areas that had a long economic history and innumerable contacts with one another, and here administrative principles were understandably less dominant than in the less developed northern regions.

Detailed consideration of one example of the distribution of towns in the Early Roman period sheds a little light on a general system (Hingley 1982). In Britain the majority of the towns were located, as were the villas, in the southern part of the country. Here the larger towns can be divided into primary tribal or regional capitals and Roman colonies, originally inhabited by veterans; in addition there was the provincial capital of London. The tribal capitals corresponded to the (large) Mediterranean 'city-states' and enjoyed a high degree of autonomy. Most of the larger and many of the smaller towns were walled. Smaller ones were more often walled when they were closer to the 'military district' of northern England or farther from large towns and therefore perhaps perceived as at risk. Small unwalled towns predominated in areas near large towns, on which they must have depended for protection. The important colony of Colchester is reckoned to have covered almost eighty hectares, another town in the area almost fifty hectares; four towns covered between thirty and fifty and ten between ten and thirty.

The size of an Early Roman town is, however, often difficult to gauge precisely, among other things because walls are relatively rare outside Britain in this period. Rome may be assumed to have had an area of more than 1,000 hectares because the third-century town walls, totalling eighteen kilometres in length, enclose an area of almost 1,400. Ephesus, contained by its Hellenistic walls, covered only a little more than 300 hectares, Alexandria more than 400. In Gaul, Nîmes and Vienne covered more than 200, Autun almost 200. London covered something more than a hundred hectares, Cologne roughly a hundred (see, e.g., Blanchet 1907; Russell 1958; Brühl 1975; Johnson 1983).

In Late Roman times nearly all towns had walls, and many of the larger ones, particularly in the west, were much reduced in size. Vienne, for example, now covered only roughly twenty hectares; Lyons, which had perhaps covered up to 160 hectares, now amounted to about 20. Autun had declined to a little more than ten hectares. On the northern frontier, however, there were still some very large towns; Trier, for example, one of the empire's capitals in the fourth century, was a little less than 300 hectares in size, while Mainz and London covered more than a hundred. Cologne covered roughly a hundred, as earlier, and Reims and Metz 60 to 70. Thus it is apparent that political, and especially military, concerns virtually dictated urban development in the zone west of the frontier. This is the more striking when one considers that agrarian settlement in this area, including villas, declined rapidly after AD 200 (though less so near the major towns to the west of the Upper Rhine). In south-western Gaul, Toulouse covered rather less than a hundred hectares, and the other large towns were far smaller; Poitiers covered less than fifty and Bordeaux only slightly more than thirty. In this area, as we have seen, there was a marked expansion of villa settlement in the fourth century, but the Late Roman towns here were of only modest size.

Among the many large towns in Late Roman times in the eastern Mediterranean was Constantinople, which on its foundation in the early fourth century covered 600 hectares but expanded early in the fifth century to 1,400 (the same as third-century Rome). Antioch in Syria, however, covered about 2,000 hectares in the early fifth century, perhaps indirectly because of the relatively small size of Constantinople. The geographical position of Constantinople within the empire was relatively marginal because of military concerns and questions of supply; thus the capital was dependent on the imperial court and did not have a particularly extensive and rich catchment area. The large size of Antioch should certainly be viewed in connection with economic power of the Levant in Late Antiquity. Against this background it is evident that in Late Roman/Late Antique times there were several different settlement systems, even in areas where agriculture predominated. One such system (which we have noted, for example, in south-western Gaul) comprised small towns, another, in the east, large ones. Of the various reasons for this diversity, we might emphasize the larger market in the east and the fact that prominent members of eastern Late Roman and Late Antique society lived mainly in towns. Rome, Constantinople, and Antioch were, however, all dwarfed by Baghdad and Samarra, each of which covered almost 9,000 hectares, and eighth-century Ch'ang-an was at least as large even without its vast imperial park and palace.

A simple technique for comparing the towns of a region according to size and assessing the character of the settlement and hence the relations between towns is rank-size analysis (Johnson 1980; cf. Paynter 1982). When the sizes of individual towns are plotted along the vertical axis and rank according to size along the horizontal one, an approximately *straight* line extending from the largest town with a downward slope of 45° indicates a well-integrated system, with a balanced distribution of functions and activities between larger and smaller towns. If the curve is *convex*, several large towns of more or less equal size are in competition with one another, and the system is relatively poorly integrated. If the curve is *concave*, one town is appreciably larger than the others, and the system is 'overintegrated', a large amount of energy being required for transport to and from the centre. A convex curve also implies that the region is peripheral, a concave one that it is centrally located in a larger system. Peripheral regions are also regions of potential growth, while central regions in a very mature system are regions of potential decline. A concave curve may also, however, represent a very immature system.

The size distribution of towns in a territory with an ancient city-state system in its primary form, such as Etruria, will be expected to produce a convex curve when it is analysed in this way. Individual main towns are relatively independent, and there are several centres of more or less the same size. Where such a system is integrated into a larger political unit, as under the Roman Republic or the Early Roman Empire, the distribution of centres at the heart of the system will produce a concave curve because the imperial capital is also the main town for the region. This pattern is probably reached through a state in which the distribution of towns produces a straight line (see Guidi 1985). Finally, a straight line can be expected in societies in an advanced state of integration – for instance, where efficient marketing systems exist and where connections with other territories, which as a rule run through the main town and tend to give it more than ordinary growth, are not unusually well developed. A good example of this situation is that of the main Danish towns around AD 1200 (Randsborg 1982b).

In testing these hypotheses the major problem is the quality of the source material. As a rule it is difficult to produce sufficient empirical (in this case archaeological) information on the areas of even the ten largest towns in any region of the Roman Empire (the north-western provinces are an exception). In addition, there are chronological difficulties because, for instance, walls were not erected simultaneously in the different towns. Finally, some older and conflicting bits of evidence have not yet been reappraised. With these reservations in mind, the following observations can be made.

The distribution of towns in Italy during the Early Empire is, as expected, concave, because the size of Rome is determined by its role as imperial capital (Russell 1958 with revisions; cf. Beloch 1898). Palermo and Capua, each covering an area of about 200 hectares, are the next-largest towns. In Spain, in contrast, the line is virtually straight, with Cadiz, covering an area of just under 400 hectares, as the largest town. The same applies to the towns of western Asia Minor, led by Smyrna (Izmir) with an area of a little less than 600 hectares (Russell 1958 with revisions). In the more peripheral regions, there are convex distributions in the Rhône Valley and Britain (Russell 1958 with revisions; cf. Hingley 1982: 46). In Gaul, in addition, there is a very important change in the pattern from Early to Late Roman times. In the latter period the largest towns lie on a straight line, which must mean that the centres of Gaul, and thus Gaul as a whole, became better integrated over time, the structure of settlement thus coming to resemble that in the Mediterranean area in the Early Roman period even though its towns were usually smaller.

In the area between the Pyrenees and the Rhine, most of the major towns lay in the north, around Trier, in Late Roman times (Blanchet 1907; Brühl 1975;

Johnson 1983; and others). For the Trier area proper, only the roughly six largest towns lie on a straight line (fig. 49); the remaining towns form a concave pattern. Thus the largest towns constitute a system of their own in a region otherwise containing only small ones. This observation corresponds excellently with our knowledge that fourth-century Trier was set up mainly to administer the areas behind the frontier and supply the army. The less fortunate economic consequences of this development are, additionally, emphasized by the fact that, as we have seen, the villa complexes and other agrarian Roman settlements in the area were declining during this period. Looking in the same way at south-western Gaul in Late Roman times, when Toulouse was the largest town, although only a third the size of Trier, we find that only the four largest towns lie on a straight line (fig. 50); the remaining towns form a convex pattern, in contrast to the situation in the north. That there are a number of medium-sized towns in competition here is probably bound up with the fact that agrarian settlement continued to be quite considerable and there were still possibilities for economic maximization, for example through the general market. A corresponding argument can be applied to the Bulgarian region, where the Late Roman/Late Antique towns form a classic convex pattern with Philippopolis (Plovdiv) covering an area of just under 80 hectares and its rival, Marcianopolis, of 70 hectares, at the top (Biernacka-Lubańska 1982) (fig. 51). Thus Bulgaria was still a peripheral area with growth potential at this time, as is also indicated by the large number of agrarian sites dating from the fifth to the seventh century and the fact that the villa structure was dominated by large complexes.

The Roman towns of the Levant around AD 400, when growth was vigorous, provide yet another rare example of a concave distribution, with Antioch as an unusually large centre that ought to have been the capital of the Eastern Empire (Russell 1958). During the Crusades the Syrian towns generally form a straight line. It appears that the Islamic world also had very considerable centres, for example in independent and relatively isolated Spain, where the towns probably had a concave distribution with Cordoba as the main centre (Russell 1958). Even the medieval provincial towns in remote Denmark were included in a highly integrated system, and their rank-size distribution is a straight line (Randsborg 1982b).

Late Roman factories

A series of Late Roman documents provides systematic information on a number of factors in Late Roman society (Seeck 1876; cf. Jones 1964, 1966). *Notitia Dignitatum*, a handbook of Roman administration, gives, for instance, the positions of the military units around AD 400 and lists the state factories that were set up in towns mainly to supply the military but also to equip the large administrative apparatus, this too partly organized along military lines. This documentary information helps us to reconstruct large parts of the geography associated with the expenditure of the late Roman state and thereby to gain a

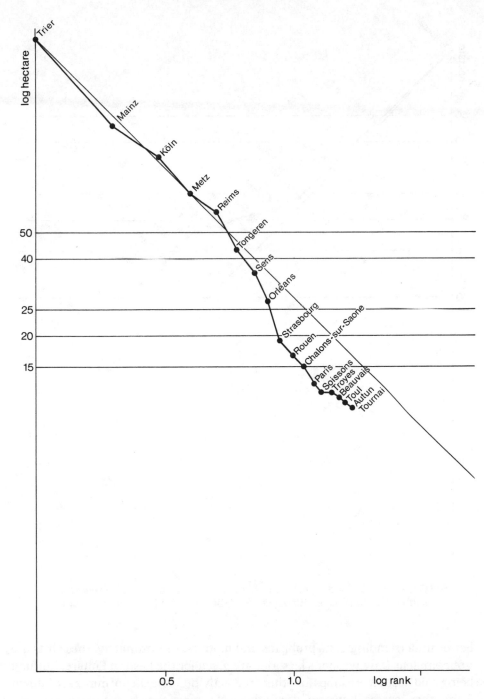

Fig. 49. Rank-size distribution of the major Late Roman walled towns in
Roman Germany and northern Gaul (*Sources*: Blanchet 1907; Brühl 1975;
Johnson 1983; and others)

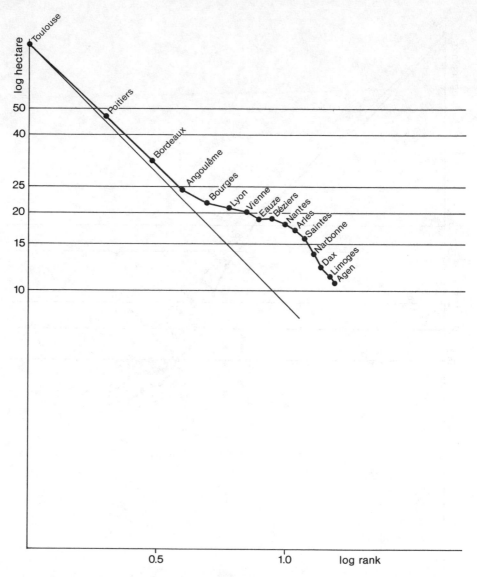

Fig. 50. Rank-size distribution of the major Late Roman walled towns in
southern Gaul (*Sources*: Blanchet 1907; Brühl 1975; Johnson 1983; and
others)

better understanding of its problems and motives. Unfortunately, these lists are
not complete. Only weapons factories are given for the Eastern Empire, nothing
being said about workshops for other craft activities. The sites of mints are known
from other sources, however, as are those of some of the other eastern factories,
for example for textiles.

The distribution of weapons factories is very informative about military
strategy, all of the factories occurring in a wide belt stretching from the Channel
across northern Italy, the Danube area, and the Bosphorus to south-eastern Asia

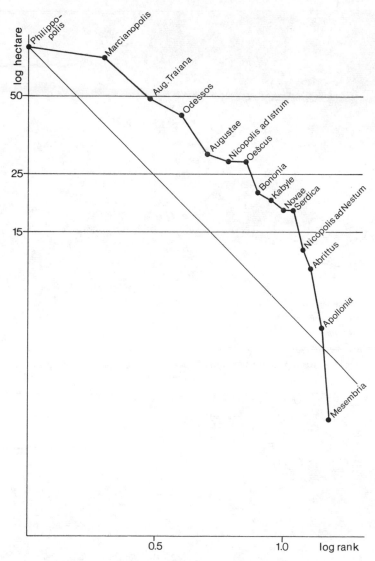

Fig. 51. Rank-size distribution of the major Late Roman/early Late
Antique walled towns in Lower Moesia and northern Thrace (present-day
Bulgaria) (*Source*: Biernacka-Lubańska 1982)

Minor and Syria (fig. 52) – close to (but probably, for security reasons, rarely
directly on) the continental northern frontier of the empire, the rivers Rhine and
Danube, or the eastern frontier in the upper reaches of the Euphrates. Factories
for woollen cloth and (along the Mediterranean coast) dye-works in particular
were concentrated in the same regions as the weapons factories (fig. 53), as also
were treasuries and mints (fig. 54). These lists reveal with almost painful clarity
what the empire's main problem was around the year AD 400: the possibility of
attack from beyond its frontiers. A very large share of the resources invested was

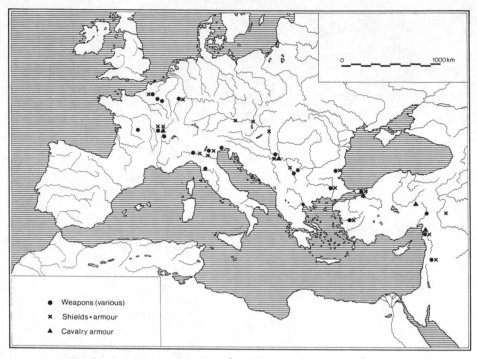

Fig. 52. Roman state weapons factories in AD 400 according to the
Notitia Dignitatum

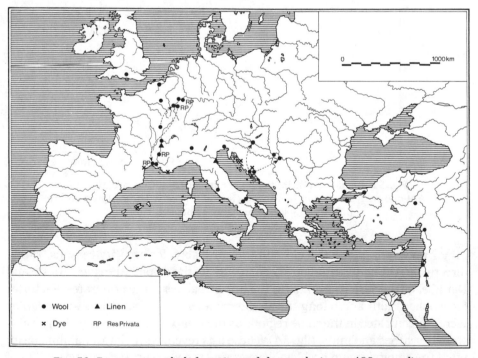

Fig. 53. Roman state cloth factories and dye-works in AD 400 according
to the *Notitia Dignitatum*. *Res privata*: imperial. Arrows indicate
movements of factories.

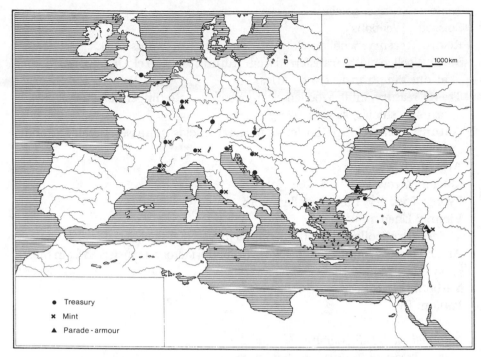

Fig. 54. Official treasuries and mints and Roman state factories producing costly parade armour at about AD 400 according to the *Notitia Dignitatum*

devoted to defence against barbarian aggression or attack by the Persians. It is hardly fortuitous that the four of five regional capitals known in the fourth century – Trier, Milan (later transferred to the well-protected Ravenna), Sirmium (near Belgrade), and Constantinople – lay within the belt of weapons factories. In addition, there was Antioch, which, although only an 'unofficial' capital, had many of the same functions as the centres just mentioned.

Certain institutions are tied by function to others. Mints occurred, of course, in places where there were treasuries and the associated administrative activities. Factories manufacturing parade armour for officers were sited only where there were also treasuries and woollen cloth factories. Weapons factories consistently coincided with cloth factories. These combinations, based on evidence relating to the Western Empire, can be used for a partial reconstruction of the situation in the east, where systematic information is available only for weapons factories and mints. The distribution by town of the various activities based on the *Notitia Dignitatum* and (for information in brackets) from other sources or logically deduced, is as follows:

Western Empire
Winchester: Woollen cloth
London: Treasure (earlier mint)
Tournai: Woollen cloth

Amiens: Swords, shields

Soissons: Weapons

Reims: Treasury, woollen cloth, parade armour, swords

Metz: Woollen cloth (transferred from Autun), woollen cloth (imperial factory at one time transferred to Arles)

Trier: Treasury, mint, woollen cloth, woollen cloth (imperial factory), parade armour, shields, siege artillery

Autun: Woollen cloth (transferred to Metz), shields, cuirasses, cavalry armour, siege artillery

Argenton: Weapons

Macon: Arrows

Lyons: Treasury, mint, woollen cloth

Vienne: Linen

Viviers (?): Woollen cloth (imperial factory)

Arles: Treasury, mint, woollen cloth, (imperial factory, transferred from Metz), parade armour

Narbonne: Dye

Toulon: Dye

Italy and the Middle Danube

Milan: Treasury, (mint), woollen cloth

Pavia (Ticinum): Bows (earlier also mint)

Cremona: Shields

Mantua: Cuirasses

Verona: Weapons, shields

Concordia (Portogruaro): Arrows

Aquileia: Treasury, mint, woollen cloth

Ravenna: Linen, (later mint and thus probably also treasury)

Lucca: Swords

Rome: Treasury, mint, woollen cloth

Canosa: Woollen cloth

Venosa: Woollen cloth

Taranto: Dye

Syracuse: Dye

'Italy': (Boots)

Balearics: Dye

Carthage: Woollen cloth, (earlier probably also treasury), (earlier mint), (later probably also treasury), (later mint)

'Africa' (Tunisia): Dye

Djerba: Dye

Pag (Cissa): Dye

Salona (Split): Treasury, woollen cloth (transferred to Petrovci [Basiana]), weapons

Split: Woollen cloth (transferred to Heténypuszta [Jovia]?)

Augsburg: Treasury

Lorch (Lauriacum): Shields

Petronell (Carnuntum): Shields

Budapest (Aquincum): Shields

Szombatheley (Savaria): Treasury

Heténypuszta (Jovia): Woollen cloth (transferred from Split?) (*Notitia Dignitatum* gives the province as 'Dalmatia', probably erroneously.)

Sisak (Siscia): Treasury, mint

Mitrovica (Sirmium): Woollen cloth, weapons, shields, saddles, etc.

Petrovci (Bassiana): Woollen cloth (transferred from Salona [Split])

Eastern Empire

Cuprija (Horreum Margi): Shields

Nis (Naissus): Weapons

Archar (Ratiaria): Weapons

Thessalonica: (Treasury), (mint), weapons

Devnya (Marcianopolis): Weapons, shields

Edirne (Hadrianopolis): Weapons, shields

Constantinople (Istanbul): (Treasury), (mint), (probably also woollen cloth), (parade armour)

Marmaraereglisi (Perinthus/Heraclea): (earlier probably treasury), (earlier mint), (woollen cloth)

Cycicus (near Bandirma): (earlier probably treasury), (earlier mint), (woollen cloth), weapons, shields, cavalry armour

Iznik (Nicaea): (Treasury)

Sardis: Weapons, shields

Kayseri (Caesarea): (Woollen cloth), cavalry armour

Maras (Irenopolis): Lances

Urfa (Edessa): Shields, (armoury for the Euphrates fleet)

Antakya (Antioch): (Treasury), (mint), (probably also woollen cloth), (parade armour), weapons, shields, cavalry armour

Damascus: Weapons, shields

Tyrus: (Woollen cloth)

Beÿt Shean (Scythopolis): (Linen)

Alexandria: (Earlier mint), (earlier probably treasury)

'Phoenicia': (Dye)

Cyprus: (Dye)

The 'Oriens' region: Parade armour (= Antioch's factory?)

The 'Asiana' region: Parade armour

The 'Pontica' region: Parade armour

The 'Thrace and Illyricum' region (?): Parade armour (= Constantinople's factory?)

Armour production was more common in the east, production of weapons, probably in the main for use by the infantry, in the west. Everywhere factories producing defensive weapons were more frequent than those producing weapons for attack. *Notitia Dignitatum* does not reflect the state's total need for weapons, cloth, etc.; state factories were probably supplementary in function and guaranteed supplies to strategic regions.

Churches, mosaics, and inscriptions

Monuments, mosaics, and inscriptions in stone offer the possibility of studying the development of Roman and other towns and centres and of making comparisons with, for example, Roman villas. Furthermore, through the study of churches insight can be gained into developments from the Late Roman period to the turn of the millennium, an interval in which statistical study is otherwise difficult. It is important to recognize, however, that these are cultural manifestations whose frequency may vary over time and from one area to another and that they are not necessarily dependent on the development of the economic system. A reduction in the number of inscriptions need not, therefore, indicate that towns or rural settlements were declining; it may just as well reflect a change in ideology or social norms. In this context it is probably the changes in the system as a whole that should interest us, but it may be useful to consider this cultural material, which in Antiquity often required the investment of large sums of money, as an economic indicator and an indicator of settlement. To a great extent a town is what it is by virtue of its monuments. Similarly, a prominent family of the first millennium was what it was by virtue of its social associations and the way in which these were expressed, in other words, the investments it made to demonstrate its status. Within a single ideological and cultural period or region, church building, for instance, can be a general indicator of economic growth and decline.

Written sources show that the number of churches built or reconstructed in Rome increased remarkably up to the second half of the fifth century (Ward-Perkins 1984; cf. Krautheimer 1980) (fig. 55). Archaeological investigations of mosaics in the churches of Rome confirm this picture, but, as might be expected, the later periods, including the Carolingian, are better represented (Marinelli 1971; cf. Guidobaldi and Guidobaldi 1983 for the preserved floors only). Between AD 500 and 700 the building and rebuilding of churches was only modest, but in the eighth century a new climax was reached, followed by a new decline that lasted until the twelfth century. This development closely follows the changes taking place in Rome and in the realms that included Rome in their sphere of interest. The earliest churches, among them the imperial buildings from Constantine times, are situated, like San Giovanni in Laterano, on the outskirts of Rome or, like Saint Peter's, immediately outside its walls. Santa Maria Maggiore, built with papal funds, and Santa Sabina, built by a bishop, date from

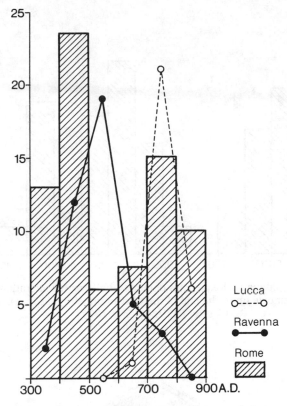

Fig. 55. Changing frequencies of church building (or alteration) in Lucca, Ravenna, and Rome, from AD 300 to 900 (*Source*: Ward-Perkins 1984)

the fifth century. The interiors of both churches remain more or less unchanged, Maggiore with its Late Antique mosaics, Sabina with its decorated wooden doors. The Carolingian churches include the well-preserved Santa Prassede, also funded by papal sources.

Ravenna, more important administratively in Late Antiquity than any other Italian town, was the scene of much church building in the fifth and sixth centuries. Many of the best-known and best-preserved buildings of the period are found here – for instance, San Vitale, built by a sixth-century banker at the cost of 36,000 solidi. The same gentleman also built the basilica on Ravenna's harbour, Sant'Apollinare in Classe, with its magnificent mosaics. In Ravenna itself Sant'Apollinare Nuovo was built by the Ostrogoth king Theodoric, whose mausoleum stands immediately outside the town. In Carolingian times Ravenna played only a minor role. The churches built in Pavia, one of the Langobardian centres, mainly date to the seventh to eighth century, the heyday of this kingdom. In Lucca the nobility built many churches in Carolingian times.

In Constantinople the first phase of church building and rebuilding lasted until the middle of the sixth century and included the best-known building of Late

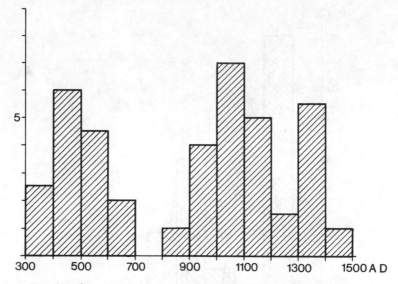

Fig. 56. Changing frequencies of church building (or alteration) in
Constantinople up to the end of the Christian metropolis in AD 1453
(*Source*: Müller-Wiener 1977)

Fig. 57. The west façade of the church of Qalblōze (Tchalenko 1953–58)

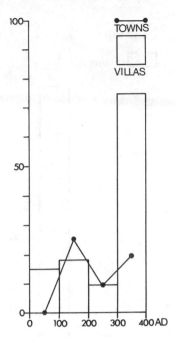

Fig. 58. Changing frequencies of Roman floor mosaics from towns and
villas in Britain (*Source*: Rainey 1973)

Antiquity, the well-preserved Sancta Sophia, whose original decoration was
badly damaged when the town was captured by the Turks in 1453 (Müller-
Wiener 1977) (fig. 56). After this first period of activity, which is the counterpart
of that at Rome and Ravenna, there was a revival of church building in the tenth
and particularly in the eleventh century, during the Middle Byzantine expansion.
This period ended with the conquest of Constantinople by the Crusaders. There
was, however, a last flowering of church building in the fourteenth century – a
Byzantine renaissance which, unlike the Italian one, had no chance to develop.
In the Levant, too, building activity was intense in Late Antiquity (Ovadiah
1970; Ovadiah and de Silva 1981, 1982) (fig. 57).

The study of floor mosaics allows comparisons between Roman villas and
towns that illuminate the development of the latter. In Britain, where there are
many mosaics in villas dating from the fourth century, contemporary mosaics in
towns are rare (Rainey 1973) (fig. 58). Around A D 200, in contrast, investment
in mosaics in towns was just as great as in villas. As in other areas, in the north-
western provinces the second to early third century saw the climax of towns. In
northern Gaul investment in mosaics culminated around A D 200 both in towns
and in rural areas (for Gaul as a whole see Stern 1957, 1960, 1967; Stern and
Blanchard-Lemée 1977; Daimon and Lavagne 1977; Barral i Altet 1980), and
the same was the case in eastern Gaul. In central Gaul, however, there was some
investment in mosaics for villas in the fourth century. In south-western Gaul

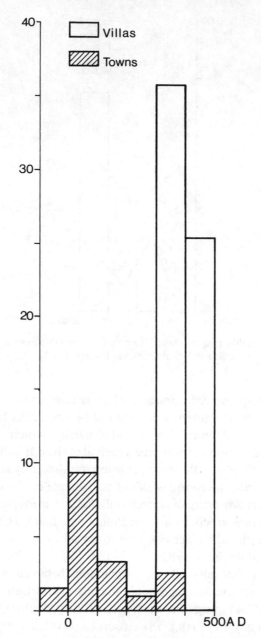

Fig. 59. Late Roman (and Late Antique) floor mosaics from towns and
villas in southernmost Aquitania (south-western France) (*Source*: Barral i
Altet 1980)

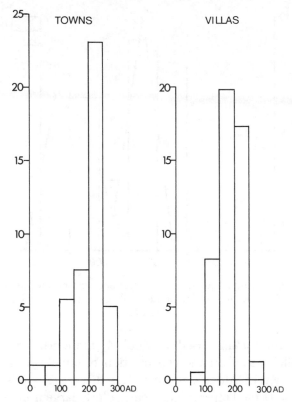

Fig. 60. Changing frequencies of Roman floor mosaics from towns and villas in Switzerland (*Source*: von Gonzenbach 1961)

mosaics in towns chiefly date from the first century and those in rural areas from the fourth and fifth (fig. 59). In south-eastern Gaul, too, the majority of mosaics in urban settings originate from the Early Roman period. Villa mosaics, and hence evidence of aristocratic life in the rural areas, are extremely rare here.

In Switzerland, as in adjacent areas in France, investment in mosaics was at its peak in both urban and rural districts around AD 200 (von Gonzenbach 1961) (fig. 60). In the Salzburg area, a similar picture emerges, but here there were also many mosaics in the fourth century in both towns and rural areas (Jobst 1982) (fig. 61). As in south-western Gaul, there must have been relatively stable conditions here. Still farther east, in Hungary, which saw a steady growth in the number of villas throughout the Roman period, investment in mosaics was remarkably modest, but there are a few finds from towns dating from around AD 200 (Kiss 1973).

In Italy the number of mosaics reached its height, for example in Anzio and Ostia, Rome's harbour town, in the second century (Becatti 1961; Scrinari and Matini 1975), but on Sardinia there were in general still many mosaics in the

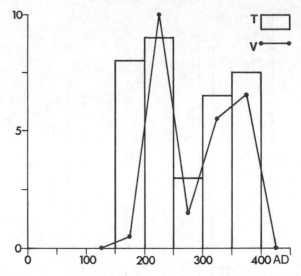

Fig. 61. Changing frequencies of Roman floor mosaics in the Salzburg area: (T) from the town of Iuvavum (Salzburg), (V) from villas (*Source*: Jobst 1982)

date from the Late Roman period, particularly the fourth century (Dunbabin 1978; cf. Lepelley 1979 on the construction of buildings in fourth-century towns). Other towns in 'Africa' show a pattern that corresponds more closely to that of Anzio and Ostia. Ephesus had a particularly large number of mosaics in the fourth century, but some date from the fifth (Jobst 1977). In Antioch the number of mosaics was considerable from about A D 100 to the sixth century, with a peak in the fifth (Levy 1947).

To sum up, we find good chronological and geographical correlation between investment in floor mosaics in towns and the general development of the Roman Empire, as, for example, at Ravenna in the fifth century (Berti 1976). At the same time, the mosaic finds in villas show that urban and rural development did not always correspond closely, for example in Britain and south-western France. Hungary provides an example of pronounced agricultural development in the Late Roman period that apparently did not give rise to much investment in floor mosaics. Perhaps this was because many of the landowners, unlike those in the Salzburg region, in south-western Gaul, in Britain, and in many areas of the Mediterranean, were absentees.

Like the mosaics, Roman inscriptions in stone may allow comparison of urban and rural areas. In the Lugo area of north-western Spain, for instance, inscriptions connected with graves are more numerous than votive inscriptions in the town, but of equal frequency in the country (Vilas, Roux, and Tranoy 1979). The number of inscriptions in the Lugo area reaches a climax in the second century; there are somewhat fewer in the third and none at all in the fourth. A larger quantity of material originates from the province of Noricum (present-day

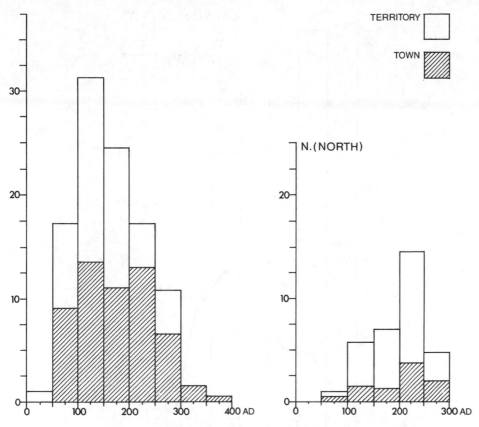

Fig. 62. Changing frequencies of Roman inscriptions in stone naming officials from towns and the countryside in (A) southern and (B) northern Noricum, showing the late development of the northern region and the absence of fourth-century inscriptions in this area (*Source*: Alföldy 1974)

Austria); here a survey of urban civil servants, for example, again points to the second century as the heyday of inscriptions, especially in the rural areas, and there are virtually no inscriptions dating from the fourth century (Alföldy 1974: appendix Xiii; cf. Leber 1972) (fig. 62). In the town and territory of Szombathely (Savaria) in Hungary the chronological picture is the same as it is in Noricum, and almost all of the relatively few Late Roman inscriptions come from the town itself (Mócsy and Szentléleky 1971). Contrary to the situation in Lugo, grave inscriptions predominate in the country but are only as frequent as votive inscriptions in the town. Thus no simple rule for the distribution of the different types of inscriptions can be observed. The many early and few late inscriptions in, for instance, Hungary, which shows considerable settlement in the fourth century, clearly prove that inscriptions in these areas are associated particularly with Early Roman society, with its pronounced status rivalry.

In Cologne, the number of inscriptions does not reach its peak until the third

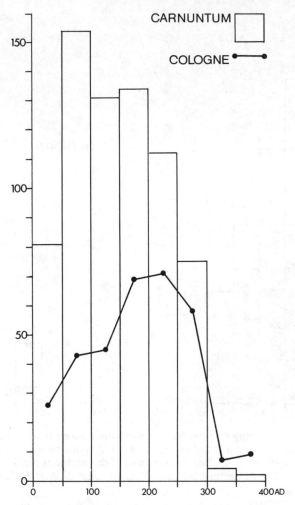

Fig. 63. Frequencies of Roman military and civil inscriptions in stone from
Carnuntum (Austria) and Cologne (*Sources*: Galsterer and Galsterer 1975;
Vorbeck 1980a and b)

century, when there are slightly more than in the second, and again there are
virtually no inscriptions dating from the fourth (Galsterer and Galsterer 1975)
(fig. 63). The Cologne material can be subclassified as military or civilian, the
latter being more conspicuous in the second to third century. Grave inscriptions
predominate in all the first-century material. In the following two centuries,
there are equal numbers of votive and grave inscriptions for both civilians and
the military.

At Carnuntum, on the Danube in Austria, the number of inscriptions reaches
its peak in the second century (Vorbeck 1980a and b) (see fig. 63). Military
inscriptions, again, are particularly frequent in the first century, civilian ones in
the second to third. There are virtually no finds dating from the fourth century.

Plate 1. The colossal, luxurious country house of the emperor Hadrian, an imaginative architectural landscape at Tivoli, east of Rome, and a significant example of the intellectual, organizational, and technical achievements of the Early Empire. The motif is from the so-called Maritime Theatre, next to the libraries, early second century AD.

Plate 2. Selected artefacts from a grave at Himlingeøje, eastern Zealand, mid-third century AD. The glasses and the silver-plated bronze dish were manufactured in the Roman Rhineland; the golden trinkets were local. The grave also contained a Roman bronze bucket, a Roman ladle and strainer, a wooden dish, a comb of bone, and fragments of clothing. The red drinking horn had been produced to the Germanic taste. (Photo National museum).

Plate 3. The city walls of Constantinople (Istanbul) erected during the reign of emperor Theodosius the Second in the early fifth century AD. The heavy double walls with ditches saved the city, and thus the eastern Roman and Byzantine empires, on several occasions. They were not scaled until the Turkish assault of AD 1453, and then only after heavy cannon fire.

Plate 4. The city of Ephesus in western Turkey as seen from its great ancient theatre (which seated 24,000). In the background is the 500-metre-long marble-covered 'Arcadian Street' named for the emperor Arcadius, from the early fifth century AD, with deep colonnades, shops, and, according to an inscription, fifty street lamps. The street led to the harbour.

Plate 5. Interior of Santa Sophia in Constantinople (Istanbul) erected in the AD 530s during the reign of emperor Justinian and in AD 1453 converted into a mosque, now a museum.

Plate 6. Highly decorated columns and capitals from the church of Saint Polyeuktos in Constantinople (Saraçhane, Istanbul) in front of the church of San Marco in Venice, where they were brought by the crusaders in the thirteenth century. (The famous porphyry statue of Late Roman emperors, also transferred from Constantinople, appear dimly at the corner.) Fragments of identical capitals and columns have recently been brought to light by the excavation of the Saint Polyeuktos, which was erected in the early sixth century and abandoned around AD 1000 (cf. fig. 74).

Plate 7. A mid-sixth-century AD wall mosaic from the church of San Vitale in Ravenna, depicting the empress Theodora, the wife of Justinian, donating a golden chalice to the church, the apse of which appears in the background.

Plate 8. Brooches of bronze – the small one tinned, the larger one gilded – from female graves at Nørre Sandegård on the island of Bornholm, Denmark, seventh century A D. The decorative, textile-like effect – often seen in mosaics – of the intentionally slightly oblique pattern on the smaller fibula is interesting. The larger fibula is decorated with two antithetical, backward-looking animals whose enlarged hind thighs and legs are intertwined and whose jaws are biting their own double-lined body as well as the hind foot. The thighs also make up the mask of a bearded man which, seen upside down, resembles a doubled-up and bound human figure (Photo National Museum).

Plate 9. Carolingian representation of villeinage in different months of the year, from an illustrated manuscript produced in Salzburg in AD 819 (Wilhelmi et al. 1985).

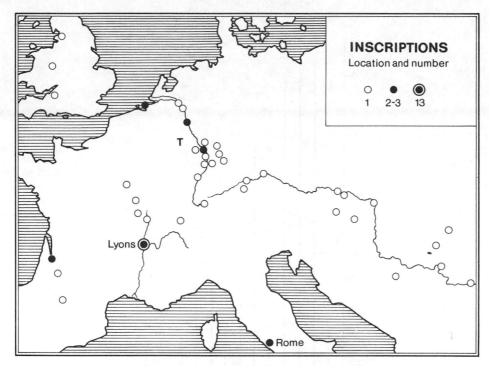

INSCRIPTIONS
Location and number

○   ●   ◎
1   2-3   13

Fig. 64. Citizens of Trier (T) mentioned in Roman inscriptions in stone
from areas outside the city territory (after Krier 1981)

Once again, grave inscriptions stand almost alone in the first century, while
votive inscriptions dominate in the second and third – the zenith of the town's
prosperity, when investment shifted from an explicit marking of the individual to
the giving of prominence to leading citizens.

A collection of inscriptions from the north-western provinces, associated with
citizens from Trier, sums up the situation in these parts of the empire (Krier 1981)
(fig. 64). Although Trier was one of the empire's capitals in the fourth century,
only one inscription dates from this century, and it was found in Rome. Almost all
of the material dates from AD 50–250, with a peak in the second century. The
'Trier inscriptions' are widely scattered, and as a rule only one has been found in
each locality. Lyon with thirteen inscriptions, Mainz, and Rome are exceptions.

In Rome and its immediate vicinity, the material is so vast that the dated
inscriptions will be used as examples. These inscriptions indicate that the first
century was the zenith for their use (Gordon 1965) (fig. 65). From then on the
number declines, most markedly in the third century. During the first three
centuries, then, circumstances in Rome correspond to those in the other towns
discussed, with the slight difference that the peak is earlier than in the provinces.
Where Rome differs is in the lesser but still considerable number of inscriptions
dating from the fourth and fifth centuries. Post-dating inscriptions elsewhere in
the Western Empire, special social significance must be ascribed to them.

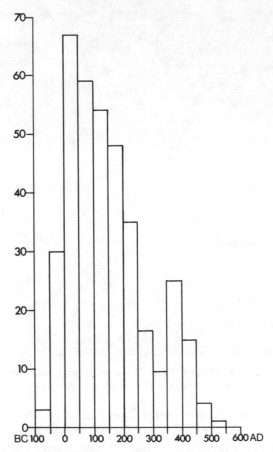

Fig. 65. Changing frequencies of dated inscriptions in stone from Rome
and its immediate vicinity. These inscriptions often have a more or less
official character (*Source*: Gordon 1965)

In the western Mediterranean, Caesarea confirms the typical picture (Leveau
1984), but here, as in Rome, the majority of inscriptions date from the first
century. There is only one dating to the fourth to fifth century. In 'Africa' the
picture differs somewhat, among other things because of some building inscriptions dating from the fourth century (Lepelley 1979; see Durliat 1981 for
inscriptions on Byzantine forts after the Justinian reconquest in the sixth century; Merlin 1944; Gsell 1922). A similar picture appears in western Libya, for
example in Leptis Magna (Reynolds and Ward-Perkins 1952). Here, as elsewhere
in this context, inscriptions on milestones are excluded. These are common in the
Late Roman period and especially in the third century. Special efforts were
evidently made at this time of crisis to maintain and develop the state communication system, presumably first and foremost for military reasons.

At Salona, near Split in Dalmatia, inscriptions in stone continue into the fourth
and even the fifth century (Brøndsted 1928). At Salonica the number of inscrip-

tions increases from 100 BC to AD 100 (Edson 1972). After a peak in the second and third centuries, the number decreases in the fourth and especially the fifth century. Votive inscriptions are common in the first century BC and in Early Roman times, rare later on. In the third century honorary inscriptions occur very frequently and can perhaps be viewed as a kind of replacement for votive inscriptions. They are associated in particular with the Greek eastern towns of the Roman Empire. Generally, grave inscriptions make up the largest group, and these are very numerous in the second century, after which their number falls very markedly.

In Sardis, western Asia Minor, the number of inscriptions increases sharply after about 200 BC and shows a marked decrease from the third to the sixth centuries (Buckler and Robinson 1932). The distribution of the various types of inscriptions over time shows no special variation apart from an unusually high frequency of grave inscriptions in the first century BC. From the same general region there is also a large body of inscriptions from Ephesus; this material is particularly rich in the second century AD, when, for instance, a number of stones bearing honorary texts were erected (cf. Knibbe and Iplikçioglu 1984). Finally, Corinth, in the western Aegean, has many Early Roman inscriptions (Kent 1966). In general the Aegean inscriptions show the same decreases in Late Roman times as do these in the provinces farther west, and as in Italy and 'Africa' there is also a small number of later inscriptions, particularly from the fourth century.

Against this background the situation in the Levant is surprising in its wealth of indications of interest in inscriptions in stone and thus of very widespread literacy. In towns such as Antioch and Apamea by far the greatest amount of dated material originates either from the fourth century or, generally, from Late Antiquity (Jalabert, Mouterde, [and Mondésert] 1955) (fig. 66). Many inscriptions date from around AD 500, when the economic position of the Levant was very strong and investment in buildings, for example monasteries and churches, considerable. As is also demonstrated by the Antioch mosaics, it seems that in the east towns were still large and rich in Late Antiquity. While these inscriptions are clearly associated in frequency with the economic development of the settlements, one should beware of reading their frequencies as a simple index of population numbers. Inscriptions associated with monuments may enhance an impression of growth and, through their absence, suggest a more dramatic recession than often was the case. Inscriptions in Britain are very few for the entire Roman period (Biró 1975).

Other late evidence of inscriptions in stone comes from the western provinces and takes the form of usually very modest, flat Christian gravestones. These inscriptions have not been included in the above comparisons. In Rome such gravestones become common around AD 400, when Christianity was gathering strength, but vanish again in the latter half of the sixth century together with Late Antique society. The same phenomenon has been recognized in Trier and

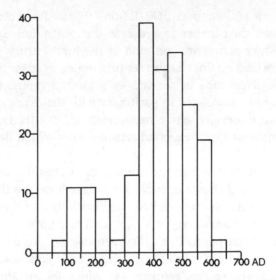

Fig. 66. Frequencies of Roman and Late Antique inscriptions in stone
with annual dates from Antioch (*Source*: Jalabert, Mouterde, [and
Mondésert] 1955)

elsewhere in the west (fig. 67), where gravestones begin to appear around AD
400, are frequent around AD 500, and then become fewer and fewer. Their
disappearance can perhaps be viewed in the light of the fact that the early-
medieval societies in Western Europe were anchored in fixed kinship structures
that required no special marking (Vives 1969; Krämer 1974; Gauthier 1975).
Thus these gravestones, which though small are still 'monuments', reflect, as do
the Levantine inscriptions, the often overlooked expansion and special character
of Late Antique society.

Roman forts

A special and historically and socially very important form of settlement in the
first millennium is represented by Roman fortified camps, fortresses, and guard
posts. Agriculture was carried on directly and indirectly from the forts, especially
the later ones, but their relationship to the state apparatus and their role in local
society make it more appropriate to deal with them in connection with centres
and towns. Alongside many forts there were townlike civilian settlements with
dwellings for the camp-followers, craftsmen, traders, and so on, who served them
and absorbed part of the wages of the soldiers or militia. Finally, the role of the
military in the process of Romanization during the Early Empire can hardly be
overestimated. Military needs had a very high priority and called for both the
transport of large quantities of commodities over both short and long distances
and large-scale production in many craft sectors. Many items, for instance tiles,
were, in addition, produced by the military themselves and could be acquired by

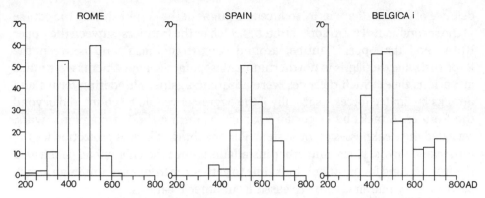

Fig. 67. Frequencies of small Christian gravestones with inscriptions from
Rome, Spain and northern Gaul (*Sources*: Vives 1969; Krämer 1974;
Gauthier 1975)

civilians. Thus the army assisted in fostering production and exchange in times
and places in which urban development had scarcely begun.

Roman forts are found particularly in the provinces and, of course, primarily in
those marginal regions whose safety was essential for production in the
heartland of the empire. A good example is provided by Britain, where forts were
concentrated in the military zones to the west and north, which were only
partially Romanized. Here permanent barriers, the best-known of which is
Hadrian's Wall, were also established to protect the empire from penetration by
peoples from Scotland, who were never pacified (see, e.g., Wacher 1978). On the
Rhine the Roman military authorities were forced to set up a defence system for
the frontier even in the phase of conquest (Luttwak 1976). In other areas,
particularly in the east, client kingdoms bore the brunt of the problems that
followed in the wake of establishing a frontier zone between two social systems.
The Germanic communities on the Rhine were not sufficiently well organized
and socially stratified to be acceptable as clients, and it was very difficult to reach
lasting agreements with them. Attempts here in the early first century to achieve
stability by advancing the frontier came to nothing, as they did in the second
century in Scotland. The result was that Roman legions had to be stationed on
the west bank of the Rhine itself and not, as elsewhere, in a strategic position
some distance from the frontier. A large number of medium-sized and small forts
erected parallel to the large legionary camps have been the object of much careful
archaeological research, making the Rhine frontier probably the best-known
such region. It is characteristic of the early imperial forts that they had a regular
perimeter, a regular plan, and a grid network of streets, in this respect resembling
the contemporary towns. They were lightly fortified; towers, for instance, were
often erected inside the walls, thus serving more as watchtowers than to protect
the ramparts. Where a continuous line of forts was set up, the ramparts and other
fortifications between them were also light.

The system embodying, as a rule, a fixed frontier and the permanent linear defence of this frontier was introduced throughout the empire during the course of the second century. On some stretches, such as the frontiers between the Upper Rhine and the Upper Danube, around conquered Dacia, and between the Euphrates and the Tigris in northernmost Mesopotamia, adjustments were made at various times. Such defences were adequate against plundering forays and attacks by limited forces, especially if the aggressors could be countered beyond the frontier. Attacks by larger forces, such as during the Marcomannic wars, revealed the weaknesses of the system. For one thing, it lacked protection for the hinterland towns, villas, and other installations once the enemy had penetrated the frontier, and for another it took time to gather the troops to counter an attack because they had first to be released from other locations.

In the third century the central political system was weakened by power struggles and civil war, inviting attacks on the empire's frontiers. On the northern one, as the Germanic communities became better organized, the area between the Upper Rhine and the Upper Danube, as well as Dacia, had to be abandoned. On the eastern frontier the Sassanids succeeded in capturing the emperor Valerian and conquering the region all the way to the Upper Euphrates. In large areas battles also had to be fought against enemy forces that had already penetrated the empire; only towards the end of the third century was the situation stabilized again. Among the many military alterations resulting from these experiences was the stationing of strong units – in particular the mobile, highly professional field armies – behind the frontier and the fortifying of all important complexes, including towns. Troops were increased perhaps to about twice their former strength, and this led to great problems of political economy, especially in the Western Empire, where the frontier was twice as long as in the economically stronger East. The western army was not only smaller than the eastern one but had a smaller percentage of frontier troops. Its field army, however, was larger. Field armies were important in struggles for political power, and while their establishment perhaps extended the life of the Roman Empire in the face of its enemies they became a useful tool in the hands of usurpers.

The military reorganization of the third and fourth centuries is observable archaeologically in many ways. All over the empire there are Late Roman and Late Antique fortresses that, in contrast to the Early Roman ones, gave relatively limited forces a good chance of withstanding a siege (fig. 68). The considerable state investment in frontier fortifications and their associated troops can be measured directly by investigating these buildings archaeologically. A general expansion of forts along the European frontier can be noted in the third century and later, in particular under the emperor Valentinian (A D 364–375). Under increasing military pressure, this emperor made an effort to maintain the credibility of the frontier, perhaps chiefly to preserve it as a 'trip wire', because forts, at any rate in Hungary, were mainly small observation posts (see e.g., Soproni 1978; cf. Soproni 1985). Along the Rhine and in its hinterland as far as northernmost Gaul, as well as along the Upper Danube, fort building appears to

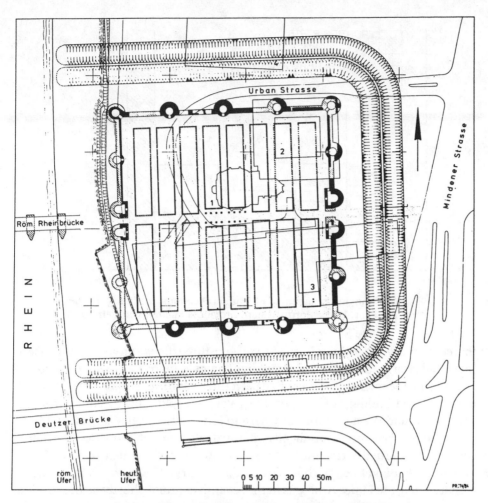

Fig. 68. The Late Roman Castellum Divitia in Cologne (Köln-Deutz), a
strongly fortified major bridgehead on the right bank of the Rhine,
connected with the town by a stone bridge. The heavy bastion towers are
typical of the period. Inside were barracks accommodating up to 1,000
troops. The fortress was evacuated at the beginning of the fifth century
and later turned into a royal compound by the Franks; a church was
erected around AD 1000 if not before (after Horn 1987)

have been considerable in the second half of the third century and in the time of
Valentinian (von Petrikovits 1971) (fig. 69). Fortification of civilian complexes
apparently occurred in the third century in particular.

Information relating to the Limes Arabicus in Jordan allows study of the whole
imperial period from before the birth of Christ to the first half of the seventh
century, when the fortifications fell to the armies of Islam (Parker 1976) (fig. 70).
Here the number of forts remained virtually the same up to about AD 200. In the
third century it doubled, particularly after the Persian attacks in the latter half of

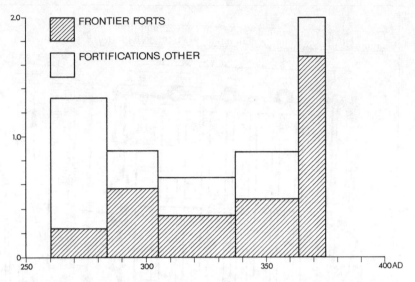

Fig. 69. Changing numbers of Roman fortifications, including frontier forts, per year, in the north-western provinces (*Source*: von Petrikovits 1971)

this century. By Valentinian's time there were three times as many forts in use as there had been in the first century and eight times as many forts were constructed and manned per century as there had been three centuries earlier. After this both manning and building of forts declined very sharply, but, in contrast to the situation in the Western Empire, where to judge from archaeological evidence the frontier was only sporadically manned after about AD 400, the Limes Arabicus continued in use until AD 640. The number of manned forts had fallen, however, to a level below that of the first century. There was some building activity along the Limes Arabicus in the seventh century, shortly before the final catastrophes.

Thus it seems clear that the Roman administration took steps to secure the frontiers of the empire in times of unrest but that these were not always sufficient. In particular, against the background of the studies on the Limes Arabicus, it seems remarkable that the frontier was allowed to decay in the fifth and sixth centuries. In the Arabian case reliance on tribal clients to patrol the areas across the frontier played a role. That there was some reconstruction around AD 500, the period of economic advance in the Eastern Empire, may indicate that part of the reason for the decay in frontier defence was financial. Another part may have been the increasing role of the field armies, which attracted men and resources and profited from their conquests (for instance, Justinian's campaigns in the west). In spite of the territorial prizes won, these forays hardly had the desired fiscal results and may have contributed catastrophically to an erosion of the empire's reserves. The crucial financial decline set in, however, only during the Persian wars, a few decades before the Islamic attack.

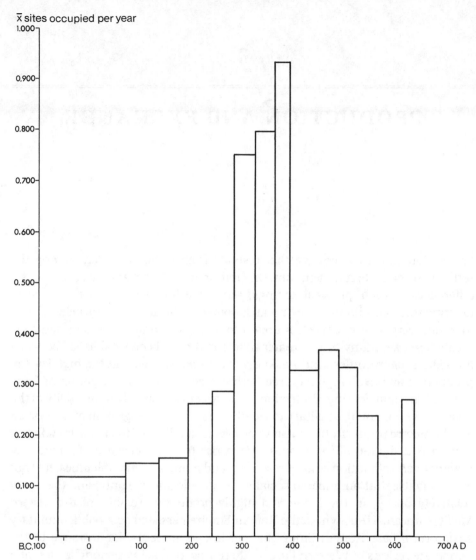

Fig. 70. Changing numbers of Roman and Late Antique frontier fortifications on the Limes Arabicus in Jordan (*Source*: Parker 1976)

6

PRODUCTION AND EXCHANGE

Production and the exchange that resulted from it varied widely among the
settlements of the first millennium. One reason for this variation was, of course,
differences in their physical settings, but more important was their widely
differing social conditions. The Roman Empire had the advantage of being able to
integrate very different types of area into a single economic system and thus
create a market many times greater than could have been established between
individual communities. One weakness of the empire was that the high level of
production and exchange required both protection and participation of large
areas on an equal footing. Protection of the system depended on the ability of the
political system and the military to weather crises. The integration of the system
was hampered primarily by transport problems that limited full participation to a
few areas and often differing ones, giving rise to crises because of a tendency
toward overexploitation of local resources and management difficulties. It is not
inconceivable that an imperial social system could survive only, and then only
relatively briefly, in the fertile and highly productive regions of the eastern
Mediterranean. Thus, where the Roman Empire persisted as a politico-military
structure in Late Roman times but had lost its impetus, for instance in the
temperate regions of Western Europe, there was increasing regionalization and
narrowing of the market. One result of this was, incidentally, the reduction of
social differences between the empire and the increasingly advanced barbarian
societies beyond its frontiers.

The Roman economy had to employ a number of distribution methods that
depended directly on the politico-military system. Many commodities were often
distributed outside the market system and subsidiary to military supplies. Pottery
is, for example, part of the cargoes, almost entirely foodstuffs, of Roman wrecks in
the Mediterranean (Fulford 1987; Parker 1984). Minting was also apparently
organized primarily with a view to the state's transactions rather than to
increasing the volume of trade (Grierson 1961; Reece, e.g., 1982a, 1985). In
spite of its magnitude, its level of production, and its ability to move large
quantities of commodities over long distances, the Roman economy was unstable

and not very well developed (Garnsey and Saller 1987). We tend to concentrate on the many conspicuous results – for instance, the monumental buildings – that reflect a 'consumer economy' or on the dense Early Roman agrarian settlement around Rome and to forget the many backward regions and the fact that the results were often short-lived.

The barbarian economies, as far as these survived the Roman expansion, were characterized by relatively low-level production and self-sufficiency. Exchange on an international level was dominated by luxury items, which through social links might be moved over very long distances with little regard to expense. We know less about regional exchange, but one thing is certain: that, influenced by relations with the empire, more advanced social systems came into being in the Late Roman period. Where exchange had earlier been general, there was now clearly a tendency towards regional monopolization of imported luxuries (Randsborg 1986). In addition, 'centres' were created – both special geographical areas of production and exchange and settlement sites with seasonal markets, craft production, and off-loading facilities, the forerunners of the later emporia. The collapse of the Roman Empire along the Rhine–Danube frontier led to a social levelling in the area, and this presented the opportunity for new partnerships in production and exchange among the barbarian and other societies, particularly after the traditions of Late Antiquity had faded.

A large share of the international trade and exchange in Carolingian times was conducted through the emporia of north-western Europe (see Hodges 1982), which represent attempts to organize production and exchange along 'imperial' lines by favouring particular sectors and thereby enhancing regional development. In Eastern Europe there were similar advances in some areas, central Czechoslovakia being one, but, perhaps with the exception of Bulgaria, on a far smaller scale. Nor did these eastern regions participate in the subsequent transformation of society in Western and Northern Europe; they followed their own path. Settlement changes were still taking place in rural Western Europe, but by the tenth century at the latest settlement had become fixed in most regions, and this created stable social and economic conditions for agriculture. Craft production and regional exchange in the form of markets became tied to towns, which showed renewed growth (Hodges 1988). Other changes – for instance, greater use of coins – also took place. At the same time, many places show less interest in large-scale international and luxury-based trading. This does not quite apply to the Mediterranean, where, because of its proximity to the world of Islam, a basis, although a modest one, was laid for the development of the interregional trading of the High Middle Ages.

Development of water transport

Widespread trade and other forms of exchange are typical of the classical world. Archaeologically this is apparent, for instance, from studies of pottery (both the amphorae used for transport of foodstuffs and the finer wares), of wrecks and their cargoes, and of metal objects, coins, etc. In addition, there is a fairly large quantity of documentary source material, although this is widely dispersed. Two groups of written sources in particular allow systematic treatment of the subject. One is the so-called Diocletian price index, dating from about AD 300, and the other the Egyptian papyri. The Diocletian index is actually an archaeological source, as all we know of it is fragmented stone tablets found in different towns in the eastern Mediterranean (for example, Aphrodisias in south-western Asia Minor), where it was publicly displayed in monumental form. Both in itself and in the way it was displayed, the index is evidence of the state's attempt to gain extensive control of society in the Late Roman period. It is also evidence of a lack of knowledge of economic forces, including inflation. The index contains a number of extremely interesting statements about services and commodities from everyday things like grain, oil, wine, and ordinary cloth to cinnamon, silk, and sealskin. Other items range from the wages of an agricultural labourer to the expenses connected with hiring a teacher of rhetoric.

An important part of the index deals with the maximum prices for transport over land and by sea, the last measured in modii or 'bushels', here probably a little less than thirteen litres (Duncan-Jones 1982: 371–2). A tabulation of specific sea routes allows us to assume that these were the main ones, at any rate for the eastern and central parts of the empire, as they are listed with an eastern or central port of shipment. Thus the list may also reflect the fact that the empire's economic centre of gravity already lay in the eastern provinces by about AD 300. The following routes are given with geographical information and transport prices in denarii per bushel (Giacchero 1974):

> From Alexandria to Rome (16), Nicomedia, an imperial capital under the emperor Diocletian (12), Byzantium, later Constantinople (12), Dalmatia (18), Aquileia (24), 'Africa' (10), Sicily (10), Ephesus (8), Salonica (12), and Pamphylia, in southern Asia Minor (6).
>
> From The Orient (the Levant) to Rome (18), Salona (16), Aquileia (22), 'Africa' (16), Spain (20), Baetica, in south-western Spain (22), Terraconensis, in north-eastern Spain (-), Lusitania (Portugal) (26), Gaul (24), Byzantium (12), Ephesus (10), and Sicily (16).
>
> From Asia (Asia Minor) to Rome (16), 'Africa' (8), and Dalmatia (12).
>
> From Africa (Tunisia) to Rome (-), Salona (18), Sicily (6), Spain (8), Gaul (4), Archaia (southern Greece) (12), Pamphylia (14).
>
> From Rome to Sicily (6), Salonica (18), Archaia (14), Spain (10), Gaul (4), and, once again, Gaul (8).
>
> From Nicomedia to Rome (18), Ephesus (6), Salonica (8), Archaia (8), Salona (14), Pamphylia (8), Phoenicia (the Levant) (12), ? (16), and (etc. ?).
>
> From Byzantium (Later Constantinople) to ? (16).
>
> From Sicily to 'Africa' (-) and Genoa (-).
>
> From Sardinia to Rome (?) (-), Genoa (?) (-), and ? (-).
>
> From Ravenna to Aquileia ($7\frac{1}{2}$ – perhaps overland transport).

From ? to Trebizond (18), Sinope (and) Tomis (= Constantia) (8), 'Africa' (-), Sicily (-), Salonica (-), Pamphylia (-), Rome (?) (-), Amastris and Sinope (8).

Some of these tariffs seem surprising, considering the distances to be travelled, but probably such factors as winds and currents and number of possible means of transport were taken into account, and these are more difficult to assess (Rougé 1966). River transportation was relatively expensive but not as expensive as transport over land, which cost 20 denarii per mile for a wagon-load of just under 400 kilogrammes (Duncan-Jones 1977:366–7; Hendy 1985: 555–6).

With respect to Egypt in the Late Roman and Late Antique periods, there are lists of sea routes starting from Alexandria (Johnson and West 1949). Seven sources give Constantinople as final destination, five mentioning Palestine, three Greece, three Italy apart from Sicily (one of which especially mentions Rome), and three Gaul (two of which mention particular Mediterranean ports). There are two sources each for Antioch, 'Africa' (one of which mentions Carthage), and Sicily. Finally, there is one source each for Libya, the Adriatic, Spain, and Britain. It is strange that there are no routes mentioning Asia Minor. Five sources name sea routes to India among routes from Egypt to countries farther east. In addition to these distant trading routes there is much information about the internal trade that increasingly prospered after about AD 500, thus confirming an increasing regionalization. Supplementary information on sea routes appears in the Egyptian papyri, which list imported goods and their origins. There are ten groups of 'eastern' goods – commodities from Ethiopia, Arabia, Persia, India, and China. Another ten originated in Syria and Palestine, fourteen in Asia Minor and Armenia, four in Constantinople and the adjacent Balkans, fourteen in Greece, one in Italy, two in North Africa, three in Spain, four in Gaul, and one in Britain. Several of the categories of commodities and routes from the Western Roman Empire reached Egypt after this part of the empire had collapsed. To sum up, we find more sea routes from Egypt to the west than there were commodities arriving from this area. For the eastern parts of the empire, on the other hand, there were more imported goods than sea routes. Many goods were imported from Asia Minor, but no mention is made of sea routes to this area. The destinations of the sea routes thus primarily reveal the identities of Egypt's export partners.

The written sources that refer to Merovingian Gaul make it possible to consider a more isolated area and to study the Mediterranean from this inverted angle (Schwärzel 1983). Here we find almost forty sources relating to internal transport routes in Gaul. Some fifteen relate to the British Isles, slightly fewer to Spain, North Africa, and Italy together (three of these mentioning Rome). Only a few sources mention connections with Norsemen or Slavs. Six sources mention transport between Gaul and Constantinople, while as many as twenty mention the Near East, where Palestine, with its holy Christian places, receives special emphasis. Thus there is much evidence of contact even with the eastern Mediterranean in the centuries following the fall of the Western Roman Empire.

Another very important source shedding light on transport patterns is the

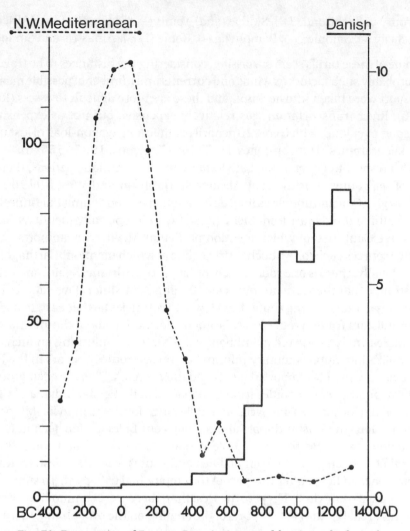

Fig. 71. Frequencies of Roman, Late Antique, and later wrecks from the
Mediterranean and of wrecks of North European ships from Danish waters
(*Sources*: Parker 1984; Crumlin-Pedersen 1981)

wrecks that are increasingly being recorded and often excavated along the
Mediterranean coasts and in North European waters (fig. 71). The majority of the
older wrecks in the Mediterranean date from the Hellenistic and Roman periods,
and therefore we must suppose that large numbers of trading vessels were sailing
the seas in these times. There are, however, two other factors that affect the
frequency of accidents at sea: putting to sea in the stormy winter months and the
design of vessels. Both these factors are of special significance in periods with a
dynamic economy.

The vast majority of the wrecks in the Mediterranean found so far are in the
northern and particularly the north-western part of it (Parker 1984). This

Table 10. *Recorded wrecks in the Mediterranean,*
c. *300 BC–AD 300*

Region	Time period			
	300–150 BC	150 BC–0	AD 0–150	AD 150–300
Western	8	10	25	5
Riviera	24	62	41	14
Western Italy	12	19	43	18
Adriatic	7	14	18	8
Southern Italy	23	20	15	22
Eastern (and Black Sea)	13	12	10	9
Total	87	139	163	87

Source: Parker 1980

reflects primarily the large number of amateur divers in southern France and Italy and the fact that marine archaeology developed early here. For the period 500 BC to AD 1500, the number of wrecks per century, is as follows: fifth BC, 25; fourth BC, 27; third BC, 44; second BC, 107; first BC, 120; first AD, 122; second AD, 98; third AD, 53; fourth AD, 39; fifth AD, 12; sixth AD, 21; seventh AD, 8; eighth AD, 1; ninth AD, 2; tenth AD, 9; eleventh AD, 2; twelfth AD, 4; thirteenth AD, 10; fourteenth AD, 6; fifteenth AD, 8. Apart from the concentration in the centuries around the birth of Christ and a slight increase in Late Antiquity, the very small number in the first half of the second millennium is notable. We know that sea transport was much used in this period, but ships must generally have put to sea in the safer months. It is certainly also significant that ships dating from the beginning of the second millennium were not – as in Antiquity – loaded with the pottery amphorae that are so conspicuous and easily datable. By far the largest amount of archaeologically identifiable material in the cargoes of the ancient wrecks consisted of foodstuff amphorae. Goods must almost certainly have been transported by sea in Antiquity at times of the year with poor weather because of the considerable pressure on the economic systems for provisions as well as for military and political reasons. Such pressures would have been considerable in the Roman Empire during its expansion phase, when, for instance, supplies for the capital's population were a constant source of transport problems. Given the decrease in frequency of wrecks from the second to the third century, it is interesting that the building of new grain stores in Ostia, Rome's port, ceased at the beginning of the second century, when the need for increased capacity apparently came to an end (Vitelli 1980). Considering now the wrecks in the Mediterranean from about 300 BC to AD 300, we find, as expected, that the majority date to 150 BC–AD 150 but there are considerable regional differences (table 10; Parker 1980). Southern Gaul shows a concentration of wrecks from the centuries around the birth of Christ, when the area constituted an important approach to the Roman provinces in the Rhine and Upper Danube regions –

where the number of wrecks in the rivers (not recorded in the table) steadily increased through time. Among the Riviera wrecks is that of a ship dating from the middle of the first century AD found at Port-Vendres; it was loaded with wine and oil from southern Spain (Colls et al. 1977; see also Parker and Price 1981). Wreck finds on the Mediterranean coasts are most frequent in the first century and a half AD, but in the period c. AD 150–300 there is a notable increase in the number of wrecks in southern Italy. There are, moreover, some important finds in this area, of wrecked ships loaded with marble. To the extent that the wrecks reflect the transport of goods from the most productive provinces, the wrecks in southern Italy may be understood as an expression of the increasingly important role of 'Africa' in Late Roman times. For the same reasons it is, moreover, characteristic that the eastern Mediterranean and the Black Sea show a very slight decrease in wreck numbers through time.

As we have seen, the eastern Mediterranean played a significant economic role in Late Antiquity, and recent investigations of wrecks lying off the south-western coast of Asia Minor enable us to make a more thorough study of the history of transport in this area. An important find is a twenty-one metres long merchantman from Yassi Ada, and with a cargo capacity of about sixty tons, that sank, according to the coins found on board, in the crucial years around AD 630 (Bass and van Doorninck 1982). Another important find from the same locality dates from the fourth century, while from near Serce Limani, to the south-east, comes an interesting eleventh-century Islamic ship among other wrecks ([Bass in] Johnstone 1980). The finds from the Serce Limani wrecks, which range in time from before 100 BC to after AD 1000, allow detailed study of the chronology in the eastern Mediterranean in particular (Slane 1982, cited by Cowin 1986; cf. Parker 1984). It appears that finds steadily increase in number throughout the whole of the first millennium BC, whereupon there is a decline, broken by a new increase in number of finds dating from the centuries around AD 500. Finally, there is a marked decline in the number of finds after AD 700. These observations thus confirm the strong position of the eastern Mediterranean in Late Antiquity, which – to confine ourselves to the maritime sector – led, for instance, to the export of prefabricated, ornamented parts for churches (Parker 1980). A shipwreck containing such a 'church' was found near Marzameni on the south-eastern coast of Sicily.

Denmark is another area where maritime archaeology developed early. Numerous wrecks have been found in Danish waters and – in contrast to the situation in the Mediterranean, except perhaps in the Levant – there is steady increase in numbers of finds, particularly from c. AD 500 to early in the second millennium (Crumlin-Pedersen 1981) (fig. 71). Here, too, there seems to be a close connection between economic and social development, on the one hand, and the development of water transport systems, on the other. The introduction of sail to North European ships around AD 500 was of crucial importance.

Roman pottery

The most important major production sector during the first millennium was agriculture, and a number of different agricultural products and their chronological and geographical distribution have already been discussed. In the simpler economies of the first millennium, the vast majority of agricultural products were transported over long distances only in small amounts. In the Roman economy, however, ships could be used to transport large amounts of foodstuffs over long distances. Without this method of transport, it is doubtful whether the empire could have been sustained.

One of the most important containers used for wine, oil, etc., in the classical world was the amphora, a large, usually pointed or round-bottomed, two-handled jar with a narrow neck. Amphorae have been the subject of thorough archaeological studies, and in a number of cases it has proved possible not only to date them extremely accurately but also to determine their provenance and their use. Thus the imports of an area can be identified on the basis of amphora finds alone. As a matter of curiosity it may be also mentioned that Roman wine amphorae have been found as far away as India (Tchernia 1986).

Besides the amphorae, the finer wares, which were often exported, have also been the subject of close study. I need only mention the traditional studies of *terra sigillata* from the northern provinces of the Early Roman Empire or the more recent work dealing with the so-called African red-slip wares (Hayes 1972). The coarser wares, apart from the amphorae, were not as a rule transported over long distances. This does not mean, however, that they are without interest in production or trading contexts. Although they have often suffered neglect, particularly by archaeologists in the Mediterranean, whose eyes, understandably enough, are more easily caught by other finds, interesting studies of them have been made in Britain. Here their distribution patterns show, for example, that water transport had greater capacity than land transport and provide information on the different marketing areas of the rival producers (Peacock 1982).

The many grave inscriptions dating from the Late Republic and Early Roman periods in Ostia and other Italian towns allow us, furthermore, to compare the production and distribution of pottery – one of the favourite topics of archaeology – with those for other crafts (Zimmer 1982). It must be added, however, that this investigation does not necessarily give a complete economic and sociological picture, since there may be differences from trade to trade, particularly with respect to the affluence of the leading practitioners and hence their ability to invest in grave monuments. It appears, however, that potters in general represent only 2 to 3 per cent of the total number of craft workers. The largest trade in numbers of workers was the foodstuffs trade, with over 20 per cent of the grave memorials; here butchers totalled 11 per cent, bakers 10 per cent. Metalworkers

Table 11. *Percentages of amphorae from various parts of the empire at Ostia, AD 50–400*

Time period	Region				
	Italy	Gaul	Spain	North Africa	Aegean
AD 50–100	28	29	31	11	1
AD 100–150	15	32	28	19	6
AD 150–200	17	19	31	29	4
AD 200–250	2	9	10	55	23
AD 300–400	4	6	10	71	10

Source: Anselmino et al. 1986

accounted for almost 20 per cent, transport workers 17 per cent, stonemasons or monument masons and weavers 10 per cent each. Carpenters and cabinet-makers, skippers, leatherworkers, and shipwrights (listed in order of decreasing frequency) have shares ranging from 10 per cent to 5 per cent each. The comb-makers whose refuse is so important for chronological research on settlements of the last half of the first millennium, amounted to only 1 per cent, but this trade hardly brought great profit to those plying it.

Ostia also provides us with a series of amphora studies covering the period from the first century BC to the fourth century AD, demonstrating considerable differences over time in the places of origin of imports. A prime import was wine, but large amounts of olive oil and fish 'sauce' (*garum*) were also imported (Tchernia 1986). The number of wine amphorae falls steadily through Early and Late Roman times, whereas that of oil amphorae in general increases. Imports of *garum*, which came mainly from Spain, were considerable in both Augustan and Late Roman times. In the first century BC Italian imports dominated, but by the early first century AD the provinces had taken over this position. At first it was Spanish foodstuffs in particular, but Gallic imports, though exclusively of wine, were already considerable by the end of the century. These latter imports decreased sharply during the latter half of the second century. Fifty years later Spanish imports were overtaken by foodstuffs from North Africa, primarily olive oil. North Africa dominated all imports from the middle of the third century onwards. In addition to a number of amphorae of unknown origin, there were significant imports of wine from the Aegean in Late Roman times. To sum up, first the wines and then the oil produced by Italy were replaced by the products of other, predominantly Mediterranean provinces. With respect to wine, it was Spain that took over, followed by Gaul, and finally the Aegean. With respect to oil, 'Africa' was of special importance. The percentages of all types of amphorae from the different areas of the empire in the various Roman phases are shown in table 11 (Anselmino et al. 1986) and the percentages of wine amphorae in table 12 (Tchernia 1986: 238).

Table 12. *Percentages of wine amphorae from various parts of the empire at Ostia, AD 0–400*

Time period	Region				
	Italy	Gaul	Spain	North Africa	Aegean
AD 0–50	63	0	33	0	3
AD 50–100	35	41	14	8	1
AD 100–150	25	55	6	4	10
AD 150–200	34	36	1	9	12
AD 200–250	4	19	0	32	45
AD 250–400	0	22	0	40	38

Source: Tchernia 1986:238
Note: Indeterminable amphorae are excluded. The African wine originated in the main from Algeria and Libya.

Another instructive example comes from the large villa at Settefinestre near Cosa, north-west of Rome, where early in the first century there was considerable production of wine. In the finds from the second and early third centuries, there are more imported amphorae (primarily Gallic and Spanish) than Italian ones (Carandini 1985), whereas only local amphorae appear among the finds dating from the first.

Around AD 500 foodstuffs from the eastern Mediterranean began to predominate, even in the west, and a few eastern amphorae travelled as far as western Britain – probably as a result of the international but not market-influenced exchange of luxuries between kings, magnates, and members of the clergy in Western Europe (Hayes 1972). In Carthage, for instance, the number of amphorae from the eastern Mediterranean increased from an insignificant percentage around AD 400 to some 50 per cent less than a hundred years later (Panella 1983; Fulford and Peacock 1984). At first glance, conquest by the Vandals appears to have made northern Africa more dependent on foreign foodstuffs, but it is, of course, quite possible to be at once an exporter of olive oil and an importer of wine. In the Barcelona area, in about AD 500 'African' amphorae amounted to almost 80 per cent, while those from the eastern Mediterranean comprised 20 per cent (Keay 1984). In Late Roman times Spanish amphorae in the Barcelona area totalled at least 20 per cent, and eastern finds were unknown. Just as in Carthage, in Rome and Naples eastern amphorae seem to make up almost half of the identifiable imports in Late Antiquity (Whitehouse et al. 1982; Arthur 1985). In Naples eastern imports, primarily from the Levant, increased between shortly after AD 400 and about AD 600 from slightly less than 20 per cent to 65 per cent, at the expense of the 'African' imports. In Ravenna, not surprisingly, eastern dominance is pronounced: two-thirds of the imported amphorae in about AD 500 originated in the Levant ([Piccoli in] Montanari 1983).

Finer pottery, often transported with foodstuffs and the next-most-frequent archaeologically identifiable maritime freight, both confirms and amplifies the picture sketched above (see Parker 1984). The removal of the *terra sigillata* factories from northern Italy to southern Gaul in the first part of the first century attests to the increasing importance of Gaul. The further expansion of the northern provinces is emphasized by the establishment of *terra sigillata* factories in central Gaul at the beginning of the second century. In the same phase, moreover, the last Italian bronze items vanish from the north-western frontier, being replaced entirely by local or Gallic products (see Kunow 1983: 67; also chapter 8 below).

In the Rhineland the marketing regions for the products of different factories making finer pottery are clearly drawn. The large factories at Rheinzabern, near the Upper Rhine, dominated this region and also exported to neighbouring and more distant areas (von Bülow 1975) (fig. 72). In Bavaria there was a branch factory at Westerndorf that distributed considerable pottery on the Upper and Middle Danube. Products from the Trier factories begin to appear on the Middle Rhine, and these clearly predominate over Rheinzabern wares in finds from regions below the Mosel–Rhine confluence. In addition to the local products, some *terra sigillata* wares came from factories in central Gaul, particularly Lezoux. These wares also penetrated into areas outside the empire. Many wares from Lezoux and Trier have been found in the northern Netherlands and along the North Sea coast as far as the mouth of the Elbe. In Moravia, Slovakia, and central Poland, there are many finds that originated in Rheinzabern and Westerndorf. The wares from these factories also dominate the Scandinavian material, despite the fact that Denmark is closer to the southern North Sea coast than it is to central Poland and, moreover, the journey could be made by sea (Hansen 1987; cf. Randsborg 1986). The *terra sigillata* finds in Free Germany therefore show that simple economic mechanisms – particularly the relationship between the amount of a commodity found at any given point and the distance to its place of production – did not neccessarily obtain here as they did within the empire.

In the Mediterranean fine wares from 'Africa' played an important part, and in the same centuries that 'African' amphorae dominated the import market for olive oil in, for instance, Italy. In Berenice in eastern Libya, as much as 80 per cent of the imports of finer pottery still came from 'Africa' in the years around AD 500 (Riley 1983). In Ravenna at the same time there is almost the same percentage of 'African' finer pottery, although the proportion of eastern products greatly increased in the sixth to the seventh century (Montanari 1983) (fig. 2). The same is the case even in Carthage at this time, thus indicating a probable collapse of 'African' production and export of finer pottery (Humphrey 1981). These products had earlier succeeded in making their mark in the Eastern Empire, too. In general, the end of Late Antiquity coincides with the cessation of the large Mediterranean 'common market' for foodstuffs and pottery. This

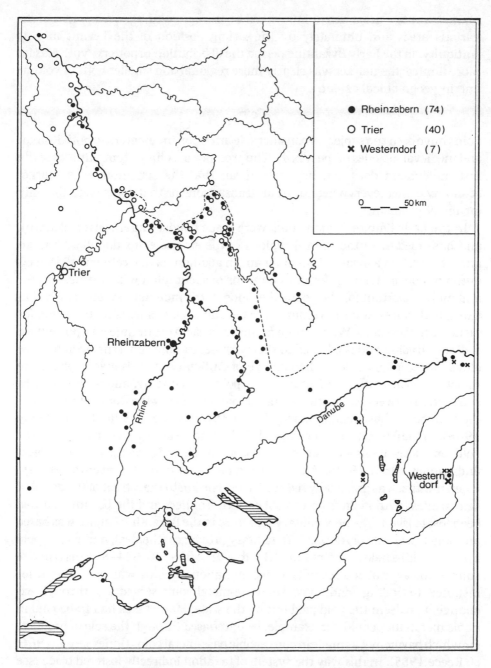

Fig. 72. Distribution of *terra sigillata* wares originating in the factories of
Trier, Rheinzabern, and Westerndorf on sites in the Rhineland and the
Upper Danube area from the second and the early third century (after
von Bülow 1975)

market was to a great extent influenced by the agricultural development of the various areas and ultimately by the strong position of the Levant in Late Antiquity. In the Early Byzantine period the distribution of pottery types was far more limited; the market was clearly more regional and smaller both in volume and in geographical extent.

Coins

Coins have been the subject of considerable attention in research on both Roman and medieval societies (appendix 4). The presence of coins in communities of the first millennium does not, however, mean that the conditions of a market economy existed everywhere or in all transactions or that coins were the only means of payment.

In the Early Empire Roman coins were made of gold (aurei), silver (denarii), and base metals. In the central regions of the empire coins doubtless had an important role as a means of payment and in addition served, rather as did jewels but in a more convenient form, as a means of accumulating a fortune. Finally, and more important for the political economy, the monetary system assisted in fixing both prices and the volume of taxes and disbursements by the state, for instance to the troops. Whereas the monetary system of our time is important for ordinary trading and is adapted to this purpose, trading concerns seem to have played a secondary role in the coinage of Antiquity. At this stage coins were struck predominantly as a feature of the political economy, and we find a close connection between, for instance, the payments made by the Roman Empire and the number of base-metal coins (Metcalf 1969; Reece 1982a, 1985; Hendy 1985). In the fifth century, for example, when state salaries were paid mainly in gold, only a few coins were struck in base metals, to judge by the archaeological finds (Jones 1964, 1966). Another example dates from the seventh century, when minting was drastically reduced in proportion to the retreat of the defeated field armies to Anatolia from the old eastern frontiers and the Levant that had been lost to Islam. The new military structure in the Byzantine Empire was based on soldier-peasants organized into military provinces (themes), and wages paid in coin could be held to a minimum (Hendy 1985: 619–20, 634–8). This is not, of course, to say that the secondary dissemination of coins was not subject, for instance, to trading conditions. The base-metal coins served too, through exchange, to redeem the gold paid out by the state. Many taxes had to be paid in noble metals that could, for example, be purchased through the sale of products for which payment was made in convertible base-metal coins (Jones 1964, 1966; cf. Reece 1985). In this way the system of taxation indirectly fostered trade (see Hopkins 1980).

The crises of the third century clearly had an effect on the political economy, for instance increasing payments to the armed forces. Among other things, this led to a reduction in the silver content of the denarius – there was no debasement of gold coins – and a levying of taxes in kind (which could, however, be converted). From the end of the third century an attempt was made to stabilize the coinage, and from the fourth century it was based on a new gold coin, the solidus, of about four and a half grammes in weight, whose value was maintained for many centuries. In addition, many base-metal coins were produced. The purchasing power of the Early Roman base-metal coins was greater than that of the lighter Late Roman issues, hence the much greater number of the latter. In the third century independent minting, enjoyed especially by many Greek towns in the eastern Mediterranean, was brought to an end, and the imperial coinage became universal.

Hoards give us a picture of the coins in circulation or used for accumulating fortunes during a given period. The coins themselves, bearing the image and name of the regent and other symbols, chiefly reflect the state's need to make payments. Settlement studies give insight into the frequency of issue, in particular for the base-metal coins often found in excavations of various types of settlement.

Base-metal coins found, for instance, at Corinth in Greece have been thoroughly studied over a very long span of time (Edwards 1933) (fig. 73). The number of coins from the Early Roman period is relatively small, but it increases in the latter half of the third century. There are many coins from the fourth century and clearly fewer from Late Antiquity. There are virtually no coin finds dating from the middle of the seventh to the middle of the ninth century, but the numbers increase again considerably in the tenth and eleventh centuries. The picture at Corinth appears with variations in many other Mediterranean settlements, particularly in eastern areas. Especially remarkable are the many base-metal coins from the late third and fourth centuries and their absence in Early Byzantine times and later. In Constantinople some base-metal coins survive, pointing to a certain continuation of the Late Antique system of administration in the capital (Harrison 1986) (fig. 74). Fifth-century coins are few; as a rule there are more sixth-century ones. Often, too, there is quite a number of coins at the beginning of the seventh century, probably connected with the crises of the Eastern Empire during the wars with Persia (see fig. 75 for Déhès in Syria). In regions abandoned early by imperial administration and the Roman forces, trends can, of course, be followed only briefly. At Colchester, one group of coins belongs to the Early Roman period, around AD 100, when this town was an important centre, and another, larger group dates from the Late Roman period, around AD 300 (Hull 1958).

Corinth lies in an area that remained within the Eastern Empire throughout the critical centuries, but in the abandoned provinces the production of new Roman base-metal coins rapidly came to an end. Gold and some silver coins continued to appear, however, as gifts or tribute payments to barbarian peoples and to the Germanic realms that had succeeded the Western Empire. In the latter areas, some coins were struck on the Eastern Roman model, and, in the early phase particularly, some of them displayed the name of the Roman emperor in

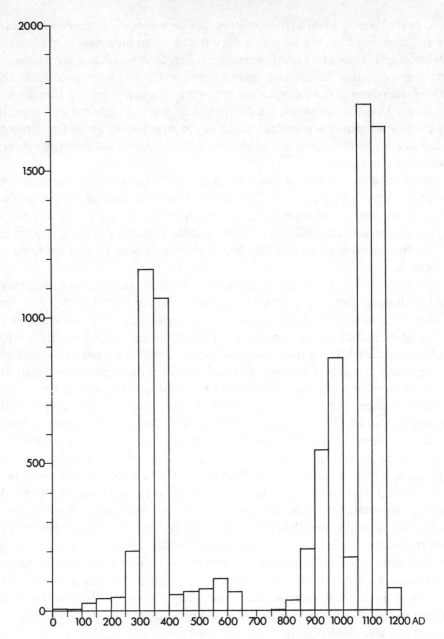

Fig. 73. Changing numbers of base-metal coins from Corinth (*Source*:
Edwards 1933)

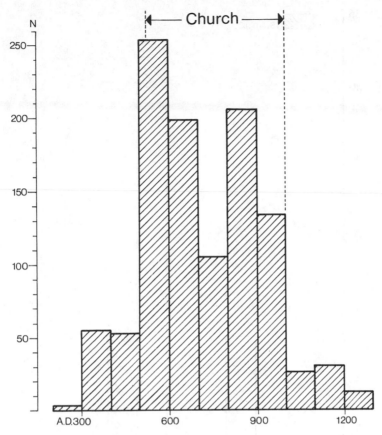

Fig. 74. Changing numbers of base-metal coins from the church of Saint
Polyeuktos, Saraçhane, Istanbul (Constantinople) (*Source*: Harrison 1986)

the east (Burnett 1977). Like the silver coins, base-metal coins were relatively
rare and largely confined to the Ostrogoths and the Vandals in, respectively, Italy
and 'Africa', where the Roman bureaucracy and other traditions survived
relatively untouched by the changes in political power.

In general, the production of gold coins was markedly reduced in the seventh
century both in the successor states in the west and in Byzantium. In the
Frankish realm, however, some coins, usually of debased gold, were struck in
central and southern Gaul (Kent 1972). These coins contained less and less gold
as time passed, and the crisis-ridden and reduced Eastern Empire also increasingly limited its minting, even of solidi. The Frankish coins reflect in part the
fragmentation of that realm, in part the demise of the ancient world by the
beginning of the seventh century at the latest. The much devalued gold coins
were replaced in the west at the beginning of the eighth century by silver coins
that were of greater use in minor transactions. With the Carolingian dynasty a
royal coinage system was recreated on the basis of silver and became the model

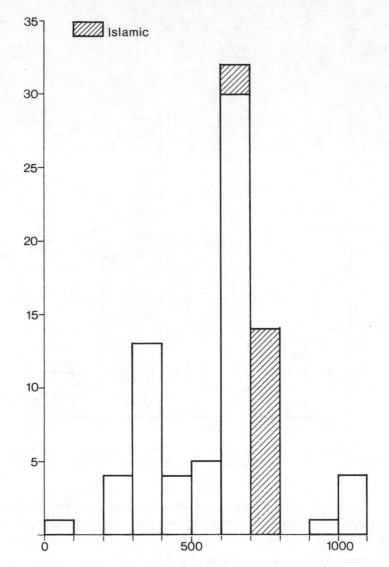

Fig. 75. Changing numbers of base-metal coins from Déhès (*Source*: Sodini
et al. 1980)

for the medieval coinage systems of Western Europe (Blackburn and Metcalf
1981). Monetary coins of silver (sceattas) continued, however, to be struck in
marginal areas on the southern North Sea coast.

The production and distribution of late Eastern Roman and Byzantine coins
can be followed by study of a number of hoards and deposits both within the
empire and elsewhere. These finds become fewer and fewer throughout Late
Antiquity and Early Byzantine times, in step with the reduction in minting
(Mosser 1935) (fig. 76). A greater number of hoards reappears in the eleventh
century. In general, the hoards from Byzantine areas show a relative increase in

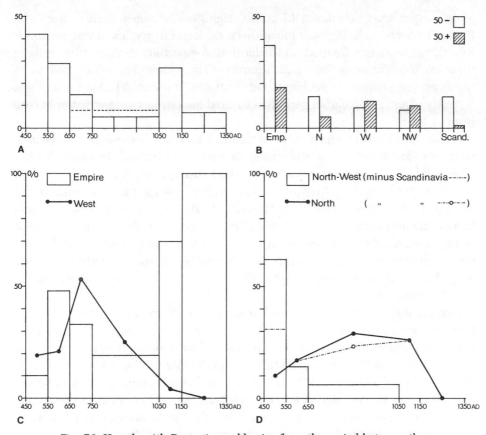

Fig. 76. Hoards with Byzantine gold coins from the period between the
late fifth and the mid-fourteenth century (*Source*: Mosser 1935): (A)
chronological distribution; (B) distribution according to size, as indicated
by number of finds with, respectively, less than fifty and fifty or more
coins, in (Emp.) the Eastern Roman or Byzantine Empire (to the east of
the Adriatic), (N) regions to the north of the empire, (W) Mediterranean
regions to the west of the heartlands of the empire, (NW) north-western
Europe, and (Scand.) Scandinavia; (C) and (D) changing frequencies (in
percentages) of hoards from the above-mentioned regions (here
Scandinavia is included among the finds from, respectively, north-western
Europe [AD 450–550] and the regions to the north of the Byzantine
Empire [AD 650–1050])

number with time, and exports therefore decrease. Most of the hoards containing
Eastern Roman or Byzantine coins from western and north-western Europe and
Scandinavia date from the (fifth and) sixth century; after this time these areas
were isolated from the Mediterranean. In the central Mediterranean regions,
including Italy, there are still relatively many hoards in the seventh century, but
thereupon they decline steadily in number. These hoards and the Western
European ones from the previous century are remarkably large, perhaps reflect-
ing the use of fine Byzantine coins for storing up the fortunes of magnates. In the
Eastern Roman heartland there are relatively many deposits dating from around
AD 600 and thereafter fewer. However, nearly all the hoards from the High

Middle Ages that contain gold coins originate, as noted earlier, from the Byzantine area itself. Deposits in southern Eastern Europe, including southern Russia, are relatively frequent in the tenth and especially the eleventh century; these are a reflection of the special interest of the Middle Byzantine realm in its northern, non-Islamic neighbours. Other studies show that Roman gold coins were also common in earlier periods of the first millennium, in particular in Late Roman times.

In Sassanid Persia coins were struck almost exclusively in silver. The Islamic states also had a widespread silver monetary standard but did not follow Persian models for the appearance of the coins. The cultural inheritance of Early Islam was predominantly Late Antique, and accordingly imitations were made of the Eastern Roman gold coins. Only around AD 700, in connection with much increased minting, did a standardized Islamic silver coin, the dirhem, come into being. It weighed slightly less than three grammes and lacked images but did display quotations from the Koran. The shape, the stamp, and perhaps also the weight of these coins influenced the silver coinage of Western Europe from the eighth century on.

Beyond these, Islamic coins are known chiefly from Northern and Eastern Europe, where hundreds of thousands of them appear in hoards and deposits of silver dating from Viking times and the Middle Slav period. These coins travelled to the Nordic area through Russia rather than the Mediterranean, where contact between Western Europe, for instance the Carolingian realm, and Islam apparently did not entail any significant use of eastern coins. The explanation probably lies in the international balance of trade: while the Nordic area and north-eastern Europe imported scarcely any Islamic products and could therefore accumulate large numbers of dirhems, the Carolingian realm had to purchase eastern goods with its stock of noble metal. It is likely that Islamic silver was introduced into the Carolingian realm in connection with exchanges of goods between the Nordic area and Eastern Europe, but such transactions have left virtually no archaeological traces. There are, however, many connections between the areas in question, and the chronological circumstances of both the coins and the hoards make it likely that there was intensive exchange, especially around AD 800 (Hodges and Whitehouse 1983; but cf. Randsborg 1981b).

Exchange in Central and Northern Europe

When the Roman Empire was extended to the Rhine–Danube line, widespread exchange had already existed for several millennia in temperate Europe. Celtic society, encountered and vanquished by the Romans, had had close associations with the Mediterranean for several centuries. Moreover, Gaul (and Britain) in particular had had close southern contacts in the period preceding Caesar's victories in these areas (Cunliffe 1981). In Central Europe many of the traditional trade and exchange routes, as well as other forms of contact, ran north–south along the great rivers Rhine, Elbe, Oder, and Vistula. Others followed the Danube. The eastern Alpine area, for instance, was an important junction for contact with the Mediterranean. Farther east and south-east in the metal-rich Balkans in the centuries prior to the Roman conquest, there was much contact with the Greek world and, via southern Russia, even more remote eastern regions.

The most advanced societies in temperate Europe before the Roman conquest were centred on large fortified settlements (*oppida*) in the area stretching from the Atlantic to the Black Sea, in Western and Central Europe ascribed in particular to the Celts. These socially stratified communities, which produced crafts, especially luxuries, to a very high standard and struck coins on Greek and later partially on Roman models, enjoyed very widespread exchange. They also had heavy ploughs with iron shares, an invention that impressed even Pliny.

North of this zone lived, among others, the Germanic peoples, who, although agriculturalists, were relatively loosely organized and still outside the direct influence of the Mediterranean societies. Their relations with the Celts had led, however, to some changes – seen, for instance, in their warrior and battle organization – as well as a very modest differentiation according to economic status that may reflect the emergence, in some tribes, of an 'aristocracy'. When the Roman frontier was established along the Rhine–Danube line, these communities rapidly came into direct contact with very sophisticated forms of organization and found themselves, after the collapse of the Celtic oppida, in an entirely novel situation with regard to social relations and exchange. Along the Rhine relations were for a long time warlike in nature, but in areas adjacent to the Danube a number of fragile alliances did come into being early in the first millennium as a result of political agreements and Roman subsidies and trade.

. With the presence of Roman military forces along the Rhine–Danube line and the economic resources this involved, the foundations were laid for further expansion or Romanization and for the establishment of the frontier areas as independent administrative units or provinces. At first this expansion involved especially the Rhine area, where the large contingents of Roman troops were stationed, but the areas east of the Alps rapidly followed. With economic expansion and military and political development, the Germanic areas beyond the frontiers were drawn into the imperial sphere. One result was that these communities obtained some of the finer products of Roman factories, chiefly in Italy, and, during the second century, from the western provinces, including silver beakers, glasses, and a number of bronze vessels (Hansen 1987). In the late second and especially the early third century many Roman weapons were introduced, along with large numbers of coins, chiefly of precious metals. In addition, there were perhaps less conspicuous products such as fibulae and textiles (Ilkjær and Lønstrup 1983; Kunow 1986; Jørgensen 1986). In areas close to the frontier these objects are almost unknown, primarily since they do not occur as grave goods and, being valuables, are of course rare in the rubbish dumps of settlements. Frontier regions are characterized by the presence of base-metal coins, reflecting both the short distance to the Roman Empire and the more irregular contacts. Even in the north-eastern Netherlands, there is a difference between the coastal area, where many base-metal coins have been found, and the interior, where finds are dominated by coins of precious metals (Randsborg 1986; van Es 1960).

The limited variety of Roman articles and their high quality make it apparent that 'imports' of Roman goods into Free Germany were governed by rather well-defined conditions, at least outside the zone of closest contact (Randsborg 1986). The articles are all of types that could be put to immediate use, and their value indicates contact between distinguished Germans and Romans of similar standing. It is natural to suppose that this contact was political in nature and that any trade agreements were subordinate to this. It has sometimes been suggested that Roman traders operated within the area, and there is sporadic evidence of this as far as the frontier zone is concerned, but no case exists of isolated trading activities (contrary to Kunow 1983). When the close contacts between the Germanic tribes revealed, for instance, by their many similarities in material culture are considered, it is probable that social relations between these communities were chiefly responsible for the dissemination of Roman objects.

Many of the Germanic graves containing valuable Roman objects have remarkably similar inventories in spite of their wide distribution (Eggers 1949–50). Weapons are virtually unknown in these graves. Among the finds are the two very valuable silver beakers, dated to the beginning of the first century, discovered in a grave at Hoby in Denmark. The composition of the grave goods may reflect the influence of the Roman Empire, since drinking and toilet sets or parts of them are common (Kunow 1983). The princely graves also reflect a remarkable social homogeneity in the Germanic communities, and even though Roman imports do not occur with the same frequency everywhere no true 'find centres' can be recognized. Each community forwarded to other communities valuable and less valuable Roman imports in the same proportion that it received them, and only between individual community members can any 'monopolization' be traced (Randsborg 1986).

This situation altered around AD 200, when, for example, in eastern Zealand, Denmark, we note a concentration of rich graves containing Roman imports, including glasses, bronze vessels, and *terra sigillata* ware. Norway and Sweden, farther north and more marginal in relation to the Roman Empire, in the same period show the same proportions of rare and more common items, and hence of valuable and less valuable imports, as does Denmark (Randsborg 1986; Hansen 1987). Although a far greater number of Roman objects has been found there than in Norway and Sweden, Denmark still supplied its Nordic partners with objects of the same quality, and in the same proportions, as itself but probably in smaller amounts than earlier.

After about the middle of the third century we find chiefly centres near harbours with craft production and seasonal markets, such as Gudme with its

harbour five kilometres away at Lundeborg (Thomsen 1986, 1987; see fig. 48).
Rare imported objects (chiefly glasses and coins of precious metals) are far more
frequent in this period in Denmark than in Norway and Sweden, suggesting that
the Danish communities monopolized their further distribution. The same
phenomenon can be noted in the latter half of the third century in Central
Europe, where certain rare Roman dishes, gold coins, etc., occur in Thuringia but
seldom elsewhere in eastern Germany (Laser 1983). There is little doubt that this
is evidence of the emergence of marked social stratification in Germanic communities, linked on a higher level to the establishment of permanent tribal confederations. Germanic society had thus moved considerably beyond what it was at the
time of Tacitus. These communities became the primary opponents of the Roman
Empire on the Rhine–Danube frontier in the late third and the fourth century.
That this development, which, as we have seen, was associated with a change in
settlement, was not without conflict is demonstrated by a number of contemporary sacrifices of battle booty in southern Scandinavia (Ilkjær and Lønstrup
1983).

In the Early Roman period a connection can be noted between the quantity of
imported goods in Free Germany and what we might call 'peaceful coexistence'
with the empire (Randsborg 1986). Correspondingly, for example during the
Marcomannic wars, a decline can be noted in exports from the empire in times of
unrest and war. In the Late Roman period and Late Antiquity, however, the
situation changed. Whereas in the written sources these periods, particularly the
latter, are characterized by bans on trade with the barbarians (Thompson 1982:
3–4), considerable quantities of Roman gold coins dating from this very time
occur in the area north of the Rhine–Danube line. Moreover, we know from
documents that considerable subsidies were paid to barbarian peoples primarily
to avert wars that might well have proved far more costly to the empire. For
example, the budget for the great campaign against the Vandals in 'Africa' in A D
468 amounted, according to various sources, to 7.3–9.4 million solidi (the
former amount being the more likely), but the last payment made to the Huns in
the A D 440s amounted to only 0.6 million solidi, of which 0.4 million represented old 'debts' (Hendy 1985). Closer study of the hoards found in the Middle
Danube area shows, furthermore, that the gold finds correspond exactly with the
times when subsidies were being paid to the peoples of this region (Kiss 1986).
We may therefore conclude that the exchange between the Romans and the
Germanic peoples, once dominated by the Romans, was in later times conducted
by them from a position of weakness despite the considerable means at their
disposal.

As early as the end of the Late Roman period there were sites in Denmark, such
as the Gudme–Lundeborg complex, with very rich imported materials, along
with traces of widespread craft production and facilities for shipping – elements
that reappear in the southern Scandinavian emporia of the end of the first
millennium. We must assume that exchange with foreign communities was

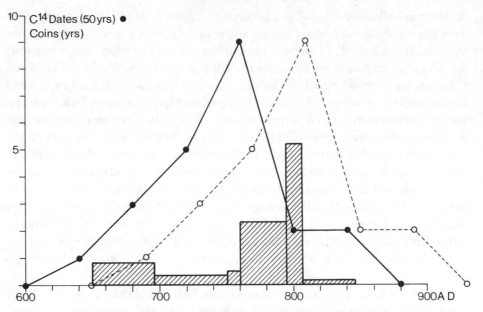

Fig. 77. Frequencies of numbers of coins per year and calibrated
radiocarbon dates per fifty-year period from the major emporium at
Dorestad. The broken line indicates the likely calendar dates (additional
calibration for the average biological age of the wood dated) (*Sources*:
Jankuhn 1976; van Es and Verwers 1980)

channelled through early centres such as Gudme and that the leaders of society
resided in them, at any rate temporarily. We are more certain of the circumstances in the later periods, when, for example, there is written evidence that the
trading and craft-producing Viking emporia were under the direct control of the
local king or his representatives (Randsborg 1980). This is not to say, however,
that there were no differences between the two periods. Viking Hedeby struck
coins in the early ninth century, had its plots of land registered, maintained a
permanent network of roads, and was far larger than earlier markets and
harbours. Like other Nordic emporia, it was fortified in the tenth century. Its
north-western European counterparts, such as Dorestad on the Rhine in the
Netherlands (van Es and Verwers 1980) (fig. 77) and Hamwih in southern
England (Hodges 1982), were by the eighth century even larger. Birka, in central
Sweden, trading with Russia and eventually with the Near East as well as in
Scandinavian products such as high-quality iron from north-central Sweden
(Dalarne) (Magnusson 1986: 226) and textiles, was second to Hedeby in size.
    Development through the almost half-millennium between the Late Roman
phase of the Gudme–Lundeborg complex and, for instance, Hedeby (established
in the eighth century) can be followed in a number of Nordic sites. Gudme
continued in existence, although the Lundeborg coastal settlement seemed to
decline into a mere landing-place, perhaps with a seasonal market but little or no

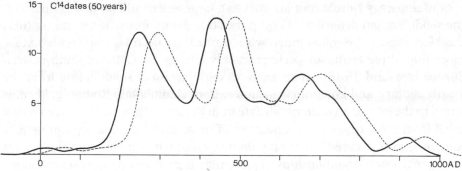

Fig. 78. Frequencies of calibrated radiocarbon dates per fifty-year period
from the emporium of Helgö. The broken line indicates the likely calendar
dates (additional calibration for the average biological age of the wood
dated) (*Source*: Kyhlberg 1986)

craft production (the latter being restricted to Gudme). Also dating from the post-
Roman period is Dankirke in south-western Jutland, where large quantities of
Frankish glass reveal that the sea route along the southern North Sea coast to
western Europe – like that across the North Sea to Britain – was in use by this time
(Jarl Hansen 1989). On Bornholm in the Baltic, very important finds of gold,
including many solidi from the late fifth century, demonstrate the existence of a
centre near the north-eastern coast of the island. Several thousand small gold-foil
figures perhaps disclose the presence here of a sanctuary as well. On the island of
Helgö in central Sweden, near Birka, there was an important craft and trading
site producing a considerable amount of jewellery and also trading in, for
instance, high-quality iron from northern Scandinavia (Jämtland) (Magnusson
1986) (fig. 78). At Helgö too there are solidi, particularly from the fifth century
(Holmqvist 1976; Kyhlberg 1986). Radiocarbon dates indicate settlement concentrated in three periods: around AD 300, the first period of 'monopolizations' of
exchange, around AD 500, the period of early Frankish, Ostrogothic, and Eastern
Roman prosperity, and, to a lesser extent, around AD 700, the first period of the
main western European emporia (Kyhlberg 1982).

  Among the Helgö finds are a 'Coptic' bronze ladle and a Buddha figure from
northern India. Both date from around AD 500 and perhaps arrived in the Baltic
area via the Rhineland, which, around 500, was in close contact with
Ostrogothic Italy (Werner 1961). A large number of Coptic (that is, eastern
Mediterranean) bronze vessels and Ostrogothic silver coins and solidi dating from
the fifth to the sixth centuries have been found in the often richly equipped
Rhineland graves. The solidi from Scandinavia, many of which were struck in
Italy, show an unusually large numer of so-called die-links and therefore cannot
have originated in ordinary trading activities (Fagerlie 1967). At least some of
them must have been included in substantial collective payments, possibly those
that the Eastern Empire made to the Ostrogoths, who from AD 473 onwards
received an annual subsidy of 144,000 solidi (Hendy 1985).

Contemporary Nordic communities to a large extent still used, together with the solidi, Roman denarii of almost pure silver dating from the second century: therefore these coins, often much worn, must have been kept in circulation for more than three centuries, perhaps mainly among the Goths of south-eastern Europe (see Lind 1988). Apart from an early group of solidi dating from the fourth century and known, for instance, from Gudme, late Roman gold coins found in the Nordic area almost all date from the late fifth century. There are few solidi from the sixth century, and most of these date from the beginning of it. Roman gold coins are thus of only limited value when it comes to the precise dating of Germanic relationships, in particular as there clearly were several kinds of 'monopolies' operating on the coins' route northward from the empire. The Rhine area and even Friesland and Thuringia, both areas under Frankish influence, where coins of the emperor Justinian (d. AD 565) are common, thus show a distribution of coins that differs from that of the Nordic area. One reason for this is probably that coins were an important part of the assets of the emerging kingdoms and more and more rarely exchanged for other goods. In eastern Central Europe, Roman gold coins vanished at the end of the fourth century, just as they did in Britain. These observations thus demonstrate once again the gradual diminution of imperial political influence and economy, with increasingly greater areas of Europe being excluded from even a marginal role. By the early seventh century, the import of gold into western Europe from the Eastern Empire was discontinued.

As we have seen, in the very early years of the Middle Ages, roughly AD 600 to 800, a western and north-western system of exchange including its own relatively modest minting was developed in relative isolation from the eastern and southern Mediterranean. In general, the use of coins greatly increased in the final centuries of the first millennium. This appears, for example, from the numbers of coin hoards found in Britain: sixth century, 0; seventh, 4; eighth, 10; ninth, 35; tenth, 64; eleventh, 47; twelfth, 41 (figures are taken, however, from a thirty-year-old survey [Thompson 1956]). The decline in numbers after AD 1000 is due to changes in patterns of saving.

In northern and eastern Europe north of the Danube, the numerous Islamic coins from the end of the eighth century show that new developments in the media of exchange were on the way. (It should not, however, be forgotten that there were media of exchange other than coins, for example, the iron bars or 'cloth money' that were widespread among the Slavs at least in the last part of the millennium [Herrmann 1985: 127ff.].) The Islamic coins arrived in two waves. The first, around AD 800, was dominated by coins from Mesopotamia – for instance, from Baghdad and Basra in the last great period of the caliphate, the time of Harun al-Rashid (Randsborg 1980, 1981a and b; Noonan 1984, 1986). The second larger wave occurred after the crisis of the caliphate in the ninth century and the subsequent marked decline of Mesopotamia and increasing independence of the Islamic provinces. The Late Islamic coins originated mainly

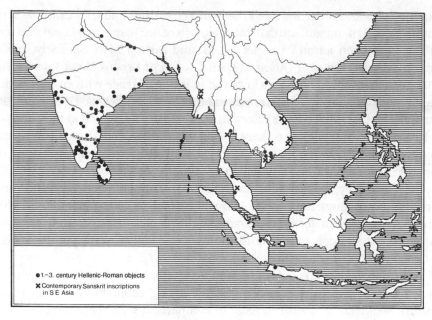

Fig. 79. Roman objects from South and South-east Asia and the
distribution of contemporary Indian inscriptions in South East Asia
(after Groslier 1985)

from the Samanid Dynasty of Turkestan, minted, for instance, in Samarkand and
Bukhara (Lombard 1971). In spite of crises, the Islamic economy proved very
strong. The Near East – for instance, the Levant and Mesopotamia, both with
very considerable settlement in Late Antiquity – can only have benefited from
this political development, which removed the old barrier between the Roman
Empire and Sassanid Persia, and the subsequent establishment of an 'imperial
economy', new both in volume and geographical extent. Moreover, this economy was associated, as was the Sassanid economy, with southern and eastern
Asia, areas that in the second half of the first millennium made great progress
(Flon 1985). The Chinese Tang dynasty opened Canton to Islamic merchants at
the end of the eighth century, and Chinese ceramics streamed westward to south-
western Asia, India, the Near East, and eastern Africa. At Siraf, on the Persian
Gulf, Chinese wares comprised 10 per cent of the finer wares around AD 800
(Hodges and Whitehouse 1983). At Manda, on the Kenyan coast, the proportion
of Chinese wares was also about 10 per cent but here of wares imported during
the whole period *c.* AD 850–1025; the other imported pottery at this site came
from the Near East (Chittick 1984).

This development led to closer economic ties between East and West than in
earlier periods, although it should not be forgotten that these contacts had
antecedents reaching back to Alexander the Great and the strong Hellenistic
influence on Central Asia itself (Flon 1985) (fig. 79). Roman wares, particularly

from the Early Roman period, are known in Yemen and India, for example at the emporium of Arikamedu, south of Madras, where, for instance, glasses and *terra sigillata* have been found (Wheeler, Gosh, and Deva 1946). Similarly, Indian pottery has been found at Quseir-al-Qadim (ancient Leucos Limen) on the Red Sea, one of the Roman harbours involved in the spice trade with eastern Africa, Arabia, and India, areas which provided other commodities too (Whitcomb and Johnson 1982; cf. Miller 1969). Even in South East Asia, which at this time was under strong Indian influence, there are definite Roman finds. In AD 166 Roman envoys reached Chinese territory, at any rate in Vietnam, carrying gifts from the emperor 'An-tun' (Antony) (Sitwell 1984). Finally, objects of precious metal (for instance, jewellery), bowls, glass, and musical instruments from Sassanid Persia were distributed along the Central Asian 'Silk Road' as far as Japan (Flon 1985). Here they were found, for example, among the objects in the Shoso-in treasury, dating from the middle of the eighth century and still preserved in the Todai-ji monastery at Nara (Hayashi 1975).

The hundreds of thousands of Islamic silver coins found in Scandinavia and eastern Europe are thus evidence of very strong economic forces in south-western, southern, and eastern Asia. In comparison with these regions, Africa and the later dominant Europe were only marginal. Nevertheless, the Islamic crisis in the ninth century and the associated cessation of the stream of silver to the Nordic area indirectly released many destructive forces in far-away Western Europe, which was subjected to continual Danish plundering forays until the second wave of Islamic silver arrived in Scandinavia shortly before AD 900. This second silver stream came to an end in the latter half of the tenth century, with the decline of the Samanid dynasty, without provoking any destructive Nordic reaction (Randsborg 1981a and b). By this time the Danish magnates, like their Frankish predecessors, were less dependent on income derived from either plunder or international trade and exchange. As a state society centred on western Denmark emerged and Christianity was introduced, leading families concentrated their efforts on agriculture and on extending their property and the rights to its use. At the same time there appeared in Denmark, in line with developments elsewhere in Western Europe, what we might call an infrastructure comprising bridges, fortifications, royal fortresses, etc., as well as a system of provincial towns to which crafts, some trade, and, for example, bishoprics and royal mints were attached.

These changes meant that to a greater degree than earlier the regional market became centred on towns, which, through their institutions, chiefly the church, at the same time acquired permanence (Randsborg 1980). Around AD 1000 Danish monetary coins were replaced by coins on a Western European model, with images of the ruler; thus the state society had found a general symbol that persists to this day. More important from an economic perspective, however, coins, all of silver, were now virtually the only medium of general exchange and investment of tangible property. The coins used for this purpose in northern

Europe might be Danish but were more often German or English, the latter dating from the first half of the eleventh century, when Danish kings ruled England, Denmark, Norway, and parts of Sweden while east-central Sweden entertained Scandinavia's last major 'prehistoric' chiefdoms or petty kingdoms.

Hoards dating from the ninth century in southern Scandinavia very rarely contain coins and generally consist of jewellery, predominantly of silver. Items of jewellery still dominated the hoards in the first half of the tenth century, but by this time they were being hacked into fragments to be used as a means of payment and measured by weight. Precious metals used as a means of payment are also known in the Nordic area in the periods corresponding to Late Antiquity. This was a time when a climax was reached in international exchange among the less developed societies in Europe and between them and the Eastern Empire; thereupon precious scrap-metal vanishes for some three hundred years. In the Viking hoards that date from the last half of the tenth century, in contrast, coins constitute more than 50 per cent by weight, and just fifty years later they dominate the hoards entirely – so swift was development in the means of exchange in the period in which Denmark was being transformed from a confederacy into a medieval state society along Western Europe lines.

Thus the last geographical area that we associate with the concept of 'early Western Europe' – the Nordic area – reached the level of development of its southern neighbours, both socially and with respect to exchange and trade, even though this transformation was as yet incomplete. The introduction of Christianity simultaneously integrated the Nordic area into the official religious ideology of Western Europe. At the end of the first millennium the eastern European confederate states were not particularly stable, and in any case they very soon became marginal in relation to the dynamic Western societies, including the Christian Mediterranean states, and even in some respects to Byzantium.

7

SOCIETY, CULTURE, AND MENTALITY

We have been examining past societies as social and cultural systems whose activities produced the material remains that can be recorded, investigated, and interpreted by means of archaeological methods. Up to now, however, we have devoted little attention to the norms that made up the core of those systems and both served as the basis of communication within and between systems and ensured their continuity. Much could be achieved here by extending the economic-historical approach adopted in the preceding chapters, for example employing an even larger corpus of archaeological material, undertaking more detailed analyses, or studying further written sources. Instead, however, we shall concentrate on a different set of material sources and on a number of related documents against the background of our general knowledge of the economy and the society of the times. There are still many limits to what can be accomplished. Archaeological method is rather undeveloped in this area, and the results are scattered and often difficult to integrate into the account.

Before going any farther, some brief explanations are needed. The first concerns the concept of 'time'. The historical concept of time is associated with events; archaeological time is measured in periods or phases, which are subdivided either in terms of an independent scale or in terms of changes in cultural norms. Because changes in norms in part dictate and in part are the consequences of other changes, the chief archaeological period boundaries may be assumed to coincide with the deeper divisions in history, society, economy – and mentality.

Cultural norms and the way in which they are expressed are often divided into public and private sectors, but too marked a distinction is, of course, absurd in the case of less developed societies such as the Germanic society of the first millennium. Therefore it may be appropriate to begin by examining certain general conditions in various social contexts. This approach can be taken, for example, in studying norms relating to the dead. Burial customs offer insight with regard to the relations between children and adults and between women and men, the

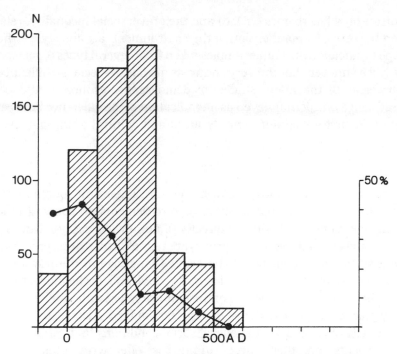

Fig. 80. Frequencies of Roman and Late Antique portrait sculptures from Anatolia (histograms), showing changing percentages of portraits of members of the imperial families (line) (*Sources*: İnan and Rosenbaum 1966; İnan and Alföldy-Rosenbaum 1979)

family (which plays a central role in the inheritance of rights, for instance, to the means of production), leaders or rulers (who sometimes but not always had very conspicuous graves), subordinates, for example slaves (who might be sacrificed on the burial of their owners), strangers, and many other matters. They may also reveal attitudes towards animals and plants, as also may the contents of dwellings (the pig, for instance, is almost unknown in Turkish Istanbul but common in Byzantine Constantinople [Morrison 1986]). Graves and other ritual and cultural expressions, for instance temples and sacrifice bogs, also provide information on ideas about the invisible.

Man's view of his surroundings is to a large extent influenced by fear and hope. Symbolic manipulation in one form or another is therefore a central aspect of everyday behaviour. When it comes to social differences between people, which have no biological basis other than distinctions of age and sex, symbolic manipulation is the psychological mechanism for maintaining the social structure. A classic example is the cult of the Roman emperors, in which symbols were used to support the imperial political system and underline the dominance of Roman or Romano-Greek culture (e.g., Price 1984; Hannestad 1986; see fig. 80). Other symbols especially related to the upper strata of society are temples and churches, art, inscriptions, and coins. In the present historical framework, we must concentrate on a few themes – death and the grave, social inequality, relations between the sexes, comprehension of the environment, art and style – that we can hope to elucidate through examples taken from several types of society. The results will be uneven, but the very contrasts may be of special significance as a counterweight to the many studies of demography, economy, and politics discussed above and perhaps even as an indication of the difference between the history of the first millennium and its social and cultural anthropology.

Burial

Graves are among archaeology's oldest and most important source materials, perhaps second in importance today only to settlements. In contrast to settlement remains, from which we can directly (if not always easily) draw conclusions about the original conditions, graves are very difficult to interpret. As a rule we have no secure knowledge of the symbol language of the past or of the connection between the layout and form of a grave and, for instance, the social status of the deceased, and the rest of the cultic area presents similar problems. The only practical approach seems, therefore, as indicated above, to be through the knowledge of economy and general social conditions that can be gathered from settlements and other sources (in our case often written ones).

In some periods and areas (for example, in Rome during the centuries around the birth of Christ), graves may take monumental form, in other periods and times not. In some periods and areas graves are provided with rich grave goods, in others (for example, Denmark in AD 300–900) not. Furthermore, these circumstances seem to vary independently. In the Rhineland Merovingian graves contain rich grave goods but are not marked by monuments (Werner 1935; Pirling 1986); in the southern Frankish realm there are no rich grave goods, but stone sarcophagi and funeral inscriptions in stone are common, particularly in towns (Gauthier 1975; James 1977, 1979). Nor are the wealth or status of the deceased closely connected with the occurrence of rich grave goods, although socio-economic differences can of course be noted within each culture-specific ritual language. For instance, in Roman graves in the north-western provinces glasses – a relatively valuable type of artefact – are found only in graves that also include many other goods (van Lith and Randsborg 1985).

There does seem, however, to be some connection between the type of society and the character of the grave. In the example from Merovingian France, it is the difference between the marginal Rhine regions, where there were many new settlements, and central and southern Gaul, where 'Roman' traditions in social structure, ownership of property, and ecclesiastical institutions were less affected by developments in the fifth century, that is reflected in the cultural material (see Werner 1961). The connection need not, however, be linear. New circumstances of power, for instance, may be either accentuated or toned down through the use of symbols and cultural expressions. Particular insight into early Frankish conditions can, moreover, be obtained from a study of the distribution of royal graves, which, once scattered from Cologne to the Bordeaux area and from Rouen to Lyons, in the mid-seventh century shifted to the north of the country, with Paris assuming the character of a ritual capital (Müller-Wille 1982).

Monumental graves, designed to be seen by succeeding generations, take many forms. In areas without stone architecture they generally appear in the first millennium in the form of the traditional earth mound. In the late tenth century, at Jelling in Jutland, the Danish royal dynasty erected the two largest barrows known in Denmark, some thirteen metres high and nearly eighty metres in diameter (Randsborg 1980, 1981c; Krogh 1982). Only the northern barrow contains a grave chamber. With this was associated the largest runic stone in the country, which lists King Harald's political achievements, including the social integration of Denmark and the introduction of Christianity. An unusually large, more than thirty-metre-long wooden church stood between the two barrows, with the runic stone on its southern side. The church contained a chamber in which a body had apparently been reburied, perhaps from the northern barrow. In terms of the symbol language of that time, these structures were impressive and unusual yet made up of traditional elements, and their erection must be viewed in the light of the emergence of the western Danish state society and the deep social and economic changes that this implied. The magnificent Jelling monument is thus an excellent example of the manipulative use of cultural symbols.

In the Early Empire, with its widespread stone and monumental architecture, graves often lay along the roads leading into a town – in Rome, for instance, along the Via Appia. Such graves are often decorated with architectural elements, sculptures, and inscriptions and may even take the form of mausoleums. Grave goods played no significant role here. With respect to the economic investment involved, these graves fall into the same class as the other edifices and decorations in the towns. For wealthy citizens many Early Roman burials were exceedingly costly affairs. It took almost a year during the first century BC to erect the twenty-seven-metre-high marble pyramid of the senator Cestius (in the third century built into Rome's town wall). These early Roman grave monuments, often both costly and imaginative, thus reveal the nature of the psychological and social environment in which they came into being as one of vast private fortunes and intense competition. The social mobility of the time is emphasized by the fact that family grave monuments from this time rarely commemorate more than one or possibly two generations (Hopkins 1983: 206). That the size of the monument seems little connected with the rank of the person commemorated underlines the openness of the system (Duncan-Jones 1982: 79, 130). In such a social environment, where, as in the West today, the extended family or lineage plays no very active part, the status of women was high. A woman could both inherit property and control it herself, though women held no political posts. Thus, half of the monumental grave inscriptions commemorate women (Huttunen 1974).

In the less open society of the Late Roman period and under the influence of

Table 13. *Percentages of grave inscriptions by category of deceased relative in imperial Rome and fifth-century north-eastern Gaul (primarily Trier)*

Location	Category of relative			
	Parent	Child	Spouse	Sibling
Rome	11	35	47	7
North-eastern Gaul (primarily Trier)	16	46	31	7

Sources: Huttunen 1974; Gauthier 1975

Christianity, monumental graves disappear, although sarcophagi (for example, in churches) and mausoleums persist. A special category of graves comprises subterranean chamber graves and catacombs, which in the present context might be classified among monumental tombs despite their more private character. The Early Roman graves in Italy and elsewhere were as a rule cremations or, more specifically, urn burials, while graves that contained corpses predominated in Late Roman times. In the early phases grave goods were often few and limited in type: perfume flasks, for instance, were virtually the only glass items (although they were extremely common [van Lith and Randsborg 1985]). Later grave goods, if any, had a more personal stamp. For instance, the glass finds now correspond to a far greater extent in type and frequency to the glasses found in settlements. One gets the impression that the personal status of the deceased, and thus his or her place in the family and society, played a greater part in Late Roman times than earlier. This is underlined by the grave inscriptions, which in some areas continued for a long time, although in a much humbler form than those of the Early Roman period (table 13 [Huttunen 1974; Gauthier 1975]). Both in imperial Rome and in Trier inscriptions dedicated to members of the nuclear family (spouse, child) predominate. The 'line of inheritance' (parent–ego–child) is a third more frequent in Trier than in Rome, where spouses (of whom wives make up 60 per cent) are the most conspicuous.

Such observations make it clear that monumental graves and grave inscriptions do not simply reflect social and biological reality but express a number of cultural norms. This is further emphasized by the Danish runic stones from the last centuries of the first millennium (Randsborg 1980, 1981c). These stones are monuments almost always to men (although Queen Thyra, mother of King Harald, is mentioned on the one at Jelling just discussed), and on the whole it was men who set them up. Not regularly associated with graves and standing in many different spots in the landscape, they must be considered 'deeds' or 'charters' recording and monumentally marking, demonstrating, and perhaps even postulating the legality of matters relating to inheritance. At all events, they are yet another example of manipulation. During the whole of the phase in which a state society was emerging in Denmark, runic stones were set up in the same province for only one or at most two generations. Those who followed evidently found it necessary only to refer to the standing stone. The dominance of men in the runic world must be related to questions of inheritance in the Viking period and, in particular, to non-traditional, less family-tied relationships in such matters as status, rank, and especially property (Randsborg 1984a).

Grave goods vary widely from area to area and period to period. In general, there is a preponderance of personal items: objects associated with clothing, weapons, and utensils for food and drink. The most valuable objects are often missing; for example, during the Danish Viking era articles of solid silver and gold, chiefly jewellery, are very common in the numerous hoards but virtually unknown in graves (Randsborg 1980, 1981c). These objects, often in daily use, apparently belonged to the lineage and therefore could not accompany the deceased to the grave. As already noted, variation in the quantity of grave goods is independent of the general level of wealth in the society, and this makes it very difficult to compare graves in different areas and of different cultural traditions.

In Scandinavia, a region with a long tradition of careful grave investigations, the inclusion of drinking glasses in grave goods is an interesting development that demonstrates how difficult it is to draw conclusions about 'real life' from the occurrence of particular items in graves (Randsborg 1988a; source Hunter 1975). In Denmark virtually no glasses occur in graves after the Roman period (AD 0–400). In Norway the same is true after AD 400–600, corresponding to Late Antiquity. Glasses first vanish from graves after AD 600–800 on the island of Gotland in the Baltic and not until after AD 800–1000/1100 on the Swedish mainland. From settlement finds we know that glasses were very common in Denmark during the post-Roman period, AD 400–600. On Gotland there are vast quantities of Arab silver coins and other traded items dating from the Viking period, and it is quite improbable that glasses should have been all but unknown. Glasses found in graves cannot, then, be used to describe changing exchange relations; it would be better to speak of an alteration in grave goods, which in the Roman period were 'rich' in glasses throughout Scandinavia but became 'poor' in them in the course of the millennium first in Denmark, then in Norway (where glasses are most common in the south), next on Gotland, and finally on the conservative Swedish mainland (where many glasses are known, for instance, from the graves of Birka).

This development might correspond to a ranking of the areas with respect to contact with the sources of the glasses. Denmark, farthest south, and southern Norway had good possibilities of contact, particularly after the middle of the first millennium when sail on ships became common. Gotland was more isolated but still centrally situated in the eastern Baltic, which played a large role in trade not only within north-western Europe but also with the Near East via Russia during the Viking period. The Swedish mainland was relatively isolated until the High Middle Ages. It is tempting to believe that glasses were less attractive as grave goods in areas and periods in which they were common. This explanation, is however, not entirely satisfactory in that it does not account for the disappearance of commoner objects at more or less the same time as glasses or the presence of many glasses in the graves of the emporium at Birka. Their geographical and chronological distribution could better be said to reflect the change in matters of ownership and inheritance introduced into Denmark in Late Roman times, parallel with the establishment of the new large Iron Age farms of the Vorbasse type and the 'monopolizing' centres. From this time grave goods become rare except in such special circumstances as those in tenth-century western Denmark (Randsborg 1982), presumably because property was being passed on to the heirs instead of accompanying the deceased into the grave. In all probability this change was associated with other alterations in use rights and the establishment of the lineage as the basis of the social structure. We have just discussed another example of this mechanism, namely the absence of objects of noble metals in Viking Age graves, an omission that is the more striking given that the hoards of the period, obviously the property of the lineage and not the individual, abounded in gold and silver (Randsborg 1980).

In one study of Roman graves, the quantitative methodology employed allows comparison of different cultural traditions (van Lith and Randsborg 1985). Because graves with glasses contain more items of other kinds, both in areas with 'poor' traditions with respect to grave goods and in areas with 'rich' ones, glasses can be attributed a greater average value than other goods. To facilitate comparison of different traditions, the method focuses on the *proportion* between the average number of glass items (A) and the average number of items ($A + B$) in different grave populations (B representing the average number of other items in the graves). It is postulated that this relationship ($A/A + B$) expresses the relative *wealth* of the population and thus of the society concerned ($[A + B]$ representing its *investment* in grave goods). Equipped with this basic tool we can, for example, measure the relationship between investment and wealth $(A + B)/A/(A + B)$. Because investment in grave goods is made under social pressure, which creates certain psychological, social, and economic problems, we postulate that this latter relationship is a measure of *social stress*. A further interesting feature is the constant (c) in the equation for the relationship between wealth (Y) and investment (X). The relationship is hyperbolic, and thus the equation takes the form $Y = c/X$ or $c = YX = A(A + B)/(A + B) = A$. A high c value is an expression of the fact that, on average, there are many glasses in the graves containing glass or, in other words, glass objects are concentrated in a few graves. The A value (derived from c) is, additionally, a measure of the degree of *social stratification* in the sampling population and thus in the society in question. From further consideration of these four constructions we note, for example, that the quantity of grave goods ($A + B$) is a product of stress and stratification and not, as is so often asserted, of stratification alone and, further, that stratification is the product of investment and wealth. Thus a society may have a high degree of stratification and few grave goods if stress is modest or has found a different means of expression – for example, as in the Early Empire, in monumental graves. Again, where a highly stratified society makes only a modest investment in grave goods its wealth must be great – and in this case too the Early Empire can serve as an example.

Among the historical information derived from this investigation is the fact that wealth in Trier increased from the first to the end of the fourth century, when the town was one of the capitals of the empire. Generally speaking, however, the town was relatively poor (though not as poor as the Roman military camps). Some agrarian sites are quite poor, others, like a number of the villas, very rich. Social stress or rivalry is high for Germanic chiefdom societies and communities, Early Frankish society (in the Rhineland), and agrarian Roman sites and low for Roman towns. In Trier the value for stress is lowest in the fourth century, but the value for stratification is high. Villas, too, are highly stratified, but other agrarian sites and military camps are not.

Social inequality

The two most marked social distinctions in all societies are those between children and adults and between men and women. Archaeology provides many examples of the different positions in society of children and adults. As a rule children were not buried as carefully and were provided with fewer grave goods. Sometimes, however, the opposite was the case, a classic instance being the burial of a Frankish prince in a grave dating from the beginning of the sixth century in the cathedral at Cologne. Although only six years of age, the boy was provided with a complete set of scaled-down weapons, and his helmet was lined with 'Coptic' – eastern Mediterranean – cloth (Werner 1961; Doppelfeld and Weyres 1980; Jørgensen 1985). Here archaeology reveals that there was distinct social differentiation in Early Frankish society and that children, through family links, could hold high rank. Age distinctions can also be seen in early Germanic society, shields and spears, the standard weapons, being associated with the graves of young men and spurs, indicating high rank, with those of older ones (Gebühr 1975). The other marked social distinction, that between men and women (Randsborg 1984a), can often be identified only through grave goods. The graves of the first millennium present a problem in that the abundant jewellery of the women often makes them more 'visible' than the men. If, however, we consider only graves containing skeletons of known sex, the situation of the sexes often proves to differ with respect to numbers. Usually it is mainly the men who have the proper graves in less developed societies. This applies, for instance, in Denmark of the Early Roman period (c. AD 0–200), when, to judge by the settlements, basically the same social conditions prevailed as in the earlier Iron Age. In the Late Roman period (c. AD 200–400), however, there are as many anthropologically determined and datable graves of females as there are of males (Sellevold, Hansen and Jørgensen 1984), and this sudden change is soon followed by a marked reduction of grave goods in all graves. Both these changes took place at the same time as the pronounced reorganization of settlement described earlier. Thus one is inclined to interpret the increase in the number of women with proper graves as an expression of the equality of the sexes with respect to burial, and this equality is probably to be understood in the light of the simultaneous establishment of large independent farms (Randsborg 1984a). This general form of agricultural management is likely to have been linked with the emergence of the lineage as the basic unit of social and economic organiza-tion. The well-defined inheritance rules that characterize the lineage would of course have applied to the personal belongings of the deceased, which, as we have seen, from Late Roman times tended to remain in the family rather than being placed in the grave. The reason for the equality of the sexes with respect to burial probably lies in inheritance through females as well as males. This is not to say, however, that the social status of women in general was equal to that of men. As we have seen, Viking runic stones show that the man was the superior in politics and warfare, official positions and duties, and matters of succession. To judge by the skeletons, the Germanic graves with grave goods in the Rhine area dating from post-Roman times or the early Middle Ages have equal numbers of men and women (Randsborg 1988a). Here we probably have another example of equality of the sexes in burial, and analogy with the northern Germanic commu-nities suggests that the same factors were involved. Finally, the Christian gravestones of Late Antiquity in Trier show largely the same number of women as men (Gauthier 1975).

The lives of women differed in a great many ways from those of men. Thus in Iron Age Denmark (*c.* 500 BC–AD 1000) we note a steady increase in average age at death for both sexes and similar fluctuations in average height, certainly determined by fluctuations in nutritional level (see chapter 8). Average age at death for women was, however, consistently lower than for men, probably because of the many dangers inherent in frequent childbearing (Randsborg 1984a; Bennike 1985). Men seem to have suffered more physical injury – for example, in battle. Archaeology has also revealed that women played only a minor economic part in the development of the early medieval towns of northern Europe; graves in these towns are for the most part those of younger men (Randsborg 1985; cf. Groenman-van Waateringe 1978). Indirectly, this also points to the socially marginal role of towns. Structurally, then, conditions for Danish women at the end of the first millennium were not as different from those for women in Rome in the Early Empire as might be imagined. The family took the leading role in both situations, but the lineage was certainly more important in the Nordic area than in imperial Rome. Both in Rome and in the Nordic area, women played no official part in politics and held practically no posts in public life. None the less, there were women in Rome who wielded vast influence by virtue of their private means, whereas in Scandinavia such influence was reserved for the married women of powerful and wealthy families, for example queens.

Outside the legal families were the slaves, of whom we know only a little for many of the societies of the first millennium. The early inscription material relating to manumitted slaves in Roman society is, however, considerable (Hopkins 1978). Although there is no doubt that slavery was widespread throughout the first millennium, there is much uncertainty about its importance. The Roman conquests and the conflict and unrest of Late Antiquity created ample opportunity for acquiring slaves for the empire and, little by little, for the production apparatuses of other societies. The slave trade was very extensive in Early Roman society, particularly in the west, just as it was in the later Islamic realm. Slaves were among the few valuables that the barbarian tribes could export to the 'civilized' realms. Thus the first time that the Danes are mentioned in written history is in connection with a slaving raid to the north-western Frankish realm at the beginning of the sixth century (Gregory of Tours 1955–6: III, 3), and Germanic slaving forays are also known from several other sources (Thompson 1982). The large quantities of Islamic silver coins in Scandinavia during the Viking period must largely represent profits from the sale of slaves.

Apparently two-thirds of the slaves and freedmen mentioned in the Roman inscriptions are men, but we are not sure whether this reflects an actual sociological situation (see, e.g., Manjarres 1971 for Spain). Judging by their names, these people were usually foreigners. In the Spain of the Early Empire, for instance, only every tenth slave was of local origin, the origins of the others being equally divided between the Western and the Eastern Empire. On average the age at death of freedmen seems to have been higher than that of slaves, who were rarely more than thirty years old. If manumission took place relatively late in the life of a slave, however, this might have influenced the situation.

In Caesarea Mauretania, the names of slaves and freedmen comprise 25 per cent of the inscription material in the first century but only 5 per cent in the second to third (Leveau 1984). It has often been assumed from this that slavery declined, but there is no way in which we can check the alternative hypothesis that the mobility and property of slaves had deteriorated and consequently they found it harder to pay for inscriptions. In any case, the slaves and freedmen named in inscriptions must have constituted a privileged group. Moreover, half of the earlier slaves and freedmen in Caesarea had Greek names. In Rome the names of slaves and freedmen comprise almost 40 per cent of the inscription material, and there are twice as many freedmen as slaves (Huttunen 1974). In the province of Noricum, too, twice as many freedmen as slaves are mentioned in inscriptions, and the percentage of slaves is highest in the Early Empire period (Alföldy 1974: 191).

Slaves were also used, sometimes in positions of trust, by the Germanic tribes, as Tacitus reports (Randsborg 1984b). There are frequent references to slaves in the Germanic laws of the latter half of the first millennium. The same applies to the Nordic sagas, but these texts are primarily associated with Iceland, where it is known that slaves comprised an unusually large percentage of the immigrant population in the Viking period. One saga, dealing with Swedish and Danish affairs around the middle of the first millennium, mentions slaves holding positions of trust under the kings, and even a slave riot.

Several cases of slaves' being sacrificed as 'grave goods' are known in the last centuries of the first millennium in Scandinavia (Randsborg 1984b). So brutal an end was hardly the fate of the slaves from the upper ranks of the social spectrum, who as freedmen could even set up runic stones and therefore held property (Randsborg 1980). The sacrifice of slaves was evidently rare but must be evaluated in the same terms as other investments in grave goods. In the earlier centuries of the first millennium, slave sacrifice was unknown in Scandinavia in connection with graves (Randsborg 1984b). Quite a number of men and women, perhaps slaves or prisoners of war, were sacrificed in the Danish bogs around the birth of Christ and before, but such sacrifice was practically unknown in the later, more advanced Iron Age society, in which a more 'economic' attitude towards valuables may be noted in connection with grave goods and was certainly also applicable to manpower. This hypothesis, which assumes the existence of Germanic slave labour, is indirectly supported by finds dating from the third to fifth centuries that consist of conspicuous and ostentatious sacrifices of the equipment of a defeated army but not of the vanquished warriors, who may have been forced into slavery (Ilkjær 1984). In passing it should be noted that these finds, along with graves, become 'poorer' with time and by the fifth century are *pars pro toto*.

As uncertain as we are about slaves and slavery in the first millennium, we are well informed when it comes to the top of the social pyramid, where demonstrations of wealth, status, power, and influence are readily observable in the archaeological material. In the present connection a detailed account of such phenomena is unnecessary in view of the extremely comprehensive literature on burials, inscriptions, monuments, etc., that we have had occasion to refer to above. It is rare for written sources from the first millennium to bring us as close to the material aspects of social inequality as archaeology does, but there are a few texts whose rich detail can compete even with the finds from Pompeii. One such document is dated 17 July AD 564 and concerns the furnishings of a house in Ravenna belonging to a relatively wealthy man, recently deceased, named Stephan and the property of a freedman, Guderit, whose effects were being sold on the same occasion (Burns 1980: 109–10). The objects listed here – household items, valuables, wearing apparel, and even a slave – might well have been found in graves from the latter half of the first millennium. In some cases the values of the various objects are also given.

The house in Ravenna
7 spoons (soup ladles)
1 large bow
1 clasp (fibula) for an apron
1 clasp for a garter
12 moulds (value of all the above items = 2 pounds of silver)
2 woven coloured tapestries (1 solidus and 1 tremissis [1/3 solidus])
1 embroidered cover (1 solidus)
1 old basket (4 gold siliquae [1/6 solidus])
1 shirt of silk and cotton in scarlet and leek-green ($3\frac{1}{2}$ solidi)
1 variegated leek-green garment ($1\frac{1}{2}$ solidi)
1 locked trunk with key
1 mixed silk shirt (short sleeves) (2 gold siliquae)
1 pair of linen trousers (1 gold siliqua)
1 pillow ($\frac{1}{2}$ solidus)
1 large copper barrel
1 small cooking pot
1 small copper pitcher
1 copper lamp with attached chain (value of the last three copper items = 12
    pounds of scrap iron)
1 vat for vinegar (1 tremissis)
1 small vat
1 barrel for grain ($2\frac{1}{2}$ gold siliquae/40 nummi)
1 small grain box with iron binding (2 gold siliquae)
1 harvesting sickle (1 gold siliqua)
4: 1 barrel, 1 hoe, 2 oil barrels
1 cabinet (4 gold siliquae)
2 twisted ropes (6 gold siliquae)
1 chair with seat of woven iron
1 chair with woven wooden seat
1 table and flat (cuttingboard) (1 gold siliqua)
2 stone mortars (1 gold siliqua)
1 wooden trough
1 pack saddle
1 lambskin blanket (2 gold siliquae)
1 slave named Proiectus.

Guderit's property
1 closed trunk (iron binding, key) (2 gold siliquae)
1 other trunk in poor condition
1 used wine vat
1 old cooking pot with iron handle (weighing $1\frac{1}{2}$ pounds)
1 broken kettle (1 pound)

1 iron cooking chain (2½ pounds)
1 seeding tool
1 whetstone with moistening oil
1 kneading-trough, broken
1 small box
1 small earthen jug
1 broken earthen pot
1 bar
1 tub
1 grain basket
1 measure
1 grain jug
1 old dyed shirt (3 gold siliquae)
1 decorated shirt (6 gold siliquae)
1 cloth
1 old coat
1 old short, thick cloak.

The objects owned by Stephan and Guderit do not differ greatly in nature, but Stephan possessed far more of them and his were of greater value and in better condition. Stephan's most costly item of apparel, a shirt of silk and cotton at 3½ solidi, is fourteen times as valuable as Guderit's best piece of clothing, an embroidered shirt. This tells us, finally, that the life-styles of these two men were not fundamentally different in spite of the distinction of riches and rank. The modern reader will also note the high value of the material items in relation to the value of food. A Roman soldier of the sixth century could be maintained and partially equipped for considerably less than ten solidi per annum (Hendy 1985: 68–9).

The visible and the invisible

In the same way that the archaeological sources provide us with information on distinguished persons from the past, they also bring us closer to past ideas about invisible powers – the gods and other forces that humans create and recreate. From the countless studies of pictures of the visible or the imagined visible in ancient times we know that classical renderings of the gods were representative; the picture was what it resembled. In contrast, the Germanic art of the Migration period and the later centuries of the first millennium was referential, signlike as is a Byzantine icon (although the latter, by virtue of the fact that we recognize the rendering, is representative too). No attempt will be made here to summarize so colossal a corpus of data. To follow the material just a step farther, however, one might point to a study of the graves that surrounded the Viking market town of Birka and, in particular, of those grave goods that could be assigned to a particular season of the year (Randsborg and Nybo 1984), which demonstrated that the graves were oriented towards the point of the horizon where the sun set on the day of burial. They lay largely east–west, as do Christian graves, but the belief underlying this arrangement must have been very different from the Christian one whereby the body 'looks' towards the rising sun and the resurrected Christ to reappear on Judgement Day. It can be shown, furthermore, that many burials took place precisely on midsummer's day. The explanation for this is probably that the chief market occurred at this time, and it explodes the myth that Birka was used as a marketplace only in winter, when the surrounding waters were frozen solid. According to the orientation of the graves, smaller markets may well have taken place in the spring and in early autumn. The different grave types also have a seasonal distribution. Burials containing simple wooden coffins are associated especially with the winter months, while the conspicuous chamber graves, often richly equipped, predominate in the summer. The latter must be evidence that prominent people visited Birka and died here particularly in the 'market season'. Simple graves without coffins were used throughout the year. Even the different burial areas seem to have a seasonal distribution. The northern one chiefly contains winter graves; perhaps Birka's relatively few permanent residents were confined to the northern part of town. The central one contains in particular graves from the equinoxes, while the southern area, near the 'fortress' and perhaps the thingstead, contains primarily summer graves, including the many from midsummer days.

The example provided by Birka is especially satisfactory because it combines the economic, social, and ideological worlds and because the ideological/symbolic dimension is so distinct. Although chamber graves were designed in such a way that onlookers might admire the many, often exotic grave goods, no attempt was made (except perhaps for a quite low, thus anonymous barrow) to set up any permanent or monumental symbol to commemorate the deceased. Those who made up the funeral procession knew, of course, who the dead person was and decided upon the form of the grave and the nature of the grave goods. Beyond this, the deceased was to be remembered only by oral tradition. In spite of the certainly highly competitive and 'cosmopolitan' milieu at Birka, it was only for a fleeting moment that such social relations were expressed.

The apparent transitoriness of the handling of the dead is notable in other aspects of barbarian societies. Dwellings often lasted only a single generation, and the signs that revealed the nature of social relationships were few and unassuming in nature. The life of most household effects was scarcely longer than that of the houses themselves, a few generations at most. Metal objects were more durable, but those made of valuable materials were often melted down. At any rate, it is rare to find very old objects together with more recent ones; the second-century Roman denarii still in use in Scandinavia in the fifth are exceptional.

The predominantly ornamental art that we know from the Germanic societies is associated almost exclusively with metal objects (plate 8); only in a few cases do we gain any insight into corresponding forms of expression in bone, wood, or stone. Monumental renderings, for example in stone, are rare except for a few places such as Gotland. As noted earlier, there are virtually no recognizable elements in the renderings, although parts of animals or fabulous beasts – rarely a whole animal – often occur. Works in this style, labelled 'Germanic animal ornamentation', have been found from northern Scandinavia to Italy and from the British Isles to Eastern Europe dating to the first millennium and the beginning of the second (Karlsson 1983). This art, whose distinct though implicit signlike nature is so evident, fits very well with the material transitoriness just described. At the same time, the art of decorating metals is often associated with objects of value and may be very elegantly and consistently carried out. Thus the signlike character of animal ornamentation is connected with the particular properties of a referential art and this in turn with a particular mental and social milieu – that of the Germanic warrior leaders, with the strong sense of lineage and family and, to us, almost exaggerated concept of honour that have come down to us in Norse literature and certain runic inscriptions. The lineage and its rights must indeed have been considered the basic element in a society with little material evidence of continuity except replication.

It is significant that Germanic animal ornamentation developed in the Late Roman period along with the new lineage farms, political centres and seasonal markets, conflicts between well-defined regions, etc. The models for such expression were, on the whole, Roman, but Roman and representative pictorial art and the plant-dominated Mediterranean ornamental style were clearly of little interest. Roman glasses, bronzes, and weapons were put to immediate use, but Roman art was either rejected or extensively reshaped. It was only after AD 400, however, that animal ornamentation came to cover the surfaces of decorated objects. The animals were compact in shape and plastic in character and, in comparison with the art of the following period (late sixth to the beginning of the eighth centuries), relatively 'naturalistic'. In general, animal ornamentation was dominated by highly harmonious interlacing from the sixth century to the eighth, when, under Carolingian influence derived from the Mediterranean, it again assumed a certain 'naturalism'. The products of this idiom can be assigned to styles, alternately simple and complex, that relatively rapidly replace one another or occur partly in parallel. In addition, there are some geographical variations, for example between the more derived and sometimes 'mixed' art of Central Europe (see Böhner 1976–7) and the 'classical' products of the Nordic area.

Development was very dynamic in the Viking Age, and different styles, which from the tenth century on were frequently used on monuments, certainly evolved in the leading political circles (for example, the Danish Jelling dynasty). At the same time, more naturalistic elements penetrated into Scandinavia from the courts of Central Europe and from ecclesiastical art. Animal ornamentation

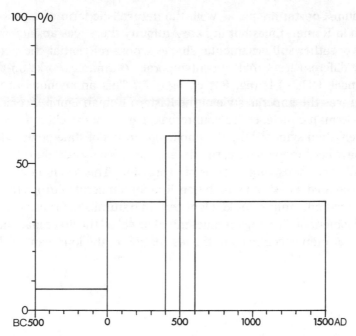

Fig. 81. Changing frequencies of stylized (or 'ornamental') versus naturalistic representations on stone from Constantinople (*Source*: Mendel 1912–14)

was, however, still in use in the High Middle Ages. Chiefly a symbol language for the dominant circles of Germanic society, it developed in step with them, thus serving, especially in its final phase, to conceal the dramatic changes of the later first and the beginning of the second millennium. At the same time, the mass production of, for instance, ornamented jewellery that began in the Viking Age helped make the styles acceptable to the population at large. This predominantly Nordic art form was, moreover, exported to other parts of Europe by means of the alliances of the Germanic princely houses, and the Vikings introduced it, for instance, to the British Isles.

The classical world was characterized by an interest in creating and decorating architectural environments – individual buildings and interiors, as well as monuments and smaller objects (plates 1–4). By Late Antiquity the focus had narrowed to the individual building and perhaps its interior decoration (plates 5–7). A number of very beautiful and valuable objects date from the Late Roman period and Late Antiquity (cover). There is a great contrast between animal ornamentation and classical art, but after the earliest phase of imperial Roman art a comparison between the northern and the southern world is not wholly inappropriate. In Late Antiquity the arts of the classical world changed dramatically in character and lost most of their former naturalism (see plate 6). On a general, highly abstract level we thus discern a dwindling of the differences between barbarian and civilized worlds. In the decoration of stone-built structures in Byzantium/Constantinople as well, the naturalistic form of expression predominated in Roman times but in Late Antiquity there was an increase in the frequency of rather stiff ornamental shapes whose referential character is not essentially different from that of contemporary Germanic works on a smaller scale (Mendel 1912–14) (fig. 81; cf. fig. 57). This anonymous ornamental decoration was the imperial style of the Eastern Roman Empire, copied by the southern Germanic societies. To counterbalance the many changes of the time and to strengthen symbolically the public apparatus of state power, deliberate use may have been made of pure, simple, and superficially rather arid – although aesthetically very satisfying – forms of expression. This levelling of north and south also created a basis on which non-Roman temperate Europe towards the end of the first millennium could adopt certain naturalistic forms of expression. This development of Carolingian times might be called the first renaissance – the first time that man succumbed to the fascination of the long-vanished ancient world.

8

ARCHAEOLOGY AND HISTORIOGRAPHY

I see mankind under two lights,
Past and future; and in two states,
Time and place. If we ask
How God accounts for this oddness
We'll get an evasive answer.
Abu al-Ala al-Ma'arri (AD 973–1057)

In the previous chapters the emphasis has been on the material remains and traces of past human activity that archaeology has brought to light, especially in recent decades. In this one, the focus is on social development and the contribution that archaeology has made to our understanding of it. Questions relating to the decline and fall of the Roman Empire are of course central, but this is only one of the points of interest here: among others are its relations with the Asiatic civilizations and especially with the northern barbarian peoples, and the foundations for the later development of Europe. Byzantium and its northern neighbours are somewhat neglected in the account, partly because, with the expansion of Western Europe, Eastern Europe came to play an increasingly marginal role (Wallerstein 1974). This bias was not, however, so pronounced in the time of Charlemagne as it became later, and I must admit, with apology, that my weighting of the material has a linguistic basis. Future archaeology in Eastern Europe will doubtless make interesting adjustments to our perceptions of the world. So many views have been expressed on the fall of the Roman Empire and the emergence of the European states that it may seem pointless to add to the debate. Few attempts have so far been made, however, to bring archaeology into the picture, just as it has been rare for the account to include not only the empire but also the barbarian societies and the developments that followed (but see Hodges and Whitehouse 1983). An account of the social changes of the first millennium and the reasons for them may allow us to view the decline and fall of the Roman Empire not simply in the light of Early Roman culture and social structure but in terms of the developments during the four centuries of the Late

Roman period and especially Late Antiquity, making it clear that the Roman Empire that fell – in the West – differed fundamentally even from the empire of Marcus Aurelius.

From the Roman Empire to the Middle Ages

A recent historical survey of treatises on the collapse of the Roman empire records some five hundred different theories devoted to this question (Demandt 1983; cf. Mazzarino 1959; Rollins 1983). Theories relating to the expansion of the empire are considerably fewer, probably because the academic western world views expansion, economic profit, and social development as natural. Here disagreement has to do more with economic structure – whether it was 'primitive' or more modern (Carandini 1986), whether trade was controlled by market forces or (perhaps more likely) administered by the state (Garnsey, Hopkins, and Whittaker 1983), whether the primary function of the ancient town was that of an economic and manufacturing centre or an object of investment for a consumer society (Ørsted 1985). Finally, because the Early Empire had much in common with previous periods, it has been easy to view the Roman Empire as the crowning achievement of development in Antiquity.

From the viewpoint of the history of research, theories concerning the reasons for the fall of the (Western) Roman Empire can be divided roughly into two groups, the first considering the reasons internal and the second external, brought about by the penetration of the Germanic peoples. The first group cites social and economic problems including population decline, political and military miscalculations, and religious apathy. Even more abstract explanations include a predestined decline of civilization and similar 'biologisms'. In the current discussion, socio-economic explanatory models have won wide acceptance, and it is indeed such a model that I tend to advocate, with the qualification that short-term decisions in crisis situations have certainly been based on concerns of political economy (see Jones 1964; Bernardi 1965). There was also, of course, a general mental frame of reference for Roman actions and norms, but it is more difficult to account for precisely.

Among recent explanatory models, Goffart's (e.g., 1980) views the settling of Germanic peoples within the empire as part of the empire's – and the landowners' – efforts to solve the problems of military recruitment and internal security. Goffart all but denies the existence of any economic or military difficulties in the Western Empire, and in this, as in his notion that what the Germanic peoples acquired was taxes rather than land, he is probably mistaken. His theory concerning a gradual 'depreciation' of the Western Empire as a solution to the state's widespread security problems, for example relating to usurpers, is very interesting, however, and a case can certainly be made for increasing political and military relations in the fourth and fifth centuries between the western Germanic peoples and tribal confederations and the Roman imperial provinces, in particular on the Rhine. Moreover, it fits in with Thompson's (1982) notion that Germanic settlement – for example, that of the Visigoths in Aquitania – was part of an attempt to counteract uprisings against the demands of state and landowners for taxes and rent (but see van Dam 1985 for a view of these uprisings as attempts to revive Roman administration). Whether these theories are 'right' or 'wrong', they do give us a more varied and perhaps more realistic picture of the fall of the Roman Empire in that they combine external and internal factors and are not tied to one or another general model. Jones (1964), in fact, combined external and internal factors twenty-five years ago by emphasizing the political economy and the military problems of the West.

Pirenne's thesis, which continues to inspire scholars (see Hodges and Whitehouse 1983), connects Carolingian development and thus (as Pirenne saw it) the birth of Western Europe with Islam's triumphal progress in the Mediterranean and the enforced isolation of the Frankish realm (Pirenne 1922). Today we realize that at any rate the Western Empire showed signs of weakening long before the rise of Islam and that the Carolingian realm was hardly totally isolated, certainly not in its relations with Islam (Lombard 1971). It is possible that the Carolingian renaissance was quite simply financed by Islamic silver acquired through trade with the Vikings (Hodges and Whitehouse 1983 [with reference to Bolin 1953, who, however, viewed the eastern trade as the financial background for the Viking raids on Western Europe; cf. Randsborg 1981a for a critique of Bolin's chronology]). Yet there were also other sources of funds for the Carolingians, among them Charles Martel's confiscation of ecclesiastical treasures, production and trade in general, economic expansion, tribute, and numerous plundering forays.

Just as there is some consensus concerning the expansion and development of the Early Empire period, there is wide agreement regarding the conditions that were of special significance for social development around AD 1000 (e.g., Duby 1974). Scholars studying this phase have tended to look for the conditions typical of the High Middle Ages, and it is therefore hardly surprising that three aspects are deemed of special importance: the development of the means of production, particularly agriculture, and the organizational changes associated with this; the urban economy, which, however, came to dominate social development only after AD 1200; and exchange and trade, in particular the development of regional markets (see, most recently, Hodges 1988).

On a general level it is agreed that social conditions stabilized after the Carolingian period and the last attacks on 'Europe' by the barbarian fringe societies. The primary reason for this was, however, the gradual dissolution of the old 'aristocratic' warrior society in the West and among the 'civilized' barbarians, including, for instance, the Danes. This society had a transregional prestige economy and a territorial rather than regional and local interest in the creation and development of estates. Archaeology has not yet been able to comment satisfactorily on the material character of the estate system of the pivotal Carolingian period as this is presented in the polyptychs of monastic estates between the Seine and the Rhine (Duby 1962; Pounds 1973). These documents do, however, suggest 'villas' comprising a demesne owned by the monastery and another part made up of dependent tenures. Ties of family and lineage left over from the old societies (here Merovingian and to some extent Carolingian) continued to constitute the basis of social structure at all levels of society. The debate concerning the transition to the High Middle Ages is thus, by comparison with that on the fall of the Roman Empire, centred upon 'minor' problems. Apart from those already mentioned, they include the forms of power, among them detailed discussion of 'feudal' relations (e.g., Poly and Bournazel 1980; Fosier 1982) and the nature of 'private life'.

In the shadow of the empire

The contribution of archaeology to the elucidation of social development under the Early Empire relates in part to the traditional work on Roman towns, villas, art, and inscriptions and in part to the (mainly) recent studies of the ecology and settlement, exchange, etc., that, for instance, make it possible to evaluate Roman society and economy in chronological and geographical detail. Of special importance among our archaeological observations is the explosion of settlement around Rome that accompanied the expansion of the empire, which shows how limited was the economic structure that supported Roman political life and the dominant culture of the capital. Archaeology has also clarified in detail the development of Rome's supply system, in which oil, wine, and even grain were transported by ship from all over the Mediterranean area, primarily from areas outside Italy. The import of foodstuffs to Rome culminated in the late second century (Anselmino et al. 1986). At the same time, settlement around Rome was reduced, from which it must be concluded that the population of the capital had begun to decline early in the Late Roman period at the latest.

In the Mediterranean area as a whole, the Early Roman period marks a high point for settlement only in the north-west. In Sicily and particularly North Africa, settlement was greatest in Late Roman times and Late Antiquity, and the same applies to the eastern Mediterranean and especially the Levant. It is tempting to regard these trends as a continuation of developments in the Mediterranean area in pre-imperial times in which the centre of gravity lay to the east and south. In Greece, for instance, there is incontrovertible evidence in a number of areas that dynamic social development in classical times was accompanied by an exponential increase in settlement that was, however, soon replaced by a decline, with pronounced erosion. This ecological-economic model, with demographic overtones, might indeed be applied to Antiquity in general, in which settlement peaks, minor and major, seem to have lasted only for a few hundred years at a time. To this picture must be added the various climatic changes, particularly in precipitation; a dry phase in the early first millennium would, for example, have been less of a calamity in the north-western than in the south-eastern Mediterranean.

In spite of the ecological problems, it is remarkable that the Early Empire did not create a basis for general economic growth. The enormous political power and control of a vast geographical area might have guaranteed a potentially vast market, but it seems that production for the broader market was relatively modest and fluctuating. The production and distribution of pottery and craft products were, moreover, linked to the development of market-oriented food production. The regional possibilities of reaching a larger market through specialization were therefore not exploited to the same extent as they would have been, for instance, in the High Middle Ages given correspondingly optimal technological conditions and transport possibilities.

Archaeology throws light, of course, on the expansion of the empire to the north and into Late Celtic society, which was in several respects also highly developed. Among the most important subjects for archaeology in this area are the military installations – for example, the Roman fortresses – and the towns, components of a 'city-state' system on the Mediterranean model that constituted the fiscal and administrative foundation of the Early Empire even north of the Alps. Architectural norms here were Mediterranean, and the knowledge of ancient values and experience thus disseminated was never to vanish entirely. The need to supply the troops along the Rhine–Danube line, coupled with the impressive ability of the very Early Empire to mobilize its resources, meant that exotic objects found their way to Central Europe. In general, the Roman political, military, and cultural system in these areas was founded on the local subsistence economy and on the plants and livestock thriving north of the Alps. Some crafts, however – building in stone and the manufacture of weapons, pottery, and glass – became Romanized. With the establishment of *terra sigillata* factories in Gaul and on the Rhine, local products dominated the markets in Gaul by AD 100, and by the second century Italian products had entirely disappeared. At the same time, in Rome for instance, there were reductions in the imports of Gallic wine, though this chiefly came from regions in southern Gaul; thus an increasing isolation of the north-western provinces of the empire can be noted. Provincial Roman commodities did, however, reach West Germany, and new relations were therefore being established farther north at the same time. The sources of Roman bronze vessels, etc., from this period in Free Germany (table 14) show some of these fundamental economic changes (Kunow 1983).

North of the Alps, the second century, particularly its latter half, constituted the zenith of Roman development; in the third century agrarian settlement declined markedly in most areas, just as it did in the vicinity of Rome. To the east and south-east, on the lower reaches of the Danube, however, it is difficult to glimpse a similar recession. In contrast, the Late Roman period in areas such as Hungary and Bulgaria was marked by progress in agriculture and settlement. The well-known 'third-century crisis' was thus not an expression of a general

Table 14. *Percentages of Roman bronze vessels from various parts of the empire in Free Germany,* AD 50–150

Time period	Region		
	Italy (including Capua)	Gaul	The Rhineland
AD 50	100	0	0
AD 100	38	62	0
AD 150	0	16	84

Source: Kunow 1983

economic recession and certainly not of a recession in agriculture. It did, however, bring profound changes in the political structure, military forces, coinage, etc., and eventually the virtual disintegration of the social structure and the urban culture of Antiquity. The crisis was accompanied and probably caused by a dramatic shift in the economic centre of gravity of the empire, affecting primarily Mediterranean food production and its market. An early prerequisite for this shift in emphasis was, however, the decline in Italian production that was reflected in the frequencies of imported amphorae of Ostia and of the bronze vessels just discussed. With the decline in Italian production that had begun in the latter half of the first century, the Roman heartland lost its dominant economic role, becoming instead dependent on the other Mediterranean regions. This led to the establishment of a degree of equality between the different areas, but, as we have seen, this was not exploited for any collective development. Nevertheless, a large Mediterranean market for foodstuffs, pottery, etc., persisted, finally collapsing only in the first half of the seventh century. Thereupon regional economies dominated ordinary commodities, and the international trade in luxuries was left to exchanges between magnates and their agents. To push this argument to its logical conclusion, we can say that the bases for the third-century crisis, and thus indirectly for the fall of the Western Empire, were established shortly after the death of the emperor Augustus.

The importance to the empire of the crisis-prone north-western provinces was greatest with regard to military supplies. The military protection of Britain and of the Rhine–Danube frontier was at the same time the safeguarding of the regional economic systems that had evolved both on the frontiers and in the hinterlands during Roman times. Thus in the fourth century, in militarily secure areas such as Britain and Aquitania, there are signs of new growth after the third-century decline. The reason the areas bordering the Lower Danube managed so well certainly lies partly in the military situation and partly in the eastward shift of the economic centre of gravity, which brought the region, which had been a relatively marginal one with late urban development (Mócsy 1970: 46), close to the new areas of economic growth in the eastern Mediterranean. In the fourth century the Balkans became a 'hinterland' for the new imperial capital at Constantinople, and Sirmium, near Belgrade, was one of its auxiliary capitals.

The end of the Pax Romana and beginning of the third-century military crisis is often traced to the Marcomannic wars. Of the Germanic tribes which inflicted these long and costly wars on the Romans, the first to break the peace came not, however, from the frontier regions in Moravia and western Slovakia inhabited by the Marcomanni and their eastern neighbours, the Quads, but from farther north, for example western Poland. Moreover, the Germanic peoples had often applied to the Romans for grants of land, which were largely denied them. Finally, the Germanic combatants often included whole families (women as well as men), perhaps the victims of internal strife among the Germanic societies on the Danube (Böhme 1975).

Knowledge of the character of the southern Germanic settlements, in Czechoslovakia for example, is relatively limited, but something is known of a number of villa-like complexes of Roman type, dated to the first half of the second century, in Moravia and western Slovakia. Perhaps these were built for Romanized Germanic leaders or even as Roman outposts with a view to trade. In the same area and from the same general period, but especially the latter half of the second and the beginning of the third century, there are considerable quantities of Roman *terra sigillata*, in the last phase clearly originating in the Rheinzabern factories on the Upper Rhine (Křížek 1961, 1966). Along with a second, contemporary concentration of *terra sigillata* in central Poland (Rutkovski 1960), these finds show that costly Roman objects in Free Germany were no longer, as earlier, relatively evenly distributed over the entire Germanic territory.

Another important concentration of finds dating from around AD 200 has come to light in eastern Denmark. This consists mainly of other types of Roman wares and only a little *terra sigillata*. It is contemporary with a number of large weapon sacrifices in the west of the country (Ilkjær 1984), evidence of the heavy fighting that may have been one result of the political and social developments expressed in positive fashion by the concentration of Roman imports in eastern Denmark (Randsborg 1986). Seen in this light, the fact that during the Marcomannic wars on the Danube some tribal groups were put to flight by others may be a negative reflection of the developments leading to a concentration of resources and social ties expressed in the clusters of, for instance, imported *terra sigillata* in central Poland and in Moravia and western Slovakia. In both the Scandinavian and the Central European cases the Romans were probably instrumental in this social development. For the Germanic tribes, the Romans acted as a strong and spatially continuous political neighbour-centre with a concentration of resources and influence.

Contemporary with the emergence of regionally concentrated distributions of imported Roman luxuries – which were a step in the direction of monopolizing centres in Free Germany – there was among the north-western Germans a change in settlement pattern towards large, independent farm complexes controlled by lineages with direct rights to the farmlands. These lineages constituted the nucleus of the new Germanic social structure and, along with the large farm complexes, persisted through the rest of the first millennium and beyond. Men and women were regarded as equals, except politically, in this structure, whereas in the earlier societies the man, as tribal warrior, had received more attention. Whether there were similar developments in the south-eastern Germanic societies is as yet unknown, but it seems likely from the organizational coherence apparent, for instance, in the Goths of the Late Roman period. We do know that the Germanic communities in these areas came to an end after around AD 500 and never attained the same regional stability as the societies of the north-west. The history of south-eastern Europe was in general dominated by emigration of various 'aristocratic' groupings and their 'peoples', particularly around the middle of the millennium.

The circumstances of the Marcomannic wars are important because the time around AD 200 saw a number of profound changes both in Germanic and in Roman society. These wars were fought, moreover, at the far end of the empire's economic 'see-saw' axis and may well have been associated with a change in the direction of Germanic economic interests in this part of Central Europe from the north-west to the south-east and thus towards the vital Roman provinces. It is, for instance, characteristic that *terra sigillata* finds dating from the period following the Marcomannic wars have come to light in the Sarmatian region of eastern Hungary, where such finds are virtually unknown from any earlier period. Political relations between the northern and western Germanic peoples and the Roman Rhineland were also strengthened in this period, however, at times becoming intimate. In the fourth century, the Franks and the Alamanni, of all Germanic tribes, played a significant role in the Roman military while tribesmen from beyond the Rhine often supported usurpers. The Late Roman period brought, in general, a weakening of the political and trading relations that had earlier dominated the contact between barbarians and Romans. It is typical that gold finds from Late Antiquity in the Middle Danube region are dated to the decades in which the Eastern Empire was paying tribute to the princes of this region (Randsborg 1986). Such payments were rewards for special services and thus made from a position of weakness.

North of the Danube and the Rhine, the Germans who had organized themselves into tribal federations during the third century became a growing problem for the empire. After the Marcomannic wars, the empire experienced increasing difficulty in maintaining, in particular, the western part of the Rhine–Danube frontier as a secure line of defence. The army of Late Roman times made considerable use of Germanic auxiliaries, however, and by serving in the regiments of imperial guards the Franks and the Alamanni achieved high posts in the fourth-century empire (Waas 1965). The relations between the Romans and the western Germanic peoples, though complex, were from the Roman viewpoint clearly centred on both countering and exploiting Germanic political and military potential. Given the limited means at their disposal, it must be said that the Romans were remarkably successful. Battles between pretenders to the throne often presented the empire with greater security problems than did the Germans

– though problems from these two quarters did not always come singly. Defence against outside enemies was, however, the litmus test of the empire, not least from the point of view of ideology. If the official defence were to have failed, it might have been tempting to seek other solutions to security problems, for instance by employing Germanic warriors, who might be given land for their services. As a last resort, the supremacy of Germanic peoples might have been accepted, a solution that would, moreover, have allowed the local or regionally resident magnates to avoid paying at least some of the taxes that had to be exacted to maintain the political and military system.

Transformation

When Constantinople was established as capital of the Roman Empire in AD 330, the Romans drew a conclusion, perhaps not entirely wittingly, from the economic situation. Despite a few frontier adjustments in the second half of the third century – for instance, the giving up to the Alamanni of the area between the Upper Rhine and Danube and the abandonment of Dacia to the Visigoths and others – attempts were still being made to maintain the Augustan extent of the empire, including the later extensions made in Upper Mesopotamia in particular. The military and many of the administrative resources of the empire were, as we have seen from the distribution of state factories, concentrated along the northern and north-eastern frontier. The archaeology is quite consistent about the development of settlement in the eastern areas of the empire, whether it is the settlements themselves that are under study or, for example, the churches. Particularly in the Levant there was a marked advance in Late Roman times and especially in Late Antiquity. In the Eastern Empire, development was also fostered by the greater precipitation and more widespread use of irrigation systems (Watson 1983:103–4). One consequence of this trend would have been to move the capital yet again, for instance to Antioch. This, of course, did not happen, but it is not without interest that the early Islamic empire, under the Umayyad dynasty, chose nearby Damascus as its capital. Baghdad, whose establishment reflects the steady eastward drift of the imperial social system and transregional imperial market economies, first became capital under the Abbasid dynasty, after the middle of the eighth century. In retrospect it is notable that the Islamic conquests were made chiefly in areas that in the seventh century still possessed vital agrarian settlement and were producing commodities for the broader market. These areas could, moreover, serve the caravan routes, a form of transport that was developing during the first millennium at the expense of road transport (Bulliet 1975). In contrast, Roman society and its northern successors in the Mediterranean relied heavily on water transport.

To judge by the archaeological evidence, the old Mediterranean towns in Late Roman times still displayed most of the features of the classical towns, such as regularity in plan, street network, and open spaces, but the number of public monuments – except, of course, churches – had declined. In the north-western empire towns were drastically reduced and then almost ceased to exist in Late Antiquity. In the Eastern Empire, in contrast, towns were still the focus of aristocratic life and thus persisted even after the Islamic conquest (Kennedy 1985). By the sixth century at the latest, however, there seem to have been difficulties in maintaining the classical town structure. New secular monuments were rare, many of the old ones had fallen into ruin, and public buildings such as baths were far smaller than in Roman times. Moreover, the town founded in Late Antiquity did not follow the classical norms, showing a more chaotic 'Islamic' aspect with narrow streets surrounding the larger buildings, for instance the churches. Such features are also known from medieval towns in the West. In some instances the streets and squares of old towns were filled in with buildings, which can only mean that legislation regulating urban construction was no longer enforced. Thus archaeology provides some insight into the administrative difficulties facing Roman society in Late Antiquity and at the same time demonstrates the limited authority that the Islamic officials had over public building. In passing it can be added that even under Islam general plans were used when new towns were founded, as was the case for Baghdad. Moreover, the new Islamic towns were often alternatives to the old Roman or Sassanid centres.

As we have seen, the towns of the Early Roman period were chiefly self-administering, but in the Late Roman period central government and its representatives took over an increasing number of local functions. Given the growing difficulties of the state, there were few funds to invest in buildings, and those that were available were generally spent on churches. The aristocracy in the Late Roman period and in Late Antiquity had close connections with the state and acted as its civil servants and regional tax collectors (Wickham 1984). The Islamic towns, like their European counterparts in the High Middle Ages, were strongly marked by craft and trading interests and less influenced by any aristocracy or state that made its presence felt through the erection of monuments.

During the Late Roman period and Late Antiquity the state had economic problems other than the financing of the classical city. An increasing burden for the empire was the vast military and the administrative cost of collecting taxes. The number of troops was scarcely increased after the reorganization of the army in the fourth century that created a permanent division into frontier troops (*limitanei*) and regional contingents of the field army (*comitatus*), including the *palatini*, the centrally stationed regiments whose job it was to shield the central administration. There were, in addition, other units such as the guard regiments. Under the emperor Justinian, in the sixth century, the expenses of the army alone amounted to more than a third of the budget (a million solidi) even in the eastern part of the empire (Hendy 1985: 168–9). Given a troop strength of more than a hundred thousand men, this meant an average annual expenditure of ten solidi per man. As has been convincingly argued, this costly arrangement enjoyed only

Table 15. *Roman military forces by region, c. AD 400*

Type of troops	Region		
	West	East	Total
Limitanei	135,000 (54%)	248,000 (70%)	383,000 (64%)
Comitatus	113,000 (46%)	104,000 (30%)	217,000 (36%)
Total	248,000	352,000	600,000

Source: Jones 1964, III:379–80

a moderate tactical advantage compared with that offered by regional forces associated exclusively with the area they were to defend (Luttwak 1976). A regional system was indeed found, for example, in the Byzantine themes of the seventh to eighth century, the expenses of which were further reduced by giving land to the troops, making them part-time peasants.

The number of troops in the Late Roman period is unknown, but there is general agreement that the eastern army was at least as large as the western and probably far larger. There is agreement, too, that frontier troops comprised a greater percentage of the army in the east than in the west, in spite of the fact that the western frontier was far longer. Moreover, the Western Empire had to face increasingly well-organized barbarian societies that were less inclined to make, and particularly to keep, diplomatic agreements than were the Persians, the main enemy in the east. According to Jones's figures for Roman military forces around AD 400 (Jones 1964, III: 379–80), the army of the west made up only 41 per cent of the total of about 600,000 Roman troops (table 15).

In the light of the weakness of the economy of the Western Empire, including the decline in settlement, it is obvious that military problems that could not be avoided through diplomacy, and a show of strength – building military installations, for instance – would have had a dramatic effect. Therefore it is hardly fortuitous that virtually all attempts at setting up rival emperors in the Late Roman period and Late Antiquity took place in the west (see Kaegi 1981). The various military emergencies, often connected with frontier attacks but not necessarily caused by them, could be avoided, with luck, by the use of force; in other instances they had to be countered by some of the scenarios discussed above.

The latest attempts in the west to maintain a static, linear defence seem to have been made under the emperor Valentinian in the latter half of the fourth century. After the battle lost to the Visigoths at Adrianople in AD 378, increasing emphasis was placed on flexible defence to supplement the various diplomatic and other measures. For reasons that must appear clear against the background of the statements made above, change was, however, inevitable, and some hundred years after the death of Valentinian the last Western Roman emperor was deposed. In the east, too, increasingly less emphasis seems to have been placed on frontier defence, perhaps because of non-aggression pacts with the Persians, but it was certainly not abandoned. By as early as the sixth century the eastern army had shrunk to perhaps less than a third of what it had been 150 years earlier. Very few troops – only about 20,000 – could now be made available for attack or counterattack. At the beginning of the seventh century the eastern frontier defences experienced a last period of reconstruction during the late Persian wars, which nevertheless ended in defeat and Persian occupation of both the Levant and Egypt. Apparently defences had not been re-established before the Islamic attacks of the AD 630s, less than ten years after the Roman reconquest. The defeat by Islamic forces at Yarmuk in Palestine led in part to apathy, in part to regional unrest within the empire, probably as a result of new state demands for taxes. In any case, the result was Muslim control of the Levant, Eyypt, and soon also Libya as the defeated Roman armies retreated to mountainous Anatolia. This was the preface to the long history of the Byzantine realm that came to an end only in AD 1453 when the Turks conquered Constantinople.

When considering the reasons for the fall of the Roman Empire, one can, of course, take as a point of departure military defeats such as Yarmuk in AD 636 or Adrianople in AD 378. One cannot, however, avoid considering matters of political economy and thus the means whereby the Late Roman state maintained itself as a military apparatus, as a political and administrative unit, and as a source of income for its dominant groups. The military defeats are indisputable. With respect to their immediate economic causes, it can be pointed out that the Western Empire was in general weaker economically than the Eastern and subject to greater problems of internal security. It had greater difficulties with populist uprisings and may therefore have been burdened with more pronounced social stratification. Moreover, it suffered more at the core from pretenders to the throne and thus almost certainly from administrative and financial problems. A similar line can be taken regarding the defeats in the Eastern Empire where the wars and associated financial difficulties of the late sixth century created a situation reminiscent of that of the Western in the fifth. In the early seventh century the situation worsened, and thus the foundations were laid for Islam to take over some of the potentially most profitable provinces of the Eastern Roman Empire.

Another line of argument begins with the decline of settlement and economy in the west by the third century and the similar developments in the east in the late sixth and seventh centuries. In this light the military and political developments in the Western Empire might be viewed as part of the general economic and social transformation of Europe. There is a problem, however, in applying this argument to the Eastern Empire, for the Levant did not suffer overall decline (the areas around Damascus illustrate this point), and relatively isolated Egypt seems to have been largely unaffected economically (Rodziewicz 1976, 1984), southern Egypt even undergoing expansion (Khatchatrian 1982). These regions of the Near East were, furthermore, incorporated into the new Islamic empire.

A general economic and socio-historical explanation of the developments in the Near East would give weight to the further eastern connections and particularly the obvious erosion of overall or state control of local matters that occurred both under the Roman Empire of Late Antiquity and under the Islamic caliphate. This is one of the reasons the Islamic armies were sometimes even regarded as liberators. It seems reasonable, however, at any rate until new (and if so probably archaeological) evidence becomes available, to view Islam's military success even with small forces and the rapid change in the status of the Levant and Egypt in the light of the contemporary politico-economic crises in the Roman Empire, as well as the associated incentives to let centrifugal forces get the upper hand – factors apparent already before Islam's victory. Seen in this way, Islam was only a catalyst, however penetrating its influence proved to be. Moreover, it could be asserted that the developments might have been delayed for, say, another hundred years, up to the point in the middle of the eighth century when agrarian settlement in the Levant collapsed and the Umayyad dynasty fell from power.

To sum up, we perceive both long and short lines in the development leading to the decline, fall, and transformation of the Roman Empire. An argument based on social history would emphasize the long lines, but in the case of the Islamic conquest of the Near East a short line seems to explain why the changes took place at that particular time.

Epilogue and prologue

Along the Danube from Pannonia to the Black Sea, imperial settlement showed no sign of weakening in the Late Roman period, and in Bulgaria, for example, settlement numbers were clearly greater in Late Antiquity and Early Byzantine times. The Roman villa as a form of organization was, however, abandoned entirely. To the south of the Drava–Danube line, the villa was replaced by a frequently fortified, architecturally irregular agrarian centre, often an estate. By the second half of the fifth century there were no agrarian settlements of even semi-Roman character north of the Drava or, for that matter, the Lower Danube. Of special interest in this connection is archaeological evidence from these south-eastern European regions of changes in agricultural technology from Roman times to the Middle Ages that can serve as a framework for discussion of developments in the last half of the first millennium.

In Pannonia the Early Roman settlement naturally adopted many of the tools and usages of Celtic society (Henning 1987). Especially characteristic here is the Celtic plough, with its triangular socketed iron share. To the south-east, in Bulgaria, there was originally a lighter, arrow-shaped iron share, probably derived from older Greek, thus Mediterranean, agricultural technology via the Black Sea colonies. A very heavy version of this arrow-shaped share was abandoned in the last centuries of the first millennium in favour of the lighter

Celtic one, which was perfect for the smaller agricultural unit not only in requiring less metal but also in being usable without the heavy ploughs and many draught animals and agricultural labourers of the major farm. Socketed shares from after about AD 700 show asymmetrical wear and can thus be demonstrated to have been used on an advanced plough, in various forms known across temperate Europe, that turned the sod.

The development from the iron tools introduced in the second half of the first millennium BC through the very heavy ones of Late Roman times and Late Antiquity to somewhat lighter and less expensive but still effective tools can also be followed in other types of implement – iron spades and hoes, for instance. Moreover, in the late centuries of the millennium the plough was the primary tool for soil preparation. At the same time, the sickle and scythe are more frequent than tools associated with cattle and sheep rearing. Finds of iron implements used in connection with livestock husbandry in the Bulgarian area (in calibrated figures) number 22 for AD 0–400, 13 for AD 400–600, and 5 for AD 600–1000. Corresponding finds of sickles and scythes (with a slightly different chronology) are 8 for AD 0–400, 23 for AD 400–700, and 40 for AD 700–1000 (Henning 1987). This development seems associated with the establishment in Late Antiquity of considerable estate-like agricultural units with large numbers of cattle and craft production. These units, which required abundant resources, disintegrated in the final days of the first millennium into smaller but relatively effective primary units concentrated on grain growing and pig rearing. The remarkable farms of Late Antiquity were based on the large Late Roman villas and show similar features, for instance craft production and, of course, very considerable numbers of workers or slaves.

In the period after AD 400, the Migration period, which in large areas of Europe is characterized by replacement or cultural transformation of the dominant groups, an estate structure of the type just sketched with relatively few 'civilized' architectural features, such as stone buildings, that would require the maintenance of the old urban trades and trading systems, would have been optimal for supporting groups of princes and their dependents. Products and livestock could have been fairly easily transported and sold, and, of prime importance, there would have been relatively little dependence on the more intensive types of farming. Given the large work- or slave force made available by incessant warfare, the Late Roman technological innovations aiming at maximization could have continued in use. To judge by the luxuries in the graves, this social milieu might furthermore have included an interest in international and interregional exchange.

This type of production seems to have come to an end in south-eastern Europe with the collapse of the world of Late Antiquity in the seventh century and, for example, the establishment of the Slavs in the Balkáns. The late, agriculturally intensive forms of management with special emphasis on grain production were associated with the Early Bulgarian and the Great Moravian realm, where a large number of iron agricultural implements of the above-mentioned types from the end of the first millennium have also been found. None of these states that came into being parallel with the Carolingian period in the west lasted for any great length of time.

In Western Europe the expansive earlier Merovingian period of estate formation and interregional economic interests, including long-distance trading, mainly in luxuries, resembles the situation in Late Antiquity in the south and east. At the transition to the Carolingian period, settlement stability was attained – in contrast with the situation in south-eastern Europe. The Carolingian realm had its centre of gravity in the northern part of old Gaul, which indicates that an attempt was now being made to exploit fully the great potential for growing grain in this area. The settlement archaeology of the region is still rather poorly developed, but written sources on Carolingian estates, some of the first economic texts on Western Europe, confirm the hypothesis of intensive cultivation of grain and a high degree of specialization (see plate 9). It is likely that the three-field system of rotation was now common. In addition, technology was improved, for instance, by the introduction of ploughs – often 'heavy' as far as this part of Europe is concerned – that turned the sod and were perhaps wheeled. Watermills were also in widespread use. From settlement grain finds it is known that rye, with its considerable requirements for soil preparation, in this case ploughing, was just then becoming popular (Randsborg 1985). Even the ordinary pottery for daily use, with its many saucepan-like pots, well suited to the cooking of grain porridges, may reflect this tendency to stake more on grain production. Settlements may also reveal this trend. In Roman times in north-western Europe they are more often located on good grain-growing soils, whereas in earlier Merovingian times they occur in areas where there was water and grazing for cattle. A little later in the millennium, however, settlements were once again concentrated in the optimal grain-growing zones of the various subregions, whereupon they remained fixed until recent times.

Similar circumstances can also be noted in southern Scandinavia, where pollen diagrams show a remarkable change around AD 1000 from an agriculture dominated by cattle raising to one in which grain production was of greatest importance. Thus this transformation took place here somewhat later than it did to the south. It is interesting, however, that the alteration apparently happened at the same time as a crisis of food supply that may have been brought about by population growth. Such a hypothesis is based on the height of the Danish 'Vikings', who were not as tall either as the people of the beginning of the first millennium or as those of the first half of the second (Bennike 1985). The average height of adults of both sexes (table 16) also suggests that more food was available in Late Roman than in Early Roman times, with the small agricultural units characteristic of the Early Iron Age. Interestingly, a second major crisis occurred in the eighteenth century, just prior to the agrarian reforms of modern times. The current average height is 179 cm for men, for women 167 cm and still rising.

In addition to information on alterations in agricultural strategy, archaeology

Table 16. *Average height
of Danish men and
women, AD 100–1900*

| Time period | Height (cm) | |
	Men	Women
AD 100	174	162
AD 300	177	162
AD 600	(178)	(156)
AD 900	171	157
AD 1300	173	161
AD 1700	174	161
AD 1850	165	154
AD 1900	169	159

Source: Bennike 1985
Note: Bracketed figures are
based on very small samples

has provided knowledge of settlement that supports the observation of a south-western to north-eastern trend in Early Medieval development (fig. 38). In the Rhineland, for example, many later agrarian sites or villages were in fact established in the late Merovingian and early Carolingian phases, the seventh to eighth century. Settlements of the High Middle Ages in Lower Saxony were mainly established in the eighth to ninth century and those in Denmark in the eleventh to twelfth. In Italy, thousands of settlements were established late in the first millennium. The Italian hill-top settlements constitute a very decisive break both with the ancient local settlement pattern and with the more recent estate system at the same time as they mark a significant intensification of the use of local resources. The latter also applies to the northern and north-western European examples just mentioned. The majority of settlements survived every-where, becoming not only the villages of the High Middle Ages but, as a rule, also those of more recent times. The founding of these settlements thus introduced a very stable system that eventually became the economic basis for the whole crucial development that made Western Europe the centre of the world in the late second millennium.

It is significant that the founding of villages in each of the three northern examples – the Rhineland, Lower Saxony, and Denmark – follows a period in which there were rich burials and thus obviously a desire to use death as an opportunity for a display of the position in society of the family and the lineage. It seems probable, therefore, that the social and economic system of these times was less stable than that later on – a supposition that has indirectly been confirmed by settlement abandonment. The example from the Rhineland concerns Frankish and other warrior groups engaged in estate formation during the Merovingian period. These peoples were heirs to the Roman estates as well as what political power could be exercised along the Rhine around AD 500. The later Carolingian graves, mainly from or around churches, had few or no grave goods, and even though this society was profoundly competitive the rivalry took a different, less personal form than in the days of early estate and society formation. Large fortunes were now spent on, for example, palaces such as Ingelheim (fig. 39), churches and monasteries, luxury craft production, and commerce. But settlement conditions were certainly more stable, and powerful technologies were put to use not only in agriculture but also in craft production, where high outputs, for instance, of ceramics from factories both in the Rhineland and in various places in northern Gaul were ensured. In Italy, for instance, mortar was again used for building, and tile making was resumed on a grand scale. The rights to the land were, moreover, fixed through permanent rules of inheritance; in addition, the church received large donations of land, the surplus of which went into impressive building programmes. Property certainly no longer accompanied the dead into the grave (Randsborg 1988a).

The Carolingian example is, however, also a little confusing, because it constitutes only a step on the way to the organization of the social and economic landscape of the High Middle Ages. We are still in a period when the interests of the 'aristocracy' and the church were concentrated on the acquisition of wealth through political agreements, alliances, trading (often over long distances), raiding, and even conquest. Only in the tenth century can archaeology – for example, urban-development studies – show that local and regional interests were predominant for the first time since the Roman era. It would, however, be a mistake to underestimate the dynamics of, for instance, Carolingian agriculture. As settlement archaeology gains momentum we should, as investigations in Scandinavia have shown, be prepared for surprises with regard to farmstead sizes, capacity and production.

Denmark provides us, as we have seen, with such an archaeological example. In the eighth and ninth centuries, the 'Carolingian' period, society here had a strong interest in trading in luxuries centred on magnate or royal estates and, in particular, major royal emporia, for instance, Hedeby, bordering on both Saxony and the Slavic lands (Randsborg 1980, 1981b, 1988a). In the eighth century the settlement shows clear signs of expanding, farmsteads, for instance, increasing in size and water-mills and other technologies being employed. Hedeby was also one of the junctions for seaborne long-distance trading, being sited strategically between the North Sea, with its connections with Western Europe, and the Baltic, which, via Russia, ultimately gave access to the Islamic markets. Under the prevailing social conditions, its location could hardly have been better. Nevertheless, the whole system was shaken by the breakdown of trade in the ninth century and the beginning of the notorious Viking forays, which must be considered a typical negative expression of this 'heroic' age. In the later tenth century there was yet another decline in long-distance trading, but this time Denmark apparently remained unshaken. The reason for this must be sought in

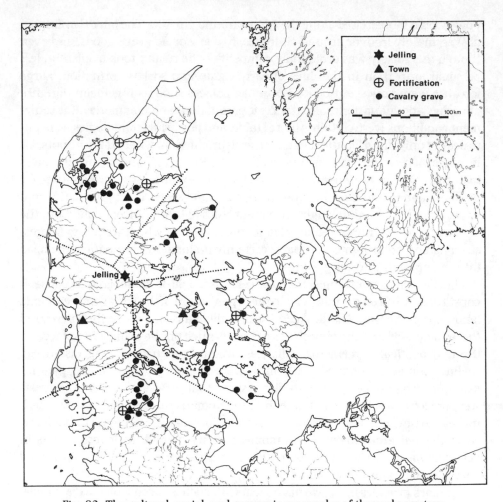

Fig. 82. The cultural, social, and economic geography of the early western Danish state society of the late tenth century: the royal centre of Jelling (*) is renowned for its colossal earthen mounds, early wooden church, and runic stones. The broken lines frame the hypothetical catchment areas of the early regional towns. The fortifications comprise the three fortresses of the Trelleborg type – the gigantic Aggersborg in the far north, the somewhat smaller Fyrkat, and, on western Zealand, Trelleborg – and the major border walls of Danevirke in the south. The horseman graves contain heavy stirrups, bits, weapons, etc., for advanced cavalry warfare; they have been found exclusively along the perimeter of the core of the western Danish realm.

the vigorous contemporary expansion of the infrastructure of the country, particularly Jutland, which at this time underwent a social process reminiscent of that in England around AD 900, which under Alfred (the 'Great') saw, for instance, the establishment of regularly spaced, fortified market centres, in fact incipient provincial towns (see fig. 82).

The most conspicuous development of the period around AD 1000 is a series of very large farmsteads (for instance, the seven complexes found at Vorbasse in Jutland) on rather marginal soils, all with magnificent halls, a wealth of other structures, and crofts up to 25,000 square metres in size. At Lejre on Zealand, even more impressive farmsteads have been found, with halls of 500 square metres and almost fifty metres in length. It seems that never before had the primary agricultural producers of the country been so well off, and, as the increase in average height implies, the system was also a highly successful one. These findings contradict much of mainstream history, which depicts the Vikings as primitives compared to the people of the High or Late Middle Ages – although admittedly farm workers at Vorbasse may have been less happy than their masters. The new settlements of the late tenth century also comprise the first small regional centres – local meeting places and markets under royal supervision, some previously emporia, to which, in the early eleventh century, the king's mints were attached. Major towns also held bishops' seats. Other installations of this period comprise royal forts of the Trelleborg type, fortifications, and bridges, a splendid example of Ravninge (near Jelling) in Jutland being almost a kilometre long and having two lanes.

In spite of its 'progressive' stamp, settlement in western Denmark in the late tenth century was focused on one central locality in Jutland, Jelling. This royal 'capital' and ritual centre had splendid, newly erected earthen mounds, the largest in the country, constructed on a prehistoric model (probably to demonstrate ancient claims to power), and a very large wooden church standing next to a series of runic stones, one of which, Denmark's largest, supported king Harald's claims to Denmark and Norway, as well as his allegiance to Christianity. This extensive settlement was, in short, a modest Nordic Aachen. The Danish royal power of the time could draw on considerable military resources, and, as the forays into Britain around AD 1000 show, the old Viking society was not completely dead. These raids were more attempts at conquest, however, than plundering expeditions. In any case, riches streamed into Denmark, for example from the notorious Danegeld tax, and the kings Svend and Canute 'the Great' succeeded in creating an admittedly short-lived and only loose-knit 'North Sea Empire' – almost a small 'Carolingian' realm – comprising England (and parts of Scotland), Denmark, Norway, and the western socially progressive provinces of Sweden.

Not until the early eleventh century were the efforts of the Jelling dynasty – inspired by Western Europe – crowned with success in southern Scandinavia. The major results, apart from a completely new distribution of land and resources, were the integration of the eastern Danish regions and continued urban development. The old emporia had given way to major and minor provincial towns, the largest one being Lund in Scania, in the eastern Danish grain region, the future seat of the archbishop of Scandinavia and of the northern Atlantic (fig. 83). The urban development led to a relative isolation of agrarian settlements, including the ancient villages found to this day in the Danish landscape. Jelling, far from the new provincial towns, was abandoned as a royal centre. Commerce,

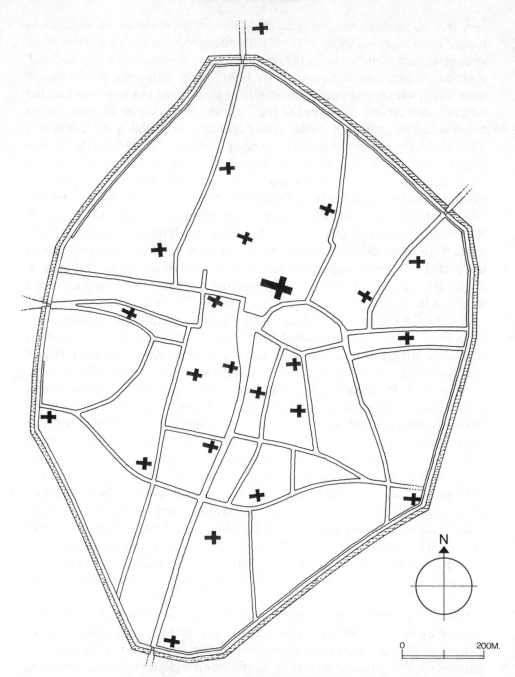

Fig. 83. The city of Lund in the late eleventh century. To the west of the
cathedral (the larger cross) were the royal palace and the mint. The
market was to the south of the cathedral, the merchants' quarter perhaps
to the west of it (after Andrén 1985 and others).

crafts and markets, royal residences, and ecclesiastical institutions, in particular the bishops' palaces, were gradually concentrated in the towns. The estates and villages came increasingly to provide the surplus necessary to ensure and continue architectural and other investments in the towns – for instance, the first stone churches, all erected by magnates of the kingdom. With this development, irreversible by the early eleventh century, local and regional interests became dominant, and soon thereafter the impact of continental or 'Roman' Christian ideology on Danish and other Nordic society can be noted. The developments of the High Middle Ages were now under way, and this area of Europe, then the northernmost, had become permanently integrated into the social and economic development of Western Europe.

To understand fully the emergence of the Roman Empire would require study of the centre–periphery relations in Europe and the Mediterranean area that emerged with the Mediterranean civilizations. Classical Antiquity destroyed the European commonwealth of the Neolithic and Bronze Ages, but without the 'villain' of Classical Antiquity the rise of Europe would not have taken place. Ideology may have it differently. The Carolingians and their contemporaries were probably the last to look seriously to the ancient Romans as models for future society, and even they did not take their discoveries literally, although with their imperfect understanding of history they may have thought that they did. This should make us cautious about viewing ideology as critical for understanding the projections of society, even today.

APPENDICES

Appendix 1: *General references for chapters 2 and 8*

Adams 1981; Alföldy 1974; Anderson 1974; Ashton 1976; Barley 1977; Bechert 1982; Bernardini 1965; Beumann and Schröder 1987; Bintliff 1984; Blazquez 1981; Boeles 1951; Böhme 1975; Böhme et al. 1981; Brandt and Slofstra 1983; Braunfels 1965; T. S. Brown 1984; P. Brown 1971; Brühl 1975; Burns 1980; Campbell 1982; Carandini 1983, 1986; Champion and Megaw 1985; Chapelot and Fossier 1980; Christlein 1978; Claude 1985; Cornell and Matthews 1982 (note references); Cunliffe 1983; [Cüppers et al] 1983; [Cüppers] 1984; Davies and Vierck 1974; Davis 1970; Demandt 1983; Dilke and Dilke 1976; Dockès 1982; Drinkwater 1983; Duby 1962, 1974; Duncan-Jones 1982; Dupuy and Dupuy 1970; Duval and Frézouls 1977; Düwel et al. 1985a, 1985b, 1987; Dzieduszycka 1985; Ermini 1961; van Es 1981; Ewig 1980; Février et al. 1980; Février and Leveau 1982; Finley 1973, 1976; Flon 1985; Foss 1977, 1979; Frere 1967; Fulford 1987; Garnsey and Saller 1987; Garnsey and Whittaker 1983; Garnsey, Hopkins, and Whittaker 1983; Giardina 1986; Gibbon 1776–88; Goffart 1980, 1981; Greene 1986; Grierson 1961, 1965, 1981; Grimm, Heinen, and Winter 1983; Groenman-van Waateringe 1980; Grünert 1975; Hansen 1987; Hendy 1985; Henig 1983; Henning 1987; Herrmann 1985; Hingley 1982; Hodges 1982; Hodges and Whitehouse 1983; Hopkins 1978, 1980; James 1979; Jankuhn, Schützeichel, and Schwind 1977; Jankuhn and Wenskus 1979; Janssen and Lohrmann 1983; Johnson and West 1949; Jones 1964, 1966; Jouffroy 1986; Kazhdan and Epstein 1985; King and Henig 1981; Köpstein 1983; Kossack, Behre, and Schmid 1984; Krautheimer 1980; Krüger 1983a, 1983b; Kunow 1983; [Lemerle] 1984; Lepelley 1979; Leveau 1983, 1984; Lewis 1978; Lombard 1971; Luttwak 1976; Macready and Thompson 1984; Malone and Stoddart 1985; Mango 1985; Manjarres 1971; Matthew 1983; Mazzarino 1959; Menghin 1985; Miles 1982; Mócsy 1974; Moss 1974; Musset 1969; Ørsted 1985; Parker 1984; Patlagean 1977; Peacock

1982; von Petrikovits 1971, 1980, 1983; Pirling 1986; Potter 1979; Pounds 1973; Randsborg 1980; Rathbone 1983; Rollins 1983; Rouche 1977, 1986; Rougé 1966; Russell 1958; Sawyer 1976, 1978; Settia 1984; Shaw 1984; Sitwell 1984; Slicher van Bath 1963; Sperber 1978; Steuer 1982; Tchalenko 1953–58; Techernia 1986; Thomas 1971; Thompson 1965, 1983; Toubert 1973; [Toubert] 1980; Udovitch 1981; Vasiliev 1952; Waines 1977; Wallerstein 1974; Ward-Perkins 1984; Werner 1956, 1961; Werner and Ewig 1979; Wickham 1981, 1984; Wielowiejski 1970; Willems 1986.

Appendix 2: *References on domestic animals (chapter 3)*

Barker 1973, 1977, 1978, (1983); Barker and Gamble 1985; Bennett 1982; Besteman 1974; Bloemers 1978; Boessneck and von den Driesch 1980; Boessneck, von den Driesch, and Stenberger 1970; Bökönyi 1974 (note references), 1984; Bortolotti 1982; Branigan 1977; Buitenhuis 1983; Carandini 1985; Carlsson 1979; Chittick 1984; Clason 1977; Clason and Buitenhuis 1978; Cunliffe 1975, 1983; Curle 1982; Demolon 1972; Donat 1984; von den Driesch 1972; van Es and Verwers 1980; Ferdière 1983; Finberg 1972; Fouet 1969; Frova 1977; Greene 1986; Gualtieri, Salvatore, and Small 1983; Harrison 1986; Henning 1987; Herrmann 1968, 1973, 1985; Hodges, Barker, and Wade 1980; Hope-Taylor 1977; Humphrey 1977, 1981; Hurst and Roskams 1984; Jarrett and Wrathmell 1981; Jones 1980; Jones and Dimbleby 1981; King 1978, 1982, 1984, 1985 (note references); Kossack, Behre, and Schmid 1984; Krüger 1983a, 1983b; Lloyd (1983); Luff 1982 (note references); Maltby 1979; Montanari 1979; Neal 1974; Pryor et al. 1985; Pyrgala 1975; Rahtz 1979; Randsborg 1980 (note references), 1985 (note references); Reese 1977, 1981; Riedel 1986; Schwartz 1984; Stead 1976; Villedieu 1984; Ward-Perkins et al. 1978; Werner 1964; Whitcomb and Johnson 1982; Whitehouse et al. 1982.

Appendix 3: *Regional settlement samples (chapter 4)*

The Mediterranean:

(1) the regions to the north of Rome (e.g., Potter 1979); (2) the Cosa region (Dyson 1978); (3) the Scarlino area (Francovich 1985a); (4) the Liri Valley (Wightman 1981); (5) the San Giovanni area (Small 1985); (6) the Monreale area (Johns 1985); (7) the region of Caesarea (Mauretania) (Leveau 1984); (8) the Barcelona region (Prevosti i Monclús 1981); (9) the Segermes region (etc.) ([Poulsen in] Ørsted 1984; Lund and Sørensen 1987; cf. Hitchner 1988); (10) the Boeotia region (Bintliff and Snodgrass 1985); (11) the southern Argolid (etc.) (van Andel and Runnels 1987; Foley 1988; etc.); (12) the Paphos region (Rupp et al. 1984, 1986); (13) the Bélus region, east of Antioch (Tchalenko 1953–58);

(14) the Aleppo region (Matthers 1981); (15) the central Israel/Palestine regions (Patlagean 1977; etc.); (16) the northern Negev (Cohen 1981); (17) the region south of the River Yarmuk (Hanbury-Tenison 1984); (18) the region north-west of Gerasa (Mittman 1970); and (19) the area around Hesbon (LaBianca 1984).

Temperate Europe:

(20) the Nijmegen area (Willems 1986); (21) the Cologne region (Gechter and Kunow in press); (22) the region east of Mainz (Schell 1964); (23) the region west of Mainz (Bayer 1967); (23A) the Alsace–Lorraine region (Poinsignon 1987); (24) the Alpine Rhine Valley region (Overbeck 1982); (25) the Le Mans area (Lambert and Rioufreyt 1982); (26) the Lion-en-Beauce area (Ferdière 1982); (27) the Upper Loire region (Vallet 1981); (28) the region east of Arles (Raynaud 1984); (29) the Cambridge region (Wilkes and Eldrington 1978); (3) the Fenlands region (Phillips 1970); (31) south-eastern England (Black 1987); southern Wales (Davies 1979); (33) the Pannonia region (Thomas 1964); (34) Pannonia (western Hungary)–Thrace (Bulgaria) (Henning 1987); (35) the northern Hessen region (Mildenberger 1972); (36) the Tollensee area (Herrmann 1985); (37) the Kruszwicka area (Dzieduszycka 1985).

Appendix 4: *References to problems of coins (chapter 6)* (less important references in brackets)

Bálint 1981; (Balty and Balty 1972); (Bass and van Doorninck 1982); Bastien and Metzger 1977; Bates 1971; (Bateson 1973); Bellinger 1938; (Bierbrauer 1975, 1987); Blackburn and Metcalf 1981; (Blazques 1978); (Boeles 1951); (von Bülow, Schieferdecker, and Heinrich 1979); Burnett 1977; Buttrey 1976, 1977; Buttrey and Hitchner 1978; Buttrey et al. 1981; Callmer 1984; Callu 1972, 1979; Casey 1980; (Chittick 1984); Crawford 1969, 1977; (Cunliffe 1975), 1981; Curina 1983; Dolley 1970; (Duncan-Jones 1982); (Düwel et al. 1985a and b, 1987); Edwards 1933; Ermini 1961; van Es 1960; Fagerlie 1967; (Foss 1976, 1979); (Fouet 1960); (Frova 1977); (Fülep 1984); Gricourt et al. 1958; Grierson 1961, 1965; Guéry, Morrison, and Slim 1982; Gumowski 1958; Gupta 1965; (Haalebos 1977); Hall and Metcalf 1972; (Harrison 1986); Hendy 1985, 1986; (Hopkins 1980); (Hull 1958); (Humphrey no date, 1976, 1977, 1978, 1981, 1982); (Hurst and Roskams 1984); (Jarrett and Wrathmell 1981); (Jones 1980); Kent 1972; Kent and Painter 1977; (King and Henig 1981); (Kiss 1986); Kolníkoková 1973; Kos 1986; Kovács 1983; (Kraeling 1938, 1962); Kropotkin 1961, (1970); Kyhlberg 1986; Laser 1980; Metcalf 1969; (Metzler, Zimmer, and Bakker 1981); Mirnik 1981; (Mócsy 1981); (Montanari 1983); Mosser 1935; (Mytum 1981); (Neal 1974); Noonan 1984; Pereira, Bost, and Hiernard 1974; (Pilet 1980); (Pirling 1979, 1986); (Planson 1982); (Randsborg 1980, 1981b); Reece 1981, 1982a and b, 1985; Spahiu 1979–80; (Stead

1976); (Steuer 1987); Thirion 1967; Thompson 1956; (Thomsen 1986, 1987); (Tushingham 1985); (Villedieu 1984); (Walke 1965); (Wendel et al. 1986); Werner 1935, (1961, 1964, 1973); (Whitehouse et al. 1982); Wielowiejski 1970, 1980; (Wilkes and Eldrington 1978); Zervos 1986.

REFERENCES

The bibliography comprises edited books, monographs, and papers, most of which are cited in the text and appendices; a few additional studies are listed for the sake of general reference. The works referred to are those judged most relevant or important for this book; many others have also been consulted but are not included.

Aaby, B. and H. Tauber. Rates of peat formation in relation to degree of humification and local environment, as shown by studies of a raised bog in Denmark. *Boreas* 4 (1975): 1ff.

Adams, R. McC. *Land behind Bagdad: A History of Settlement of the Diyala Plains.* Chicago: University of Chicago Press, 1965.
　Heartland of Cities: Surveys of Ancient Settlement and Land Use of the Central Floodplain of the Euphrates. Chicago: University of Chicago Press, 1981.

Agache, R. La campagne à l'époque romaine dans les grandes plaines du Nord de la France d'après les photographies aériennes. *Aufstieg und Niedergang der römischen Welt* 2, no. 4 (1975): 658ff.

Ahrens, C. (ed.). *Sachsen und Angelsachsen.* Veröffentlichungen des Helms-Museums 32 (1978).

Alcock, L. Early historic fortifications in Scotland, in Guilbert, pp. 150ff.
　Cadbury–Camelot: a fifteen-year perspective. *Proceedings of the British Academy* 68, (1982): 355ff.

Alexander, M. A. and M. Ennaifer. *Utique, Insulae,* vols. 1–3: *Région de Ghar el Melh (Porto Farina).* Atlas archéologique de la Tunisie 7 (1) = Corpus des Mosaïques de Tunisie 1 (1973).

Alexandrescu-Vianu, M. Les stèles funéraires de la Mésie inférieure. *Dacia* n. 5., 29, nos. 1–2 (1985): 93ff.

Alföldy, G. *Noricum.* London: Routledge & Kegan Paul, 1974.

Andel, T. H. van and C. Runnels. *Beyond the Acropolis: A Rural Greek Past.* Stanford: Stanford University Press, 1987.

Andel, T. H. van, C. N. Runnels, and K. O. Pope. Five thousand years of land use and abuse in the southern Argolid, Greece. *Hesperia* 55, no. 1 (January–March 1986): 103ff.

Anderson, P. *Passages from Antiquity to Feudalism.* London: New Left Books, 1974.

Andrén, A. *Den urbana scenen. Städer och samhälle i det medeltida Danmark.* Acta Archaeologica Lundensia, series in 8°, 13 (1985).

Angiolillo, S. *Sardinia: Mosaici antichi in Italia.* Rome: Istituto Poligrafico, 1981.

Anselmino, L., C. M. Coletti, M. L. Ferrantini, and C. Panella. Ostia: Terme del Nuotatore, in Giardina, pp. 45ff.

d'Archimbaud, G. D. *Les Fouilles de Rougiers (Var.): contribution à l'archéologie de l'habitat rural médiéval en pays mediterranéen.* Publication de l'U.R.A. 6, Archéologie médiévale mediterranéenne, Mémoire 2 (1980).

Aricescu, A. *The Army in Roman Dobrudja.* British Archaeological Reports International Series 86 (1980).

Arrhenius, B. *Merovingian Garnet Jewellery: Emergence and Social Implications.* Stockholm: Almqvist and Wiksell, 1985.

  Helgö as a border post between Uppland and Södermanland. *Acta Archaeologica* 58 (1987): 137ff.

Arthur, P. Naples: Notes on the economy of a Dark Age city, in Malone and Stoddart, vol. 4, pp. 247ff.

Arwidsson, G. *Valsgärde 7: Die Gräberfunde von Valsgärde,* vol. 3. Acta Musei Antiquitatum Septentrionalium Regiae Universitatis Upsaliensis 5 (1977).

Ashtor, E. *A Social and Economic History of the Near East in the Middle Ages.* London: Collins, 1976.

Ayi-Yonah, M. The economics of Byzantine Palestine. *Israel Exploration Journal* 8, no. 1 (1958): 39ff.

Axboe, M. The Scandinavian gold bracteates. *Acta Archaeologica* 52 (1981): 1ff.

Baldry, J. *Textiles in Yemen: Historical References to Trade and Commerce in Textiles in Yemen from Antiquity to Modern Times.* British Museum Occasional Paper 27 (1982).

Bálint, C. Einige Fragen des Dirhems-Verkehrs in Europa. *Acta Archaeologica Hungarica* 33 (1981): 105ff.

Balty, J. and J. C. Balty (eds.). *Apamée de Syrie: Bilan des recherches archéologiques 1969–1971, Actes du colloque tenu a Bruxelles les 15, 17 et 18 avril 1972.* Fouilles d'Apamée de Syrie Misc. Fasc. 7 (1972).

Bang, M. *Die Germanen im römischer Dienst bis zum Regierungsantritt Constantins I.* Berlin: Weidmann, 1906.

Barker, G. The economy of medieval Tuscania: the archaeological evidence. *Papers of the British School at Rome* 41 (1973): 155ff.

  L'economia del bestiame a Luni, in Frova, pp. 725ff.

  Informazioni sull'economia medievale e postmedievale di Pavia: le ossa dello scavo, in Ward-Perkins et al., pp. 249ff.

  Economic life at Berenice: the animals and fish bones, marine molluscs, and plant remains, in Lloyd, pp. 1ff.

Barker, G. and C. Gamble (eds.). *Beyond Domestication in Prehistoric Europe: Investigations in Subsistence Archaeology and Social Complexity.* London: Academic, 1985.

Barker, G. and R. Hodges (eds). *Archaeology and Italian Society: Prehistoric, Roman, and Medieval Studies.* British Archaeological Reports International Series 102 (1981).

Barker, G., J. Lloyd and J. Reynolds (eds.). *Cyrenaica in Antiquity.* British Archaeological Reports International Series 236 (1985).

Barley, M. W. (ed.). *European Towns: Their Archaeology and Early History.* London: Academic, 1977.

Barral i Altet, X. *Province d'Aquitaine,* vol. 1: *Partie méridionale (Piémont pyrénéen).* Recueil général des mosaïques de la Gaule, 10th supplement to *Gallia,* 4, no. 1 (1980).

Bass, G. F. and H. F. van Doorninck, Jr. *Yassi Ada I (A Tenth-Century Byzantine Shipwreck).* College Station: Texas A & M University Press, 1982.

Bastien, P. and C. Metzger. *Le Trésor de Beaurains (dit d'Arras).* Numismatique Romaine 10 (1977).

Bates, G. F. *Byzantine Coins.* Archaeological Exploration of Sardis 1. Cambridge, Mass: Harvard University Press, 1971.

Bateson, J. D. Roman material from Ireland: a re-consideration. *Proceedings of the Royal Irish Academy* 73, section C, 2 (1973): 21ff.

Bayer, H. Die ländliche Besiedlung Rheinhessens und seiner Randgebiet in römischer Zeit. *Mainzer Zeitschrift* 62 (1967): 125ff.

Becatti, G. *Mosaici e pavimenti marmorei.* Scavi di Ostia 4 (1961).

Bechert, T. *Römisches Germanien zwischen Rhein und Maas: Die Provinz Germania Inferior.* München: Hirmer, 1982.

Beck, H. and P. C. Bol (eds.). *Spätantike und frühes Christentum.* Frankfurt a.M: Liebieghaus, 1983.

Beck, H., D. Denecke and H. Jankuhn (eds.). *Untersuchungen zur eisenzeitlichen und frühmittelalterlichen Flur in Mitteleuropa und ihrer Nutzung.* 2 vols. Abhandlungen der Akademie der Wissenschaften in Göttingen, Philologisch-historische Klasse, Series 3, no. 115 (1979).

Becker, B. Fällungsdaten römischer Bauhölzer. *Fundberichte aus Baden-Württemberg* 6 (1981): 369ff.

  Dendrochronologie und paläoökologische subfossiler Baumstämme am Flussablagerungen: Ein Beitrag zur nacheiszeitlichen Auenentwicklung im südlichen Mitteleuropa. Mitteilungen der Kommission für Quartärforschung der österreichischen Akademie der Wissenschaften 5 (1982).

Becker, C. J. (ed.). Viking-Age settlements in western and central Jutland: recent excavations. *Acta Archaeologica* 50 (1979): 89ff.

Beckwith, J. *Early Medieval Art.* Rev. edn. London: Thames and Hudson, 1969.

Bell, G. *The Churches and Monasteries of the Tur 'Abdin.* London: Pindar, 1982.

Bellinger, A. R. Coins, in Kraeling, pp. 497ff.

Beloch, G. Le città dell'Italia antica. *Atene e Roma* 1, no. 6 (November–December 1898): 257ff.

Bennett, P. (ed.). *Exavations at Canterbury Castle.* The Archaeology of Canterbury 1 (1982).

Bennike, P. *Palaeopathology of Danish Skeletons: A Comparative Study of Demography, Disease, and Injury.* Copenhagen: Akademisk, 1985.

Bergengruen, A. *Adel und Grundherrschaft im Merowingerreich: Siedlungs- und Standesgeschichtliche Studie zu den Anfängen des fränkischen Adels in Nordfrankreich und Belgien.* Vierteljahrschrift für Sozial- und Wirtschaftgeschichte 41 (1958).

Berglund, B. E. Vegetation and human influence in south Scandinavia during prehistoric times. *Oikos* (Suppl.) 12 (1969): 9ff.

Bernardi, A. *The Economic Problems of the Roman Empire at the Time of its Decline.* Studia et Documenta Historiae et Iuris 31 (1965).

Bernhard, H. Zur Diskussion um die Chronologie rheinzaberner Relieftöpfer. *Germania* 59, 1 (1981): 79ff.

Bersu, G. *Das Wittnauer Horn.* Monographien zur Ur- und Frühgeschichte der Schweiz 4 (1945).

Berti, F. *Ravenna 1, Regione Ottava: mosaici antichi in Italia.* Rome: Istituto Poligrafico, 1976.

  Lucerne, in Montanari, pp. 147ff.

Beševliev V. and J. Irmscher (eds.). *Antike und Mittelalter in Bulgarien.* Berliner byzantinistische Arbeiten 21 (1960).

Besteman, J. C. Carolingian Medemblik. *Berichten van de Rijksdienst voor het Oudheidkundig Bodemonderzoek* 24 (1974): 43ff.

Beumann, H. and W. Schröder (eds.). *Die transalpinen Verbindungen der Bayern, Alemannen und Franken bis zum 10. Jahrhundert.* Nationes 6 (1987).

Bierbrauer, V. *Die ostgotischen Grab- und Schatzfunde in Italien.* Biblioteca degli 'Studi Medievali' 7 (1975).

  Frühmittelalterliche Castra im östlichen und mittleren Alpengebiet: Germanische Wehranlagen oder romanische Siedlungen? Ein Beitrag zur Kontinuitätsforschung. *Archäologisches Korrespondenzblatt* 15 (1985): 497ff.

Invillino-Ibligo in Friaul, vols. 1 and 2, *Die römische Siedlung und das spätantik-frühmittelalterliche Castrum* and *Die spätantiken und frühmittelalterlichen Kirchen*. Münchner Beiträge zur Vor- und Frühgeschichte 33–34 (1987).

Biernacka-Lubańska, M. *The Roman and Early Byzantine Fortifications of Lower Moesia and Northern Thrace*. Bibliotheca Antiqua 17 (1982).

Bintliff, J. *European Social Evolution: Archaeological Perspectives*. Bradford: University of Bradford Press, 1984.

Bintliff, J. L. and A. M. Snodgrass. The Cambridge/Bradford Boeotian Expedition: the first four years. *Journal of Field Archaeology* 12, no. 2 (Summer 1985): 123ff.

Bintliff, J. L. and W. van Zeist (eds.). *Palaeoclimates, Palaeoenvironments, and Human Communities in the Eastern Mediterranean Region in Later Prehistory*. 2 vols. British Archaeological Reports International Series 133 (1982).

Biraben, J.-N. and J. Le Goff. The Plague in the early Middle Ages, in B. Forster and O. Ranum (eds.), *Biology of Man in History: Selections from the Annales: Economies, Societies, Civilisations*. Baltimore: Johns Hopkins University Press, 1975.

Bíro, M. The inscriptions of Roman Britain. *Acta Archaeologica Hungarica* 27 (1975): 13ff.

Black, E. W. *The Roman Villas of South-East England*. British Archaeological Reports 171 (1987).

Blackburn, M. S. A. and D. M. Metcalf (eds.). *Viking-Age Coinage in the Northern Lands*. 2 vols. British Archaeological Reports International Series 122 (1981).

Blagg, T. F. C., R. F. J. Jones, and S. J. Keay (eds.). *Papers in Iberian Archaeology*. 2 vols. British Archaeological Reports International Series 193 (1984).

Blagg, T. F. C. and A. C. King. *Military and Civilian in Roman Britain: Cultural Relationships in a Frontier Province*. British Archaeological Reports (1984).

Blanchet, A. *Les Enceintes romaines de la Gaule*. Paris: Leroux, 1907.

Blau, P. M. and R. K. Merton (eds.). *Continuities in Structural Inquiry*. London: Sage, 1981.

Blazquez, J. M. *Economia de la Hispania Romana*. Bilbão: Najera, 1978.

Mosaicos romanos de Córdoba, Jaén y Malaga. Corpus de Mosaicos de España 3. Madrid: Instituto Español de Arqueología, 1981.

Bloemers, J. H. F. *Rijswijk (Z. H.) 'De Bult': Eine Siedlung der Cananefaten*. 3 vols. Nederlandse Oudheden 8 (1978).

Bloemers, J. H. F., L. P. Louwe Kooijmans, and H. Sarfatij (eds.). *Verleden Land: Archeologische opgravingen in Nederland*. Amsterdam: Meulenhoff, 1981.

Boeles, P. C. J. A. *Friesland tot de elfde eeuw zijn vóór- en vroege geschiedenis*. 2nd edn. s' -Gravenhage: Martinus Nijhoff, 1951.

Boessneck, J. and A. von den Driesch. Knochenfunde aus dem römischen Munigue (Mulva). *Studien über frühe Tierknochenfunde von der iberischen Halbinsel* 7 (1980): 160ff.

Boessneck, J., A. von den Driesch, and L. Stenberger (eds.). *Eketorp, Befestigung und Siedlung auf Öland/Schweden: Die Fauna*. Stockholm: Almqvist and Wiksell, 1979.

[Bogaers, J. E. (ed.)]. *Noviomagus: Auf den Spuren der Römer in Nijmegen*. Nijmegen: Rijksmuseum Kam, (1979).

Böhme, H. W. Archäologische Zeugnisse zur Geschichte der Markomannenkriege (166–80 N.Chr.). *Jahrbuch des römisch-germanischen Zentralmuseums Mainz* 22 (1975): 153ff.

Böhme, H. W., K. Böhner, M. Schulze, K. Weidemann, G. Waurick, F. Baratte, and F. Vallet (eds.). *A l'aube de la France: la Gaule de Constantin à Childéric*. Paris: Réunion des Musées nationaux, 1981.

Böhner, K. Die Reliefplatten von Hornhausen, *Jahrbuch des römisch-germanischen Zentralmuseums Mainz* 23–24 (1976–77): 89ff.

(ed.). *Les Relations entre l'empire romain tardif, l'empire franc et ses voisins*. Colloque XXX, IXe Congrès, Union Internationale des Sciences Préhistoriques et Protohistoriques, Nice 1976.

Bojadziev, S. L'architecture monumentale à Pliska. *Berichte über den II. Internationalen Kongress für Slawische Archäologie, Berlin 24.–28. August 1970*, vol. 1, pp. 354ff. Berlin: Akademie, 1970.

Bökönyi, S. *History of Domestic Mammals in Central and Eastern Europe*. Budapest: Akadémiai, 1974.

   Animal Husbandry and Hunting in Tác-Gorsium: the Vertebrate Fauna of a Roman Town in Pannonia. Studia Archaeologica 8(1984).

Bolin, S. Mohammed, Charlemagne and Rurik. *Scandinavian Economic History Review* 1 (1953): 5ff.

Borg, K., U. Näsman, and E. Wegraeus (eds.). *Eketorp, Fortification and Settlement on Öland/Sweden: The Monument*. Stockholm: Almqvist and Wiksell, 1976.

Borger, H. *Die römischen Steininschriften aus Köln*. Wissenschaftliche Kataloge des römisch-germanischen Museums Köln 2. Köln: Greven and Bechtold, 1975.

Borkovsky, I. *Die Prager Burg zur Zeit der Premyslidenfürsten*. Prague: Academia, 1972.

Bortolotti, I.M. *Økonomiske forhold i det romerske imperium, specielt med henblik på landbruget i Pannonien*. Unpublished paper, University of Copenhagen, 1982.

Bott, G. (gen. ed.). *Germanen, Hunnen und Awaren, Schätze der Völkerwanderungszeit: Die Archäologie des 5. und 6. Jahrhunderts an der mittleren Donau und der östlichmerowingische Reihengräberkreis*. Nürnberg: Germanisches Nationalmuseum, 1987.

Bottema, S. Palynological investigations in Greece with special reference to pollen as an indicator of human activity. *Palaeohistoria* 24 (1982): 257ff.

Bouras, C. City and village: urban design and architecture. XVI. Internationaler byzantinistenkongress, Akten 1, no. 2. *Jahrbuch der österreichischen Byzantinistik* 31 no. 2 (1981): 611ff.

Bowen, R. LeB. Jr and F. P. Albright. *Archaeological Discoveries in South Arabia*. Baltimore: Johns Hopkins University Press, 1958.

Brachmann, H. Zum Ursprung und zur Entwicklung des feudalen Befestigungsbaues. *Zeitschrift für Archäologie* 16 (1982): 165ff.

Brandt, R. and J. Slofstra (eds). *Roman and Native in the Low Countries: Spheres of Interaction*. British Archaeological Report International Series 184 (1983).

Branigan, K. *Gatcombe Roman Villa*. British Archaeological Reports 44 (1977).

Braudel, E. *The Mediterranean and the Medditerranean World in the Age of Philip II*. 2 vols. London: Collins, 1972.

Braunfels, W. (ed.). *Karl der Grosse*. 5 vols. Düsseldorf: Schwann, 1965–68.

Breda, A. and G. P. Brogiolo. Piadena, loc. Castello, scavo 1984, lotti 2 e 3. *Archeologia Medievale* (1984): 181ff.

Brown, P. *The World of Late Antiquity: From Marcus Aurelius to Muhammad*. London: Thames and Hudson, 1971.

Brown, T. S. *Gentlemen and Officers: Imperial Administration and Aristocratic Power in Byzantine Italy A.D. 554–800*. Rome: British School at Rome, 1984.

Brozzi, M. Zur Topographie von Cividale im frühen Mittelalter. *Jahrbuch des römisch-germanischen Zentralmuseums Mainz* 15 (1968): 134ff.

Bruce-Mitford, R. *Recent Archaeological Excavations in Europe*. London: Routledge & Kegan Paul, 1975.

Brühl, C. *Palatium und Civitas: Studien zur Profantopographie spätantiker Civitates vom 3. bis zum 13, Jahrhundert*. Köln: Böhlau, 1975.

Brøndsted, J. La basilique des cinq martyrs à Kapljuc. *Recherches à Salone* 1 (1928): 33ff.

Buchet, L. (ed.). *Le Phenomène des grands 'invasions': actes des premières journées anthropologiques de Valbonne (16–18 Av. 1981)*. Centre de Recherches Archéologiques, Notes et Monographies Techniques 12 (1983).

Buck, D. J. and D. J. Mattingly (eds.). *Town and Country in Roman Tripolitania*. British Archaeological Reports International Series 274 (1985).

Buckler, W. H. and D. M. Robinson. *Greek and Latin Inscriptions*, vol. 1, *Sardis 7*. Leiden: Brill, 1932.

Buckley, D. G. (ed.). *Archaeology in Essex to A.D. 1500*. Council for British Archaeology Research Report 34 (1980).

Buitenhuis, H. The animal remains of Tell Sweyhat, Syria. *Palaeohistoria* 25 (1983): 131ff.

Bulliet, R. *The Camel and the Wheel*. Cambridge, Mass.: Harvard University Press, 1975.

Bülow, G. von, Die Keramikproduktion, in R. Günther and H. Köpstein (eds.), *Die Römer an Rhein und Donau: Zur politischen, wirtschaftlichen und sozialen Entwicklung in den römischen Provinzen an Rhein, Mosel und oberer Donau im 3 und 4. Jahrhundert*, pp. 230ff. Veröffentlichungen des Zentralinstituts für Alte Geschichte und Archäologie der Akademie der Wissenschaften der DDR 3 (1975).

Bülow, G. von, D. Schieferdecker, and H. Heinrich (sub-eds.). *Iatrus-Krivina, Spätantike Befestigung und frühmittelalterliche Siedlung an der unteren Donau*, vol. 1: *Ergebnisse der Ausgrabungen 1966–1973*. Berlin: Ost, 1979.

Burnett, A. *The Coins of Late Antiquity A.D. 400–700*. London: British Museum, 1977.

Burns, J. R. and B. Denness. Climate and social dynamics: the Tripolitanian example, 300 BC–AD 300, in Buck and Mattingly, pp. 201ff.

Burns, T. S. *The Ostrogoths: Kingship and Society*. Historia 36 (1980).

Buttrey, T. V. The coins, in Humphrey 1976, pp. 157ff.

The coins, in Humphrey 1977, pp. 335ff.

Buttrey, T. V. and R. B. Hitchner. The coins, in Humphrey 1978, pp. 99ff.

Buttrey, T. V., A. Johnston, K. M. MacKenzie, and M. L. Bates. *Greek, Roman and Islamic Coins from Sardis*. Archaeological Exploration of Sardis, Monograph 7. Cambridge, Mass.: Harvard University Press, 1981.

Butzer, K. W. Civilization: organisms or systems? *American Scientist* 68 (September–October 1980): 517ff.

Callmer, J. The archaeology of Kiev *ca.* A.D. 500–1000: a survey, in Zeitler, pp. 29ff. *Sceatta Problems in the Light of the Finds from Åhus*. Scripta Minora, Regiae Societatis Humaniorum Litterarum Lundensis, 1983–1984, no. 2.

Callu, J.-P. Remarques numismatiques: les monnaies romaines d'Auguste à Anastase trouvées dans les fouilles d'Apamée de Syrie (1966–1971), in Balty and Balty, pp. 159ff.

Les Monnaies Romaines: fouilles d'Apamée de Syrie 8, no. 1. Monnaies Antiques (1966–1971) 2 (1979).

Campbell, J. (ed.). *The Anglo-Saxons*. Oxford: Phaidon, 1982.

Carandini, A. Columella's vineyard and the rationality of the Roman economy. *Opus* 2, no. 1 (1983): 177ff.

(ed.) *Settefinestre, una villa schiavistica nell'Etruria romana*. 3 vols. Modena: Panini, 1985.

Il mondo della tarda antichità visto attraverso le merci, in Giardina, pp. 3ff.

Carlsson, D. *Kulturlandskapets utveckling på Gotland: En studie av jordbruks- och bebyggelsesförändringar under järnåldern*. Kulturgeografiska Institutionen, Stockholms Universitet, B 49 (1979).

Casey, P. J. (ed.). *The End of Roman Britain*. British Archaeological Reports 71 (1979). *Roman Coinage in Britain*. Shire Archaeology 12. Aylesbury: Shire, 1980.

Casson, L. *Ships and Seamanship in the Ancient World*. Princeton: Princeton University Press, 1971.

Champion, T. C. and J. V. S. Megaw (eds.). *Settlement and Society: Aspects of West European Prehistory in the First Millennium B.C.* Leicester: Leicester University Press, 1985.

Chapelot, J. and R. Fossier. *Le Village et la maison au Moyen Âge*. Paris: Hachette, 1980.

Chapman, R., I. Kinnes, and K. Randsborg. *The Archaeology of Death*. Cambridge: Cambridge University Press, 1981.

Chevallier, R. (ed.). *Actes du Collège: La ville romaine dans les provinces du nord-ouest*. Caesarodunum 17 (1982).

Chittick, N. *Manda: Excavations at an Island Port on the Kenya Coast*. British Institute in Eastern Africa Memoir 9 (1984).

Christlein, R. *Die Alamannen*. Stuttgart: Theiss, 1978.

Chropovsky, B. (ed.). *Archaeological Research in Slovakia*. Nitra: Archaeological Institute, 1981.

Clack, P. A. G. The northern frontier: farmers in the military zone, in Miles, pp. 377ff.

Clack, P. and S. Haselgrove (eds.). *Rural Settlement in the Roman North*. Durham: Department of Archaeology, University of Durham, 1982.

Clarke, G. *The Roman Cemetery at Lankhills*. Pre-Roman and Roman Winchester 2/ Winchester Studies 3 (1979).

Clason, A. T. *Jacht en veeteelt van prehistorie tot middeleeuwen*. Haarlem: Fibula-van Dishoeck, 1977.

Clason, A. T. and H. Buitenhuis. A preliminary report on the faunal remains of Nahr el Homr, Haidi, and Ta'as in the Tabqa Dam region in Syria. *Journal of Archaeological Science* 5 (1978): 75ff.

Claude, D. *Die byzantinische Stadt im 6. Jahrhundert*. Byzantinisches Archiv 13 (1969). *Der Handel im westlichen Mittelmeer während des Frühmittelalters: Untersuchungen zu Handel und Verkehr der vor- und frühgeschichtlichen Zeit in Mittel- und Nordeuropa*, vol. 2. Abhandlungen der Akademie der Wissenschaften in Göttingen, Philologisch-historische Klasse, series 3, no. 144 (1985).

Clavel, M. *Béziers et son territoire dans l'Antiquité*. Centre de Recherches d'Histoire Ancienne, Annales Littéraires de l'Université de Besançon 2 (1970).

Cohen, R. *Archaeological Survey of Israel, Map of Sede Boqer-East (168) 13–03*. Jerusalem, 1981.

Colls, D., R. Étienne, R. Lequément, B. Liou, and F. Mayet. *L'épave Port-Vendres II et le commerce de la Bétique a l'époque de Claude*. Archaeonautica 1 (1977).

Cornell, T. and J. Matthews. *Atlas of the Roman World*. Oxford: Phaidon, 1982.

Coscarella, A. Lucerne di 'tipo mediterraneo' o 'africano', in Montanari 1983, pp. 155ff.

Cowin, M. M. Artifacts recovered off the southwestern Turkish coast by the Institute of Nautical Archaeology Shipwreck Surveys in 1973 and 1980. Unpublished thesis, Texas A & M University, 1986.

Crawford, D. J. Imperial estates, in Finley 1976, pp. 35ff.

Crawford, M. H. *Roman Republican Coin Hoards*. London: Royal Numismatic Society, 1969.

  Republican denarii in Romania: the suppression of piracy and the slave-trade. *Journal of Roman Studies* 67 (1977): 117ff.

Crickmore, J. (ed.) *Romano-British Urban Defenses*. British Archaeological Reports 126 (1984).

Crumlin-Pedersen, O. Skibe på havbunden: Vragfund i danske farvande fra perioden 600–1400. *Handels- og Søfartsmuseet på Kronborg* 40 (1981): 28ff.

Cunliffe, B. *Excavations at Portchester Castle*, vol. 1, *Roman*. Society of Antiquaries of London, Reports of the Research Committee 32 (1975).

  Coinage and Society in Britain and Gaul: Some Current Problems. Council for British Archaeology Research Report 38 (1981).

  Danebury: Anatomy of an Iron Age Hillfort. London: Batsford, 1983.

[Cüppers, H. (ed.)]. *Trier, Augustusstadt der Treverer: Stadt und Land in vor- und frührömischer Zeit*. Mainz: von Zabern, 1984.

[Cüppers, H., G. Collot, A. Kolling, and G. Thill (eds.)]. *Die römer an Mosel und Saar*. Mainz: von Zabern, 1983.

Curina, R. Le monete, in Montanari 1983, pp. 204ff.

Curle, C. L. *Pictish and Norse Finds from the Brough of Birsay 1934–74*, Society of Antiquaries of Scotland Monograph Series 1 (1982).

Daimon, J.-P. and H. Lavagne. *Province de Lyonnaise*, pt.3: *Partie centrale*. Recueil général des mosaïques de la Gaule, 10th supplement to *Gallia*, 4, no. 3 (1977).

Dam, R. van. *Leadership and Community in Late Antique Gaul.* Berkeley: University of California Press, 1985.

Dauphin, C. A new method of studying early Byzantine mosaic pavements (coding and computed cluster analysis) with special reference to the Levant. *Levant* (1976): 113ff.

  Mosaic pavements as an index of prosperity and fashion. *Levant* 12 (1980): 112ff.

Davies, W. Roman settlements and post-Roman estates in south-east Wales, in Casey 1979, pp. 153ff.

Davies, W. and H. Vierck. The contexts of tribal hidage: social aggregates and settlement patterns. *Frühmittelalterliche Studien* 8 (1974): 223ff.

Davis, R. H. C. *A History of Medieval Europe: From Constantine to Saint Louis.* London: Longman, 1970.

Delorme, A and H.-H. Leuschner. Dendrochronologische Befunde zur jüngeren Flussgeschichte von Main, Fulda, Lahn und Oker. *Eiszeitalter und Gegenwart* 33 (1983): 45ff.

Demandt, A. Erklärungsversuche zur Auflösung des römischen Reiches. *Mitteilungen des deutschen archaeologischen Instituts, Römische Abteilung* 90, no. 1 (1983): 211ff.

Demolon, P. *Le village mérovingien de Brebières (VIe–VIIe siècles).* Mémoires de la Commission Départementale des Monuments Historiques du Pas-de-Calais 14 (1972).

Dilke, O. A. W. and M. S. Dilke. Perception of the Roman world. *Progress in Geography* 9 (1976): 41ff.

Dockes, P. *Medieval Slavery and Liberation.* London: Methuen, 1982.

Dolley, M. *Anglo-Saxon Pennies.* London: British Museum, 1970.

Donat, P. *Haus, Hof und Dorf in Mitteleuropa vom 7.–12. Jahrhundert.* Schriften zur Ur-und Frühgeschichte 33 (1980).

  Die Mecklenburg: Eine Hauptburg der Obodriten. Schriften zur Ur- und Frühgeschichte 37 (1984).

Donat, P. and H. Ullrich. Einwohnerzahlen und Siedlungsgrösse der Merowingerzeit: Eine methodischer Beitrag zur demographischen Rekonstruktion frühgeschichtlicher Bevölkerungen. *Zeitschrift fur Archäologie* 5 (1971): 234ff.

Doorninck, F. H. van, Jr. An 11th-century shipwreck at Serçe Liman, Turkey: 1978–81 (Report No. 8). *International Journal of Nautical Archaeology* 11, no. 1 (1982): 7ff.

Doppelfeld, O. and W. Weyres. *Die Ausgrabungen im Dom zu Köln.* Kölner Forschungen 1. Mainz: von Zabern, 1980.

Dorigo, W. *Venezia origini: fondamenti, ipotesi, metodi.* Milan: Electa, 1983.

Douglas, D. C. and G. W. Greenaway (eds.). *English Historical Documents.* Vol. 2. London: Eyre and Spottiswoode, 1953.

Driesch, A. von den. *Osteoarchäologischen Untersuchungen auf der iberischen Halbinsel.* Studien über frühe Tierknochenfunde von der iberischen Halbinsel 3 (1972).

Drinkwater, J. F. *Roman Gaul: The Three Provinces 58 BC–AD 260.* London: Croom Helm, 1983.

Duby, G. *L'Economie rurale et la vie des campagnes dans l'Occident Médiéval.* Paris: Aubier, 1962.

  The Early Growth of the European Economy: Warriors and Peasants from the Seventh to the Twelfth Century. Ithaca: Cornell University Press, 1974.

  (ed.). *Histoire de la France urbaine,* vol. 1. Paris: Seuil, 1980.

Dunbabin, K. M. D. *The Mosaics of Roman North Africa.* Oxford: Clarendon, 1978.

Duncan-Jones, R. *The Economy of the Roman Empire: Quantitative Studies.* 2nd edn. Cambridge: Cambridge University Press, 1982.

Dupuy, R. E. and T. N. Dupuy. *The Encyclopedia of Military History, from 3500 B.C. to the Present.* New York: Harper, 1970.

Durliat, J. *Les Dédicaces d'ouvrages de défense dans l'Afrique byzantine.* Collection de l'Ecole Française de Rome 49 (1981).

Duval, P.-M. and E. Frézouls (eds.). *Thèmes de recherches sur les villes antiques d'Occident.*

Colloques Internationaux du Centre National de la Recherche Scientifique 542 (1977).

Düwel, K., H. Jankuhn, H. Siems, and D. Timpe (eds.). *Untersuchungen zu Handel und Verkehr der vor- und frühgeschichtlichen Zeit in Mittelund Nordeuropa*, vol. 1, *Methodische Grundlagen und Darstellungen zum Handel in vorgeschichtlicher Zeit und in der Antike*. Abhandlungen der Akademie der Wissenschaften in Göttingen, Philologisch-historische Klasse, series 3, no. 143 (1985a).

(eds.). *Untersuchungen zu Handel und Verkehr der vor- und frühgeschichtlichen Zeit in Mittelund Nordeuropa*, vol. 3, *Der Handel des frühen Mittelalters*. Abhandlungen der Akademie der Wissenschaften in Göttingen, Philologisch-historische Klasse, series 3, no. 150 (1985b).

(eds.). *Untersuchungen zu Handel und Verkehr der vor- und frühgeschichtlichen Zeit in Mittelund Nordeuropa*, vol. 4, *Der Handel der Karolinger- und Wikingerzeit* Abhandlungen der Akademie der Wissenschaften in Göttingen, Philologisch-historische Klasse, series 3, no. 156 (1987).

Dyson, S. L. Settlement patterns in the Ager Cosanus: the Wesleyan University Survey, 1974–1976. *Journal of Field Archaeology* 5 (1978): 251ff.

Dzieduszycka, B. Demographic and economic transformations in the area surrounding Early Medieval Kruszwicka. *Archaeologia Polana* 24 (1985): 73ff.

Earle, T. A reappraisal of redistribution: complex Hawaiian chiefdoms, in T. Earle and J. Ericson (eds.), *Exchange Systems in Prehistory*, pp. 213ff. New York: Academic, 1977.

Eckstein, D., S. Wrobel and R. W. Aniol (eds.). *Dendrochronology and Archaeology in Europe*. Mitteilungen der Bundesforschungsanstalt für Forst- und Holzwirtschaft Hamburg 141 (1983).

Eddy, J. A. The case of the missing sunspots. *Scientific American* 236, no. 5 (May 1977): 80ff.

Edmondson, J. C. *Two Industries in Roman Lusitania: Mining and Garum Production*. British Archaeological Reports International Series 362 (1987).

Edson, C. *Inscriptiones Thessalonicae et viciniae: Inscriptiones Macedoniae*. Inscriptiones graecae 10, 2, no. 1 (1972).

Edwards, K. M. *Coins 1896–1929*. Corinth 6. Cambridge, Mass.: Harvard University Press, 1933.

Eggers, H. J. Lübzow: Ein germanischer Fürstensitz der älteren Kaiserzeit. *Prähistorische Zeitschrift* 34–5 (1949–50): 58ff.

Der römische Import im freien Germanien. Atlas der Urgeschichte 1 (1951).

Zur absoluten Chronologie der römischen Kaiserzeit im freien Germanien. *Jahrbuch des römisch-germanischen Zentralmuseums Mainz* 2 (1955): 196ff.

Eickhoff, E. *Seekrieg und Seepolitik zwischen Islam und Abendland: Das Mittelmeer unter byzantinischer und arabischer Hegemonie (650–1040)*. Saarbrücken: Universität des Saarlandes, 1966 (reprint, Berlin).

Ermini, G. (ed.). *Moneta e scambi nell'alto Medioevo*. Settimane di Studio del Centro Italiano sull'Alto Medioevo 8 (1961).

Es, W. A. van *De romeinse muntvondsten uit de drie noordelijke provincies, een periodisering der relaties*. Scripta Academica Groningana (1960).

Wijster, a Native Village beyond the Imperial Frontier 150–425 A.D. Palaeohistoria 11 (1967).

De Romeinen in Nederland. Haarlem: Fibula-van Dishoeck, 1981.

Es, W. A. van and W. J. H. Verwers. *Excavations at Dorestad*, vol. 1, *The Harbour. Hoogstraat 1, Kromme Rijn Projekt 1*. Nederlandse Oudheden 9 (1980).

Evans, A. D. *The Sutton Hoo Ship Burial*. London: British Museum, 1986.

Ewig, E. *Frühes Mittelalter*. Rheinische Geschichte 1, 2, Altertum und Mittelalter. Düsseldorf: Schwann, 1980.

Fagerlie, J. M. *Late Roman and Byzantine Solidi found in Sweden and Denmark*. Numismatic Notes and Monographs 157 (1967).

Fentress, E. Caesarian reflections. *Opus* 3, no. 2 (1984): 487ff.

Ferdière, A. Archéologie et histoire socio-économique, apport de la prospection systématique à l'étude de l'habitat rural gallo-romain; l'example de Lion-en-Beauce, in Février and Leveau, pp. 43ff.

(ed.). *Un site rural gallo-romain en Beauce: Dambron.* Orléans: Fédération Archéologique du Loiret, 1983.

Février, P. A., M. Fixot, C. Goudineau, and V. Kruta. La ville antique, des origines au IXe siècle. *Histoire de la France urbain,* vol. 1. Paris: Seuil, 1980.

Février, P. A. and P. Leveau (eds.). *Villes et campagnes dans l'empire romain: actes du colloque organisé à Aix-en-Provence (1980).* Aix-en-Provence: Lafitte, 1982.

Fiedler, U. Zur Datierung der Langwälle der mittleren und unteren Donau, *Archäologisches Korrespondenzblatt* 16 (1986): 457ff.

Finberg, H. P. R. (ed.). *The Agrarian History of England and Wales,* vols. 1 and 2, A.D. *43–1042.* Cambridge: Cambridge University Press, 1972.

Finley, M. I. *The Ancient Economy.* London: Chatto and Windus, 1973.

(ed.). *Studies in Roman Property.* Cambridge: Cambridge University Press, 1976.

Fitz, J. (ed.). *Der römische Limes in Ungarn.* Az István Király Múzeum Közlemenyei, series A, 11 (1976).

Flon, C. (ed.). *Le Grand Atlas de l'archéologie.* Paris: Encyclopedia Universalis, 1985 / *The World Atlas of Archaeology.* London: Mitchell Beazley, 1985.

Foley, F. *The Argolid 800–600 B.C.: an Archaeological Survey, together with an Index of Sites from the Neolithic to the Roman Period.* Studies in Mediterranean Archaeology 80 (1988).

[Forsström, M. (ed.)]. *Den medeltida staden.* Bebyggelsehistorisk tidskrift 3 (1982).

Fosier, R. *Enfance de l'Europe, Xe–XIIe siècles: aspects économiques et sociaux.* Nouvelle Clio 17. Paris: Presses Universitaires de France, 1982.

Foss, C. *Byzantine and Turkish Sardis.* Archaeological Exploration of Sardis, Monograph 4. Cambridge, Mass.: Harvard University Press, 1976.

Archaeology and the 'Twenty Cities' of Byzantine Asia. *American Journal of Archaeology* 81 (1977a): 469ff.

Late Antique and Byzantine Ankara. *Dumbarton Oaks Papers* 31 (1977b): 27ff.

Ephesus after Antiquity: A Late Antique, Byzantine, and Turkish City. Cambridge: Cambridge University Press, 1979.

Fouet, G. *La Villa gallo-romain de Montmaurin.* 20th supplement to *Gallia* (1969).

Francovich, R. (ed.). *Scarlino I, storia e territorio.* Ricerche di Archeologia Altomedievale e Medievale 9/10 (1985a).

(ed.). Un villaggio di minatori e fonditori di metallo nella Toscana del medioevo: San Silvestro (Campiglia Marittima). *Archeologia Medievale* 12 (1985b): 313ff.

Frank, R. I. *Scholae Palatinae: The Palace Guards of the Later Roman Empire.* Papers and Monographs of the American Academy in Rome 23 (1969).

Freed, J. San Giovanni di Ruoti: cultural discontinuity between the Early and Late Roman Empire in southern Italy, in Malone and Stoddart, vol. 4, pp. 179ff.

Frenzel, B. (ed.). *Dendrochronologie und postglaziale Klimaschwankungen in Europa.* Erdwissenschaftliche Forschungen 12 (1977).

Frere, S. *Britannia: A History of Roman Britain.* London: Routledge & Kegan Paul, 1967.

Verulamium Excavations, vol. 1. Society of Antiquaries of London, Reports of the Research Committee 28 (1972).

Frova, A. (ed.). *Scavi di Luni,* vol. 2, *Relazione delle campagne di scavo 1972–1973–1974.* Rome: Bretschneider, 1977.

Frye, R. M. Byzantine and Sasanian trade relations with north-eastern Russia. *Dumbarton Oaks Papers* 26 (1972): 263ff.

Fülep, F. *Sopianae: The History of Pécs during the Roman Era and the Problem of the Continuity of the Late Roman Population.* Archaeologia Hungarica, n.s., 50 (1984).

Fulford, M. G. *New Forest Pottery.* British Archaeological Reports 17 (1975).

Economic interdependence among urban communities of the Roman Mediterranean. *World Archaeology* 19, no. 1 (June 1987): 58ff.

Fulford, M. G. and D. P. S. Peacock. *The Avenue du President Habib Bourguiba, Salammbo: The Pottery and Other Ceramic Objects from the Site Excavations at Carthage*: The British Mission 1, no. 2. Sheffield: Department of Archaeology, Sheffield University, 1984.

Gabler, D. Die Sigillaten von Gebiete der Hercules-Villa in Aquincum. *Acta Archaeologica Academiae Scientiarum Hungaricae* 28 (1976): 3ff.

Differences between imported pottery in the western and Danubian provinces of the Roman Empire. *Acta Archaeologica Hungarica* 38 (1986): 93ff.

Gabler, D., F. Patek, and I. Vörös. *Studies in the Iron Age of Hungary*. British Archaeological Reports International Series 144 (1982).

Gabler, D. and A. H. Vaday. *Terra Sigillata im Barbaricum zwischen Pannonien und Dazien*. Fontes Archaeologici Hungariae (1986).

Galsterer, B. *Die Grafitti auf der römischen Gefässkeramik aus Haltern*. Bodenaltertümer Westfalens 20 (1983).

Galsterer, B. and H. Galsterer. *Die römischen Stein-Schriften aus Köln*. Wissenschafftliche Katalogue des römisch-germanischen Museums Köln II (1975).

[Garbrecht, G. (ed.)]. *Vorträge der Tagung historische Wassernutzungsanlagen im östlichen Mittelmeeraum*. Leichtweiss-Institut für Wasserbau der Technischen Universität Braunschweig Mitteilungen 82 (1984).

Garnsey, P., K. Hopkins, and C. R. Whittaker (eds.). *Trade in the Ancient Economy*. London: Chatto and Windus, Hogarth, 1983.

Garnsey, P. and R. Saller. *The Roman Empire: Economy, Society, and Culture*. London: Duckworth, 1987.

Garnsey, P. and C. R. Whittaker (eds.). *Trade and Famine in Classical Antiquity*. Cambridge Philological Society, supplementary vol. 8 (1983).

Gascou, J. *Inscriptions latines*. Inscriptions antiques du Maroc 2. Paris: Centre National de la Recherche Scientifique, 1982.

Gauthier, N. *Première Belgique*. Recueil des inscriptions chrétiennes de la Gaule antérieures à la Renaissance carolingienne 1 (1975).

Gebühr, M. Versuch einer statistischen Auswertung von Grabfunden der römischen Keiserzeit am Beizpiel der Gräberfelder von Hamfelde und Kemnitz. *Zeitschrift für Ostforschung* 24 (1975): 433ff.

Gechter, M. Die Anfänge des Niedergermanischen Limes. *Bonner Jahrbücher* 179 (1979): 1ff.

Gechter, M. and J. Kunow. Zur ländlichen Besiedlung des Rheinlandes vom 1. Jahrhundert v. bis ins 5. Jahrundert n.Chr.Geb. *Bonner Jahrbücher* (in press).

Gehrig, U. *Hildesheimer Silberschatz*. 2nd edn. Berlin: Staatliche Museen, 1980.

Geraty, L. T. and Ø. S. LaBianca. The local environment and human food-procuring strategies in Jordan: the case of Tell Hasban and its surrounding region, in Hadidi 1985, vol. 2, pp. 323ff.

Giacchero, M. (ed.). *Edictum Diocletiani et Collegarum de pretiis rerum venalium*. Genova: Istituto di storia Antica e Scienze Ausiliare, 1974.

Giardina, A. (ed.). *Le merci, gli insediamenti*. Società Romana e Impero Tardoantico 3. Rome: Laterza, 1986.

Gibbon, E. *The Decline and Fall of the Roman Empire*. London, 1776–88 (etc.).

Gilles, K.-J. *Spätrömische Höhensiedlungen in Eifel und Hunsrück*. Trierer Zeitschrift 7 (1985).

Gissel, S., E. Jutikkala, E. Österberg, J. Sandnes, and B. Teitsson. *Desertion and Land Colonization in the Nordic Countries 1300–1600*. Comparative Report, Scandinavian Project on Deserted Farms and Villages, Publications Series II. Stockholm, 1981.

Glasbergen, W. Terra Sigillata uit de provincie Groningen: Bijdrage tot de geschiedenis van den handel in den romeinschen tijd. *Jaarverslag van de Vereeniging voor Terpenonderzoek* 25–8 (1940–44): 317ff.

De romeinse castella te Valkerburg Z.H.: Opgravningen 1962. Cingvla 1. Groningen: Wolters-Noordhoff, 1972 (1967).

Glasbergen, W. and W. Groenmann-van Wateringe. *The Pre-Flavian Garrisons of Valkenburg Z. H.: Fabriculae and Bipartite Barracks.* Cingvla 2. Amsterdam: North-Holland, 1974.

Godłowski, K. *The Chronology of the Late Roman and Early Migration Periods in Central Europe.* Zeszyty Naukowe Universytet Jagiellonskiego 217 / Prace Archeologiczne 11 (1970).

Der römische Handel in der Germania libera aufgrund der archäologischen Quellen, in Düwel et al. (1985a), pp. 337ff.

Goffart, W. From Roman taxation to medieval seigneurie: three notes (pts. 1 and 2). *Speculum* 47 (1972): 165ff, 373ff.

Caput and Colonate: Towards a History of Late Roman Taxation. Phoenix, supplementary vol. 12 (1974).

Barbarians and Romans, A.D. 418–584: The Techniques of Accommodation. Princeton: Princeton University Press, 1980.

Rome, Constantinople, and the barbarians. *American Historical Review* 86 (April 1981): 275ff.

Gonzenbach, V. von *Die römischen Mosaiken der Schweiz.* Monographien zur Ur- und Frühgeschichte der Schweiz 13 (1961).

Goody, J. *Production and Reproduction.* Cambridge Studies in Social Anthropology 17. Cambridge University Press, 1976.

Gordon, A. E. *Album of Dated Latin Inscriptions (Rome and the Neighborhood)*, vol. 4. *Indexes.* Berkeley: University of California Press, 1965.

Goyon, G. *Les Inscriptions et grafitti des voyageurs sur la grande pyramide.* Cairo: Société royale de géographie, 1944.

Grant, C. P. *The Syrian Desert: Caravans, Travel, and Exploration.* London: Black, 1937.

Greene, K. *The Archaeology of the Roman Economy.* London: Batsford, 1986.

Gregory of Tours (Gregorius Turonensis) Gregorii episcopi Turonensis Historiarum Libri Decem, in R. Buchner (ed.), *Ausgewählte Quellen zur deutschen Geschichte des Mittelalters*, vols. 2 and 3. Berlin: Rütten and Leoning, 1955–56.

Gricourt, J., G. Fabre, M. Mainjonet, and J. Lafaurie. *Trésors monétaires et plaques-boucles de la Gaule romaine: Bavai, Montbouy, Chécy.* 12th supplement to *Gallia* (1958).

Grierson, P. Coinage and money in the Byzantine Empire 498–c. 1090, in Ermini, pp. 411ff.

Money and coinage under Charlemagne, in Braunfels, pp. 501ff.

The Carolingian Empire in the eyes of Byzantium. *Settimane di Studio del Centro Italiano sull'Alto Medioevo* 27 (1981): 885ff.

Grimm, G., H. Heinen, and E. Winter (eds.). *Das römisch–byzantinische Ägypten: Akten des internationalen Symposiums 26–30. September 1978 in Trier.* Aegyptiaca Treverensia 2 (1983).

Gringmuth-Dallmer, E. Zur Kulturlandschaftentwicklung in frühgeschichtlicher Zeit im germanischen Gebiet. *Zeitschrift für Archäologie* 6 (1972): 64ff.

Die Entwicklung der frühgeschichtlichen Kulturlandschaft auf dem Territorium der DDR unter besonderer Berücksichtigung der Siedlungsgebiete. Schriften zur Ur- und Frühgeschichte 35 (1983).

Groenman-van Waateringe, W. Shoe sizes and Paleodemography? *Helinium* 28 (1978): 184ff.

Urbanization and the north-west frontier of the Roman Empire, in Hanson Keppie, pp. 1037ff.

Groslier, P. The 'Indianization' of Southeast Asia, in Flon, pp. 254ff.

Grosse, R. *Römische Militärgeschichte von Gallienus bis zum Beginn der byzantinischen Themenverfassung.* Berlin: Weidmann, 1920.

Grünert, H. (ed.). *Römer und Germanen in Mitteleuropa.* Berlin: Akademie, 1975.

Gsell, S. *Inscriptions de la proconsulaire*. Inscriptions latines de l'Algérie 1. Paris: Honoré Champion, 1922.

Gualtieri, M., M. Salvatore, and A. Small (eds.). *Lo scavo di S. Giovanni di Ruoti ed il periodo tardoantico in Basilicata: Atti della Tavola Rotonda, Roma 4 luglio 1981*. Pubblicazioni del Centro Accademico Canadese 1. [Bari: (Adriatica)], 1983.

Guéry, R., C. Morrison, and H. Slim. *Le Trésor de monnaies d'or byzantines: recherches archéologiques franco-tunisiennes à Rougga*, vol.3. Collection de l'Ecole Française de Rome 60 (1982).

Guidi, A. An application of the rank size rule to protohistoric settlements in the middle Tyrrhenian area, in Malone et al. 1985, vol. 3, pp. 217ff.

Guidobaldi, F. and A. G. Guidobaldi. *Pavimenti marmorei di Roma dal IV al IX secolo*. Studi di Antichità Cristiana 36 (1983).

Guilbert, G. (ed.). *Hill-Fort Studies: Essays for A. H. A. Hogg*. Leicester: Leicester University Press, 1981.

Gumowski, M. Moneta rzymska w Polsce. *Przeglad Archaeologiczny* 10 (1958): 85ff.

Gupta, P. L. *Roman Coins from Andhra Rradesh*. Andhra Pradesh Government Museum Series 10 (1965).

Haalebos, J. K. *Zwammerdam – Nigrum Pullum: Ein Auxilliarkastell am Niedergermanischen Limes*. Cingula 3. Amsterdam: Instituut voor Prae- en Protohistorie, 1977.

Haarnagel, W. *Die Grabung Feddersen Wierde: Methode, Hausbau, Siedlung und Wirtschaftformen sowie Sozialstruktur*. Feddersen Wierde 2. Wiesbaden: Franz Steiner, 1979.

Hadidi, A. (ed.). *Studies in the History and Archaeology of Jordan*. 2 vols. Amman: Department of Antiquities, 1985.

Haendler, G. *Die abendländische Kirche im Zeitalter der Völkerwanderung*. Kirchengeschichte in Einzeldarstellungen 2, no. 5. Berlin: Evangelische, 1980.

Hall, E. T. and D. M. Metcalf (eds.). *Methods of Chemical and Metallurgical Investigation of Ancient Coinage*. Royal Numismatical Society Special Publication 8 (1972).

Halstead, P. Traditional and ancient rural economy in Mediterranean Europe: plus ça change? *Journal of Hellenic Studies* 107 (1987): 77ff.

Hammer, C. V., H. B. Clausen, and W. Dansgaard. Greenland ice sheet evidence of post-glacial volcanism and its climatic impact. *Nature* 288, no. 5788 (20 November 1980): 230ff.

Hanbury-Tenison, J. W. Wadi Arab Survey 1983. *Annual of the Department of Antiquities (Amman)* 28 (1984): 385ff.

Hannestad, N. *Roman Art and Imperial Policy*. Jutland Archaeological Society Publications 19 (1986).

Hansen, H. Jarl. Dankirke, in Randsborg 1989.

Hansen, U. L. Das Gräberfeld von Harpelev, Seeland: Studien zur jüngeren römischen Kaiserzeit in der seeländischen Inselgruppe. *Acta Archaeologica* 47 (1976): 91ff.
    Römischer Import im Norden: Warenaustausch zwischen dem Römischen Reich und dem freien Germanien während der Kaiserzeit unter besonderer Berücksichtigung Nordeuropas. Nordiske Fortidsminder, serie B, 10 (1987).

Hanson, W. S. and L. J. F. Keppie (eds.). *Roman Frontier Studies 1979*. British Archaeological Reports International Series 71 (1980).

Harck, O. Undersøgelser af bosætningskontinuitet fra romertid til tidlig middelalder belyst ved eksempler fra Nedresaksen og Mellemslesvig (Sild), in Thrane 1977, pp. 55ff.

Harding, A. F. (ed.). *Climatic Change in Later Prehistory*. Edinburgh: Edinburgh University Press, 1982.

Harrison, R. M. *Excavations at Saraçhane in Istanbul*, vol. 1. Princeton: Princeton University Press, 1986.

Hartyányi, B. P. and G. Noyáki. Samen- und Fruchtfunde in Ungarn von der Neusteinzeit bis zum 18. Jahrhundert. *Agrártörténeti Szemle*, supplement, 1975, pp. 1ff.

Haversath, J.-B. *Dir Agrarlandschaft im römischen Deutschland der Kaiserzeit (1.-4. Jh. n. Chr.)*. Passau: Universitätsverlag, 1984.

Hayashi, R. *The Silk Road and the Shoso-in*. Heibonsha Survey of Japanese Art 6. Tokyo: Heibonsha, 1975.

Hayes, J. W. *Late Roman Pottery*. Rome: British School at Rome, 1972.

The Villa Dionysos excavations, Knossos: the pottery. *Annual of the British School at Athens* 78 (1983): 97ff.

Hedeager, L. Besiedlung, soziale Struktur und politische Organisation in der älteren und jüngeren römischen Kaiserzeit Ostdänemarks. *Prähistorische Zeitschrift* 55 (1980): 38ff.

Heidinga, H. A. *De Veluwe in de vroege Middeleeuwen: Aspecten van de nederzettings-archeologie van Kootwijk en zijn buren*. Amsterdam: Instituut voor Prae- en Protohistorie (1984).

Hendy, M. F. *Studies in the Byzantine Monetary Economy c. 300–1450*. Cambridge: Cambridge University Press, 1985.

The coins, in Harrison 1986, 278ff.

Henig, M. (ed.). *A Handbook of Roman Art*. Oxford: Phaidon, 1983.

Hennig, R. *Katalog bemerkenswerter Witterungsereignisse von den ältesten Zeiten bis zum Jahre 1800*. Abhandlungen des Königlich Preussischen meteorologischen Instituts 2, no. 4 (1904).

Henning, J. *Südosteuropa zwischen Antike und Mittelalter*. Schriften zur Ur- und Frühgeschichte 42 (1987).

Hensel, W., L. Leciejewicz, E. Tabaczynsca, and S. Tabaczynscy. Polskowloskie badania nad poczatkami Wenecji. *Polski Archeologia* 10, no. 2 (1966): 600ff.

Herrmann, J. *Siedlung, Wirtschaft und gesellschaftliche Verhältnisse der slawischen Stämme zwischen Oder/Neisse und Elbe*. Deutsche Akademie der Wissenschaften zu Berlin, Schriften der Sektion für Vorund Frühgeschichte 23 (1968).

Die germanischen und slawischen Siedlungen und das mittelalterliche Dorf von Tornow, Kr. Calau. Schriften zur Ur- und Frühgeschichte 26 (1973).

(ed.). *Archäologie als Geschichtwissenschaft*. Schriften zu Ur- und Frühgeschichte 30 (1977).

Probleme der Fruchtwechselwirtschaft im Ackerbau des 8. bis 9. Jh. am Beispiel ausgewählter schriftlicher und archäologischer Quellen. *Zeitschrift für Archaologie* 15 (1981): 1ff.

Tendenzen und Grundlinien der Produktivkraftentwicklung an der Wende von der Antike zum Mittelalter, in Herrmann et al. 1982, pp. 525ff.

(ed.). *Die Slawen in Deutschland: Geschichte und Kultur der slawischen Stämme westlich von Oder und Neisse vom 6. bis 12. Jahrhundert*. 2nd edn. Veröffentlichungen des Zentralinstituts für Alte Geschichte und Archäologie 14 (1985.)

Herrmann, J. and I. Sellnow (eds.). *Produktivkräfte und Gesellschaftsformationen in vorkapitalistischer Zeit*. Veröffentlichungen des Zentralinstituts für Alte Geschichte und Archäologie 12 (1982).

Hingley, R. Roman Britain: the structure of Roman imperialism and the consequences of imperialism on the development of a peripheral province, in Miles, pp. 17ff.

Hinz, H. *Kreis Bergheim: Archäologische Funde und Denkmäler des Rheinlandes*, vol. 2. Düsseldorf: Rheinisches Landesmuseum Bonn, 1969.

Hitchner, R. B. The Kasserine Archaeological Survey. *Antiquités Africaines* 24 (1988): 7ff.

Hodges, R. *Dark Age Economics: The Origins of Towns and Trade A.D. 600–1000*. London: Duckworth, 1982.

Primitive and Peasant Markets. Oxford: Blackwell, 1988.

The rebirth of towns in the early Middle Ages, in Hodges and Hobley, pp. 1ff.

Hodges, R., G. Barker, and K. Wade. Excavations at D85 (Santa Maria in Civita): an early medieval hilltop settlement in Molise. *Papers of the British School at Rome* 48 (1980): 70ff.

Hodges, R. and B. Hobley (eds.). *The Rebirth of Towns in the West.* Council for British
    Archaeology Research Report 68 (1988).
Hodges, R. and J. Mitchell (eds.). *San Vincenzo al Volturno: The Archaeology Art, and
    Territory of an Early Medieval Monastery.* British Archaeological Reports Inter-
    national Series 252 (1985).
Hodges, R., J. Moreland, and H. Patterson. San Vincenzo al Volturno, the Kingdom of
    Benevento, and the Carolingians, in Malone and Stoddart, vol. 4, pp. 261 ff.
Hodges, R. and D. Whitehouse. *Mohammed, Charlemagne and the Origins of Europe:
    Archaeology and the Pirenne Thesis.* London: Duckworth, 1983.
Hodges, R. and C. Wickham. The evolution of hilltop villages in the Biferno Valley, Molise,
    in Barker and Hodges, pp. 305ff.
Hohlfelder, R. L. (ed.). *City, Town, and Countryside in the Early Byzantine Era.* East European
    Monographs 120, Byzantine Series 1 (1982).
Hollstein, E. *Mitteleuropäische Eichenchronologie.* Trierer Grabungen und Forschungen 11
    (1980).
Holmqvist, W. Die Ergebnisse der Grabungen auf Helgö (1954–74). *Prähistorische
    Zeitschrift* 51 (1976): 127ff.
Hope-Taylor, B. *Yeavering: An Anglo-British Centre of Early Northumbria.* Department of
    the Environment Archaeological Reports 7 (1977).
Hopkins, K. *Conquerors and Slaves.* Sociological Studies in Roman History 1. Cambridge:
    Cambridge University Press, 1978.
    Taxes and trade in the Roman Empire (200 B.C.–A.D. 400). *Journal of Roman Studies*
    70 (1980): 101ff.
    Death and Renewal. Sociological Studies in Roman History 2. Cambridge: Cambridge
    University Press, 1983.
Horedt, K. *Siebenbürgen in Frühmittelalter.* Antiquitas, series 3 (in 4°), 28 (1986).
Horeth, L. *Siebenbürgen in Spätrömischer Zeit.* Bucharest: Kriterion, 1982.
Horn, H. G. (ed.). *Die Römer in Nordrhein-Westfalen.* Stuttgart: Theiss.
Hrala, J. (ed.). *Nouvelles archéologiques dans la République socialiste Tchèque.* Prague/Brno:
    Archaeological Institute, Prague, 1981.
Hübener, W. and V. Lobbedey. Zur Struktur der Keramik in der späteren Merowingerzeit.
    Bonner Jahrbücher 164 (1964): 88ff.
Hudson, P. J. and M. C. La Rocca Hudson. Lombard immigration and its effects on North
    Italian rural and urban settlement, in Malone and Stoddart, vol. 4, pp. 225ff.
Hull, M. R. *Roman Colchester.* Society of Antiquaries, Reports of the Research Committee
    10 (1958).
Humphrey, J. H. (ed.). *Apollonia, the Port of Cyrene: Excavations by the University of
    Michigan 1965–1967.* Supplement to *Libya Antiqua* 4 (no date).
    (ed.). *Excavations at Carthage 1975 Conducted by the University of Michigan,* vol. 1. Ann
    Arbor: Kelsey Museum, 1976.
    (ed.). *Excavations at Carthage 1976 Conducted by the University of Michigan,* vol. 3. Ann
    Arbor: Kelsey Museum, 1977.
    (ed.). *Excavations at Carthage 1976 Conducted by the University of Michigan,* vol. 4. Ann
    Arbor: Kelsey Museum, 1978.
    (ed.). *Excavations at Carthage 1977 Conducted by the University of Michigan,* vol. 6. Ann
    Arbor: Kelsey Museum, 1981.
    (ed.). *Excavations at Carthage 1978 Conducted by the University of Michigan,* vol. 7. Ann
    Arbor: Kelsey Museum, 1982.
Hunter, J. R. Glasses from Scandinavian burials in the first millennium A.D. *World
    Archaeology* 7, no. 1 (June 1975): 79ff.
Hurst, H. R. and S. P. Roskams. *The Avenue du President Habib Bourguiba, Salammbo: The
    Site and Finds Other than Pottery.* Excavations at Carthage: The British Mission 1, no.
    1. Sheffield: Department of Archaeology, Sheffield University, 1984.

Huttunen, P. *The Social Strata in the Imperial City of Rome*. Acta Universitatis Ouluensis, series B, Humaniora 3, Historica 1 (1974).

Hvass, S. Die völkerwanderungszeitliche Siedlung Vorbasse, Mitteljütland. *Acta Archaeologica* 49 (1979): 61ff.

Hodde: Et vestjysk landsbysamfund fra ældre jernalder. Arkæologiske Studier 7 (1985).

Vorbasse: Eine Dorfsiedlung während des 1. Jahrtausends n. Chr. in Mitteljütland, Dänemark. *Berichte der römisch–germanische Kommission* 67 (1986): 529ff.

Hyenstrand, Å. *Centralbygd – Randbygd: Struktuella, ekonomiska och administrativa huvudlinger i mellensvensk yngre järnålder*. Studies in North-European Archaeology 5. Stockholm: Almqvist and Wiksell, 1974.

Ilkjær, J. Mosefundene i går og i dag, in P. Mortensen (ed.). *Fra Stamme til Stat: Symposium på Sostrup Kloster 23.-25. maj 1984*. Højbjerg: Moesgaard [1984].

Ilkjær, J. and J. Lønstrup. Der Moorfund im Tal der Illerup-Å bei Skanderborg in Ostjütland (Dänemark). *Germania* 61 (1983): 95ff.

İnan, J. and E. Alföldi-Rosenbaum. *Römische und frühbyzantinische Porträtplastik aus der Türkei: Neue Funde*. Mainz: von Zabern, 1979.

İnan, J. and E. Rosenbaum. *Roman and Early Byzantine Portrait Sculpture in Asia Minor*. Oxford: Oxford University Press, 1966.

Jalabert, L., R. Mouterde (and C. Mondésert). *Inscriptions greques et latines de la Syrie*, vol. 4. Institut Français d'Archéologie de Beyrouth, Bibliothèque Archéologique et Historique 61. Paris: Paul Geuthnen, 1955.

James, E. *The Merovingian Archaeology of South-West Gaul*. 2 vols. British Archaeological Reports International Series 25 (1977).

Cemeteries and the problem of Frankish settlement in Gaul, in Sawyer 1979, pp. 55ff.

Jankuhn, H. *Haithabu, Ein Handelsplatz der Wikingerzeit*. 6th edn. Neumünster: Karl Wachholz, 1976.

Jankuhn, H., W. Schlesinger, and H. Steuer (eds.). *Vor- und Frühformen der europäischen Stadt im Mittelalter*. 2 vols. Abhandlungen der Akademie der Wissenschaften in Göttingen, Philologisch-historische Klasse, series 3, nos. 83–84 (1973–74).

Jankuhn, H., R. Schützeichel, and F. Schwind (eds.). *Das Dorf der Eisenzeit und des frühen Mittelalters*. Abhandlungen der Akademie der Wissenschaften in Göttingen, Philologisch-historische Klasse, series 3, no. 101 (1977).

Jankuhn, H. and R. Wenskus (eds.). *Geschichtswissenschaft und Archäologie: Untersuchungen zur Siedlungs-, Wirtschafts- und Kirchengeschichte*. Vorträge und Forschungen 22 (1979).

Janssen, W. *Studien zur Wüstungsfrage im fränkischen Altsiedelland zwischen Rhein, Mosel und Eifelnordrand*. 2 vols. Köln: Rheinland, 1975.

Some major aspects of Frankish and medieval settlement in the Rhineland, in Sawyer 1976, pp. 41ff.

Dorf und Dorfformen des 7 bis 12. Jahrhunderts im Lichte neuer Ausgrabungen in Mittel- und Nordeuropa, in Jankuhn, Schützeichel, and Schwind, pp. 285ff.

Die Importkeramik von Haithabu. Die Ausgrabungen in Haithabu 9 (1987).

Janssen, W. and D. Lohrmann (eds.). *Villa – curtis – grangia: Landwirtschaft zwischen Loire und Rhein von der Römerzeit zum Hochmittelalter*. Beihefte der Francia 1 (1983).

Jarrett, M. G. and S. Wrathmell. *Whitton: An Iron Age and Roman Farmstead in South Glamorgan*. Cardiff: University of Wales Press, 1981.

Jelgersma, S. and J. F. van Regteren Altena. An outline of the geological history of the coastal dunes in the western Netherlands. *Geologie en Mijnbouw* 48, no. 3 (1969): 335ff.

Jeppesen, T. G. *Middelalderlandsbyens opståen: Kontinuitet og brud i den fynske agrarbebyggelse mellem yngre jernalder og tidlig middelalder*. Fynske Studier 11 (1981).

Jobst, W. *Die Hanghäuser des Embolos: Römische Mosaiken aus Ephesos*. Forschungen in Ephesos 8 no. 2 (1977).

Römische Mosaiken in Salzburg. Wien: Bundesverlag, 1982.

Johns, J. The Monreale Survey: indigenes and invaders in medieval West Sicily, in Malone and Stoddart, vol. 4, pp. 215ff.

Johnson, A. C. and L. C. West. *Byzantine Egypt: Economic Studies.* Princeton University Studies in Papyrology 6. Princeton: Princeton University Press, 1949.

Johnson, G. A. Rank-size convexity and system integration: a view from archaeology. *Economic Geography* 56, no. 3 (July 1980): 234ff.

Johnson, S. *Late Roman Fortifications.* London: Batsford, 1983.

Johnstone, P. *The Sea-craft of Prehistory.* London: Routledge & Kegan Paul, 1980.

Jones, A. H. M. *The Later Roman Empire.* 3 vols. Oxford: Blackwell, 1964.

The Decline of the Ancient World. London: Longman, 1966.

Jones, D. M. *Excavations at Billingsgate Buildings 'Triangle', Lower Thames Street. 1974.* London and Middlesex Archaeological Society Special Paper 4 (1980).

Jones, M. and G. Dimbleby (eds.). *The Environment of Man: The Iron Age and the Anglo-Saxon Period.* British Archaeological Reports 87 (1981).

Jones, R. F. J. [J. H. F. Bloemers, S. Dyson, and M. Biddle] (ed(s).). *The First Millennium.* British Archaeological Reports International Series 401 (1988).

Jones, R. F. J., S. J. Keay, J. M. Nolla, and J. Tarrús. The Late Roman villa of Vilauba and its context: a first report on field-work and excavation in Catalunya, North-East Spain, 1978–81. *Antiquaries Journal* 62, no. 2 (1982): 245ff.

Jouffroy, H. *La Construction publique en Italie et dans l'Afrique romaine.* Groupe de Recherche d'Histoire romaine de l'Université des Sciences humaines de Strasbourg, Études et Travaux 2 (1986).

Jørgensen, L. B. *Forhistoriske textiler i Skandinavien.* Nordiske Fortidsminder, serie B, 9 (1986).

Kaegi, W. E. Jr. *Byzantine Military Unrest 471–843: An Interpretation.* Amsterdam: Hakkert, 1981.

Kajanto, I. The disappearance of classical nomenclature in the Merovingian period. *Classica et Mediaevalia, Dissertationes* 9 (1973): 383ff.

Kaltofen, A. *Studien zur Chronologie der Völkerwanderungszeit im südostlichen Mitteleuropa.* British Archaeological Reports International Series 191 (1984).

Karlsson, L. *Nordisk Form: Om djurornamentik.* Museum of National Antiquities, Stockholm, Studies 3 (1983).

Kaul, F. Priorsløkke, in Randsborg 1989.

Kazhdan, A. P. and A. W. Epstein. *Change in Byzantine Culture in the Eleventh and Twelfth Centuries.* Berkeley: University of California, 1985.

Keay, S. J. *Late Roman Amphorae in the Western Mediterranean, a Typology and Economic Study: The Catalan Evidence.* 2 vols. British Archaeological Reports International Series 196 (1984).

Keller, D. R. and D. W. Rupp. *Archaeological Survey in the Mediterranean Area.* British Archaeological Reports International Series 155 (1983).

Kennedy, H. From polis to madina: urban change in Late Antique and early Islamic Syria. *Past and Present* 106 (1985): 3ff.

Kenrick, P. Fine wares of the Hellenistic and Roman periods, in Matthers vol. 2, pp. 439ff.

Kent, J. H. *The Inscriptions 1926–1950.* Corinth 8, no. 3. Princeton: Princeton University Press, 1966.

Kent, J. P. C. Gold standards of the Merovingian coinage, in Hall and Metcalf, pp. 69ff.

Kent, J. P. C. and K. S. Painter (eds.). *Wealth of the Roman World* AD *300–700.* London: British Museum, 1977.

Khatchatrian, A. *Origine et typologie des baptistères paléochrétiens.* Mulhouse: Centre de Culture chrétienne, 1982.

King, A. A comparative survey of bone assemblages from Roman sites in Britain. *Bulletin of the Institute of Archaeology* 15 (1978): 207ff.

The animal bones, in Bennett, pp. 193ff.

Animal bones and the dietary identity of military and civilian groups in Roman Britain, Germany, and Gaul, in Blagg and King, pp. 187ff.

I resti animali, in Carandini 1985, pp. 278ff.

King, A. and M. Henig (eds.). *The Roman West in the Third Century: Contributions from Archaeology and History*. British Archaeological Reports International Series 109 (1981).

Kirwan, L. P. Rome beyond the southern Egyptian frontier. *Proceedings of the British Academy* 63 (1977): 13ff.

Kiss, A. *Roman Mosaics in Hungary*. Budapest: Akadémiai, 1973.

Die Goldfunde des Karpatenbeckens vom 5.–10. Jahrhundert: Angaben zu den Vergleichsmöglichkeiten der schriftlichen und archäologischen Quellen. *Acta Archaeologica Academiae Scientiarum Hungaricae* 38 (1986): 105ff.

Kiszely, I. *The Anthropology of the Lombards*. 2 vols. British Archaeological Reports International Series 61 (1979).

Knibbe, D. and B. Iplikçioglu: *Ephesos im Spiegel seiner Inschriften*. Wien: Schindler, 1984.

Kochavi, M. (ed.). *Judaea, Samaria, and the Golan: Archaeological Survey 1967–68*. Publication of the Archaeological Survey of Israel 1 (1972).

Koenig, G. G. Schamane und Schmid, Medicus und Mönch: ein überblick zur Archäologie der merowingerzeitlichen Medizin im südlichen Mitteleuropa. *Helvetia Archaeologica* 51/52 (1982): 75ff.

König, I. *Die Meilensteine der Gallia Narbonensis: Studien zum Strassenwesen der Provincia Narbonensis*, Itinera Romana 3. Bern: Kümmerly and Frey, 1970.

Köpstein, H. (ed.). *Besonderheiten der byzantinischen Feudalentwicklung: Eine Sammlung von Beiträgen zu den frühen Jahrhunderten*. Berliner byzantinistische Arbeiten 50 (1983).

Kolendo, J. Les influences de Rome sur les peuples de l'Europe centrale habitant loin des frontières de l'Empire: l'exemple du territoire de la Pologne. *Klio* 63 (1981): 453ff.

Kollwitz, J. and H. Herdejürgen. *Die Ravennatischen Sarkophage: Die Sarkophage der westlichen Gebiete des Imperium Romanum*, vol. 2. Die Antiken Sarkophagreliefs 8, no. 2 (1979).

Kolník, T. Römische Stationen im slowakischen Abschnitt des nordpannonischen Limesvorlandes. *Archeologické Rozhledy* 38, no. 4 (1986): 411ff.

Kolníkoková, E. Ku Konfrontácii Nálezov Mincí s Vysledkami Bádania o Dobe Rímskej na Slovensku. *Slovenská Archeológia* 20, no. 1 (1973): 167ff.

Kooijmans, L. P. L. Archaeology and coastal change in the Netherlands, in Thompson 1980, 106ff.

Kos, P. *The Monetary Circulation in the Southeastern Alpine Region ca. 300 B.C.–A.D. 1000*. Situla 24 (1984–85).

Kossack, G., K.-E. Behre, and P. Schmid (eds.). *Archäologische und naturwissenschaftliche Untersuchungen an ländlichen und frühstädtischen Siedlungen im deutschen Küstengebiet vom 5. Jahrhundert v.Chr. bis zum 11. Jahrhundert n.Chr.*, vol. 1. Weinheim: Chemie, 1984.

Kovács, L. Byzantinische Münzen im Ungarn des 10. Jahrhunderts. *Acta Archaeologica Hungarica* 35, nos. 1–2 (1983): 133ff.

Kraeling, C. H. (ed.). *Gerasa: City of the Decapolis*. New Haven: American Schools of Oriental Research, 1938.

Ptolemais: City of the Libyan Pentapolis. University of Chicago Oriental Institute Publications 90 (1962).

Krämer, K. Die frühchristlichen Grabinschriften Triers. *Trierer Grabungen und Forschungen* VIII (1974).

Krautheimer, R. *Early Christian and Byzantine Architecture*. Harmondsworth: Penguin, 1965.

Rome: Profile of a City, 312–1308. Princeton: Princeton University Press, 1980.

Krier, J. *Die Treverer ausserhalb ihrer Civitas: Mobilität und Aufstieg*. Trierer Zeitschrift 5 (1981).

Křížek, F. Nové nálezy terra sigillaty na Slovensku. *Slovenská Archeológia 9* (1961): 301ff.
Nové nálezy terra sigillaty na Slovensku (2). *Slovenská Archeológia 14* (1966): 97ff.

Krogh, K. The Royal Viking-Age monuments at Jelling in the light of recent archaeological excavations. *Acta Archaeologica 53* (1982): 183ff.

Kropotkin, V. V. *Klady rimskich monet na territorii SSSR*. Archeologia SSSR, Svod
archeologičeskich istočnikov, G4-4 (1961).
Rimskije importnyje izdelija v vostočnoj Evrope (II v. do n.e.-V v. n. e.). Archeologia SSSR,
D1–27 (1970).

Krüger, B. (ed.). *Die Germanen: Geschichte und Kultur der germanischen Stämme in
Mitteleuropa.*, vol. 1, *Von den Anfängen bis zum 2. Jahrundert unserer Zeitrechnung*. 4th
edn. Veröffentlichungen des Zentralinstituts für Alte Geschichte und Archäologie 4,
no. 1 (1983a).
Die Germanen: Geschichte und Kultur der germanischen Stämme in Mitteleuropa, vol. 2, *Die
Stämme und Stammesverbände in der Zeit vom 3. Jahrhundert bis zur Herausbildung der
politischen Vorherrschaft der Franken*. Veröffentlichungen des Zentralinstituts für Alte
Geschichte und Archäologie 4, no. 2 (1983b).

Kunow, J. *Der römische Import in der Germania libera bis zu den Markomannenkriegen:
Studien zu Bronze- und Glasgefäen*. Göttinger Schriften zur Vor- und Frühgeschichte
21 (1983).
Bemerkungen zum Export römischer Waffen in das Barbaricum, in C. Unz (ed.), *Studien
zu den Militärgrenzen Roms*, vol. 3. 13. *Internationaler Limeskongress Aalen 1983*.
Forschungen und Berichte zur Vor- und Frühgeschichte in Baden-Wurttemberg 20
(1986), pp. 740ff.

Kunst, M. Arm und Reich – Jung und Alt: Untersuchungen zu socialen Gruppierungen
auf dem Gräberfeld vom Hamfelde, Kreis Herzogtum Lauenburg. *Offa 35* (1978):
86ff.

Kyhlberg, O. Chronological and topographical analysis of the cemeteries and settlements.
Excavations at Helgö 8 (1982): 13ff.
Late Roman and Byzantine solidi: an archaeological analysis of coins and hoards.
Excavations at Helgö 10 (1986): 13ff.

LaBianca, Ø. S. *Objectives, Procedures, and Findings of Ethnoarchaeological Research in the
Vicinity of Hesbon in Jordan*. Annual of the Department of Antiquities 28 (1984).

LaMarche, V. C. Jr. Paleoclimatic inferences from long tree-ring records. *Science 183*, no.
4129 (15 March, 1974): 1043ff.

Lamb, H. H. *Climate: Present, Past, and Future*, vol. 2, *Climatic History and the Future*.
London: Methuen, 1977.
Climate, History, and the Modern World. London: Methuen, 1982.

Lambert, C. and J. Rioufreyt. Habitats indigènes, villas gallo-romaines et structures
agraires antiques dans le Maine, in Chevallier, pp. 141ff.

Lamm, J. P. and H.-Å. Nordström (eds.). *Vendel Period Studies: Transactions of the Boat-
Grave Symposium in Stockholm, February 2–3, 1981*. Museum of National Antiquities, Stockholm, Studies 2 (1983).

Lang, M. *Graffiti and Dipinti*. The Athenian Agora 21 (1976).

Lange, E. *Botanische Beiträge zur mitteleuropäischen Siedlungsgeschichte* Schriften zur Ur-
und Frühgeschichte 27 (1971).
Grundlagen und Entwicklungstendenzen der frühgeschichtlichen Agrarproduktion
aus botanischer Sicht. *Zeitschrift für Archäologie 10* (1976): 75ff.

Laser, R. *Die römischen und frühbyzantinischen Fundmünzen auf dem Gebiet der DDR*.
Schriften zur Ur- und Frühgeschichte 28 (1980)
Römisch–germanische Beziehungen im 3. Jahrhundert, in Krüger 1983b, pp. 32ff.

Lassère, J.-M. *Vbique Popvlvs: peuplement et mouvement de population dans l'Afrique romaine
de la chute de Carthage à la fin de la dynastie des Sévères (146 a. C. – 235 p. C.)*. Paris:
Centre National de la Recherche Scientifique, 1977.

Lassus, J. *Inventaire archéologique de la region au nord-est de Hama.* 2 vols. Documents d'études orientales 4. Damascus: Institut Français de Damas, (no date [*c.* 1935]).

László, G. and I. Rácz. *Der Goldschatz von Nagyszentmiklós.* Budapest: Corvina, 1977.

Lavagne, H. *Province de Narbonnaise,* vol. 1, *Partie centrale.* Recueil général des mosaïques de la Gaule. 10th supplement to *Gallia,* 3, no. 1 (1979).

Leber, P. S. *Die in Kärnten seit 1902 gefundenen römischen Steinin-schriften.* Aus Kärntens römischer Vergangenheit 3. Klagenfurt: Johannes Heyn, 1972.

Leciejewicz, L., E. Tabaczynska, and S. Tabaczynski. *Torcello: scavi 1961–62.* Istituto Nazionale d'Archeologia e Storia dell'Arte, Monografie 3 (1977).

Leday, A. *La Campagne à l'époque romaine dans le centre de la Gaule/Rural Settlement in Central Gaul in the Roman Period.* 2 vols. British Archaeological Reports International Series 73 (1980).

Lefort, J., C. Morrisson, and J.-P. Sodini. Expansion and crisis: the end of Byzantium, in Flon, pp. 142ff.

Lehtosalo-Hilander, P.-L. *Luistari III: A Burial-Ground Reflecting the Finnish Viking Age Society.* Suomen Muinaismuistoyhdistyksen Aikakauskirja 82, no. 3 (1982).

[Lemerle, P. (ed.)]. *Villes et peuplement dans l'Illyricum protobyzantin.* Collection de l'École Française de Rome 77 (1984).

Lepelley, C. *Les cités de l'Afrique romaine au Bas-Empire.* 2 vols. Paris: Études Augustiniennes, 1979.

Leube, A. Die Sachsen, in Krüger 1983, pp. 443ff.

Leveau, P. La ville antique et l'organisation de l'espace rural: villa, ville, village. *Annales: Economies, Sociétés, Civilisations* 38, no. 4 (July–August 1983): 920ff.

  Caesarea de Maurétanie: Une ville romaine et ses campagnes. Collection de l'Ecole Française de Rome 70 (1984).

Levy, D. *Antioch Mosaic Pavements.* 2 vols. Princeton: Princeton University Press, 1947.

Lewis, A. Mediterranean maritime commerce: A.D. 300–1100 shipping and trade. *Settimane di Studio del Centro Italiano di Studi sull'Alto Medioevo* 25, nos. 1–2 (1978): 481ff.

[Lilliu, G. (ed.)]. *L'archeologia romana e altomedievale nell'Oristanese: Atti del Convegno di Cuglieri (22–23 giugno 1984).* Mediterraneo Tardoantico e Medievale, Scavi e Ricerche 3. Taranto: Scorpione, 1986.

Lind, L. *Romerska denarer funna i Sverige.* Stockholm: Rubicon, 1988.

Lith, S. van and K. Randsborg. *Roman Glass in the West: A Social Study.* Berichten van de Rijksdienst voor het Oudheidkundig Bodemonderzoek 35 (1985).

Lloyd, J. A. (ed.). *Excavations at Sidi Khrebish Benghazi (Berenice),* vol. 2. Supplements to *Libya Antiqua* 5, no. 2, (no date [1983]).

Lombard, M. *L'Islam dans sa première grandeur.* Paris: Flammarion, 1971.

Longworth, I. and J. Cherry (eds.). *Archaeology in Britain since 1945.* London: British Museum, 1986.

Lough, J. M., T. M. L. Wigley, and J. P. Palutikof. Climate and climate impact scenarios for Europe in a warmer world. *Journal of Climate and Applied Meteorology* 22, no. 10 (October 1983): 1673ff.

Love, J. The character of the Roman agricultural estate in the light of Max Weber's economic sociology. *Chiron* 16 (1986): 99ff.

Luff, R.-M. *A Zooarchaeological Study of the Roman North-western Provinces.* British Archaeological Reports International Series 137 (1982).

Luttwak, E. N. *The Grand Strategy of the Roman Empire: from the First Century A.D. to the Third.* Baltimore: Johns Hopkins University Press, 1976.

Lund, J. and Z. W. Sørensen. *Segermes Survey 1987, Project Africa Procounsularis, Foreløbig rapport over 1987 survey-kampagnen i Segermesregionen.* København: (no publisher), 1987.

Macready, S. and F. H. Thompson. *Cross-Channel Trade between Gaul and Britain in the Pre-Roman Iron Age*. Society of Antiquaries of London Occasional Paper, no. 5, 4 (1984).

Macready, S. and F. H. Thompson (eds.). *Archaeological Field Survey in Britain and Abroad*. Society of Antiquaries of London Occasional Paper, no. 5, 6 (1985).

Maehler, H. Häuser und ihre Bewohner in Fayüm in der Kaiserzeit, in Grimm, Heinen, and Winter, pp. 119ff.

Magnusson, G. *Lågteknisk järnhantering i Jämtlands Län*. Jernkontorets Bergshistoriska Skriftserie 22 (1986).

Maioli, M. G. La ceramica fine da mensa (terra sigillata), in Montanari 1983, pp. 87ff.

Malleret, L. *L'archéologie du delta du Mékong*, vol. 3. Paris: de Boccard, 1962.

Malone, C. and S. Stoddart (eds.). *Papers in Italian Archaeology*. 4 vols. *The Cambridge Conference*. British Archaeological Reports International Series 243–7 (1985).

Maloney, J. and B. Hobley (eds.). *Roman Urban Defences in the West*. Council for British Archaeology Research Report 51 (1983).

Maltby, M. *The Animal Bones from Exeter: Faunal Studies on Urban Sites*. Exeter Archaeological Reports 2. Sheffield: Department of Archaeology, Sheffield University, 1979.

Manacorda, D. *Archeologia urbana a Roma: Il progetto della Crypta Balbi*. Biblioteca Archeologia Medievale 2. Firenze: all'Insegna del Giglio, 1982.

Mango, C. *Le développement urbain de Constantinople (IVe–VIIe siècles)*. Collège de France, Travaux et Mémoires du Centre de Recherche d'Histoire et Civilisation de Byzance, Monographies, 2 (1985).

Manjarres, J. M. *Esclavos y libertos en la España romana*. Acta Salmanticensia, Filosofia y Letras 62 (1971).

Mannoni, T. Materia prima e scarti di produzione dei recipienti in pietra ollare. *Rivisti di Studi Liguri* 52 (1986): 155ff.

Marinelli, G., *Les Mosaiques chrétiennes des églises de Romes, III–XIV* siècles. Rome: Istituto Editoriale, no date (*c.* 1971).

Matini, M. L. M. *Roma, Regione X Palativm, regione prima: mosaici antichi in Italia*. Rome: Consiglio Nazionale delle Ricerche, 1967.

Matthers, J. (ed.). *The River Qoueiq, Northern Syria, and its Catchment: Studies arising from the Tell Rifa' at Survey 1977–79*. 2 vols. British Archaeological Reports International Series 98 (1981).

Matthew, D. *Atlas of the Medieval Europe*. Oxford: Phaidon, 1983.

Maurin, L. *Saintes antique*. Saintes: Musée Archéologique, 1978.

Mayhew, B. H. and P. T. Schollaert. A structural theory of rank differentation, in Blau and Merton, pp. 287ff.

Mazzarino, S. *La fine del mondo antico*. Milan: Aldo Garzanti, 1959.

Mendel, G. *Catalogue des sculptures grecques, romaines et byzantines des Musées imperiaux ottomans*. 3 vols. Constantinople, 1912–14.

Menghin, W. *Die Langobarden*. Stuttgart: Theiss, 1985.

Merlin, A. *Inscriptions latines de la Tunisie*. Paris: Presses Universitaires, 1944.

Mertens, J. Urban wall-circuits in Gallia Belgica in the Roman period, in Maloney and Hobley, pp. 42ff.

Metcalf, D. M..*The Origin of the Anastasian Currency Reform*. Amsterdam: Hakkert, 1969.

Metzler, J., J. Zimmer, and L. Bakker. *Ausgrabungen in Echternach*. Luxembourg: Ministère des Affaires Culturelles et Ville d'Echternach, 1981.

Mierow, C. C. (ed.). *The Gothic History of Jordanes*. Princeton: Princeton University Press, 1915.

Mildenberger, G. *Römerzeitliche Siedlungen in Nordhessen*. Kasseler Beiträge zur Vor- und Frühgeschichte 3 (1972).

    Germanische Burgen. Veröffentlichungen der Altertumskommission im Provinzialinstitut für westfälische Landes- und Volksforschung 6 (1978).

Miles, D. (ed.). *The Romano-British Countryside: Studies in Rural Settlement and Economy*. 2 vols. British Archaeological Reports 103 (1982).

Miller, J. Innes *The Spice Trade of the Roman Empire 29 B.C.–A.D. 641*. Oxford: Clarendon, 1969.

Milojčíc, V. Zu den spätkaiserzeitlichen und merowingischen Silberlöffeln. *Bericht der römisch-germanischen Kommission* 49 (1968): 111ff.

Der runde Berg bei Urach: Ergebnisse der Untersuchungen von 1967–1974. *Ausgrabungen in Deutschland* 2 (1975): 181ff.

Mirnik, I. A. *Coin Hoards in Yugoslavia*. British Archaeological Reports International Series 95 (1981).

Mitchell, S. *The Inscriptions of North Galatia: The Ankara District*. British Archaeological Reports International Series 135 (1982).

Mittmann, S. *Beiträge zur Siedlungs- und Territorialgeschichte des nördlichen Ostjordanlandes*. Abhandlungen des deutschen Palästinavereins. Wiesbaden: Harrassowitz, 1970.

Mócsy, A. *Gesellschaft und Romanisation in der römischen Provinz Moesia Superior*. Amsterdam: Hakkert, 1970.

Pannonia and Upper Moesia: a History of the Middle Danube Provinces of the Roman Empire. London: Routledge & Kegan Paul, 1974.

Die spätrömische Festung und das Gräberfeld von Tokod. Budapest: Akadémiai, 1981.

Mócsy, A. and T. Szentléleky (eds.). *Die römischen Steindenkmäler von Savaria*. Amsterdam: Hakkert, 1971.

Prevosti i Monclús, M. *Cronologia i poblament a l'àrea rural d'Iluro*. 2 vols. Barcelona: Dalmau, 1981.

Montanari, G. B. *Ravenna e il porto di Classe: venti anni di richerche archeologiche tra Ravenna e Classe*. Realità regionale, Fonti e Studi 7. Bologna: University of Bologna Press. 1983.

Montanari, M. *L'alimentazione contadina nell'alto Medioevo*. Naples: Liguori, 1979.

Moss, J. R. The effects of the policies of Aetius on the history of Western Europe. *Historia* 22, no. 4 (1974): 711ff.

Mosser, S. McA. *A Bibliography of Byzantine Coin Hoards*. New York: American Numismatic Society, 1935.

Muckelroy, K. *Archaeology under Water: An Atlas of the World's Submerged Sites*. New York: McGraw-Hill, 1980.

Müller-Wiener, W. *Bildlexikon zur topographie Istanbuls, Byzantion-Konstantinopolis-Istanbul bis zum Beginn des 17. Jahrhunderts*. Tübingen: Wasmuth, 1977.

Müller-Wille, M. Königsgrab und Königskirche: Funde und Befunde in frühgeschichtlichen und mittelalterlichen Nordeuropa. *Bericht der römisch-germanischen Kommission* 63 (1982): 349ff.

Müller-Wille, M. and J. Oldenstein. Die ländliche Besiedlung des Umlandes von Mainz in spätrömischer und frühmittelalterlicher Zeit. *Bericht der römisch-germanischen Kommission* 62 (1981): 261ff.

Musset, L. *Les Invasions: les vagues germaniques*. 2nd edn. Nouvelle Clio 12. Paris: Presses Universitaires, 1969.

Myhre, B. Settlements of southwest Norway during the Roman and Migration periods. *Offa* 39 (1982): 197ff.

Mytum, H. Ireland and Rome: the maritime frontier, in King and Henig, pp. 445ff.

Näsman, U. *Glas och handel i senromersk tid och folkvandringstid: En studie kring glas från Eketorp–II, Öland, Sverige*. Archaeological Studies, Uppsala University Institute of North-European Archaeology 5 (1984).

Näsman, U. and E. Wegraeus (eds.). *Eketorp, Fortification and Settlement on Öland/Sweden: The Setting*. Stockholm: Almqvist and Wiksell, 1976.

Neal, D. S. *The Excavation of the Roman Villa in Gadebridge Park, Hemel Hempstead 1963–8*. Society of Antiquaries of London, Reports of the Research Committee 31 (1974).

Nikolov, D. *The Roman Villa at Chatalka, Bulgaria*. British Archaeological Reports International Series 17 (1976).

Noonan, T. S. Why Dirhams first reached Russia: the role of Arab–Khazar relations in the development of the earliest Islamic trade with Eastern Europe. *Archivum Eurasiae Medii Aevi* 4 (1984): 151ff.

Why the Vikings first came to Russia. *Jahrbücher für Geschichte Osteuropas* 34 (1986): 321ff.

Northedge, A. Selected Late Roman and Islamic coarse wares, in Matthers, vol. 2, pp. 459ff.

Ovadiah, A. *Corpus of the Byzantine Churches in the Holy Land.* Theophaneia 22 (1970).

Ovadiah, A. and C. G. de Silva. Supplementum to the *Corpus of the Byzantine Churches in the Holy Land* (pt. 1): Newly discovered churches. *Levant* 13 (1981): 200ff.

Supplementum to the *Corpus of the Byzantine Churches in the Holy Land* (pt. 2): Updated material on churches discussed in the *Corpus. Levant* 14 (1982): 122ff

Overbeck. B. *Das Alpenrheintal in römischer Zeit,* vol. 2. Münchner Beiträge zur Vor- und Frühgeschichte 21 (1973).

Das Alpenrheintal in römischer Zeit, vol. 1. Münchner Beiträge zur Vor- und Frühgeschichte 20 (1982).

Painter, K. S. *The Mildenhall Treasure: Roman Silver from East Anglia.* London: British Museum, 1977.

(ed.). *Roman Villas in Italy: Recent Excavations and Research.* British Museum Occasional Paper 24 (1980).

Panella, C. Le anfore di Cartagine: nuovi elementi per la ricostruzione dei flussi commerciali del Mediterraneo in età imperiale romana. *Opus* 1 (1983):53f.

Parker, A. A ships' graveyard off Sicily, in Muckelroy, pp. 60ff.

Roman wrecks in the western Mediterranean, in Muckelroy, pp.50ff.

Shipwrecks and ancient trade in the Mediterranean. *Archaeological Review from Cambridge* 3, no. 2 (Autumn 1984): 99ff.

Parker, A. J. and J. Price. Spanish exports of the Claudian period: the significance of the Port Vendres II wreck reconsidered. *International Journal of Nautical Archaeology* 10, no. 3 (1981): 221ff.

Parker, S. T. Archaeological survey of the Limes Arabicus: a preliminary report. *Annual of the Department of Antiquities (Amman)* 21 (1976): 19ff.

Patlagean, E. *Pauvreté économique et pauvreté sociale à Byzance 4e–7e siècles.* Civilisations et Sociétés 48. Paris: Mouton, 1977.

Patzelt, G. Der zeitliche Ablauf und das Ausmass postglazialer Klimaschwankungen in den Alpen, in Frenzel, pp. 248ff.

Paynter, R. *Models of Spatial Inequality: Settlement Patterns in Historical Archaeology.* New York: Academic, 1982.

Peacock, D. P. S. (ed.). *Pottery and Early Commerce: Characterization and Trade in Roman and Later Ceramics.* London: Academic, 1977.

Pottery in the Roman World: An Ethnoarchaeological Approach. London: Longman, 1982.

Pearson, M. P. Economic and ideological change: cyclical growth in the pre-state societies of Jutland, in D. Miller and C. Tilley (eds.), *Ideology, Power, and Prehistory,* pp. 69ff. Cambridge: Cambridge University Press, 1984.

Pereira, I., J.-P. Bost, and J. Hiernard. *Les Monnaies.* Fouilles de Conimbriga 3 (1974).

(Perin, P. [ed.]). *Lutèce: Paris de César à Clovis.* Paris: Musée Carnavalet, 1984.

Perlzweig, J. *Lamps of the Roman Period, First to Seventh Century after Christ.* The Athenian Agora 7 (1961).

Pescheck, C. *Die germanische Bodenfunde der römischen Kaiserzeit in Mainfranken.* Münchner Beiträge zur Vor- und Frühgeschichte 27 (1978).

Petré, B. *Bebyggelsearkeologisk analys: Arkeologiska undersökningar på Lovö,* vol. 4. Studies in North-European Archaeology 10. Stockholm: Almqvist and Wiksell, 1984.

Petrikovits, H. von. Fortifications in the north-western Roman Empire from the third to the fifth centuries A D. *Journal of Roman Studies* 61 (1971): 178ff.

Die Rheinlände in römischer Zeit. Düsseldorf: Schwann, 1980.

Die römischen Provinzen am Rhein und an der oberen und mittleren Donau im 5. Jahrhundert n.Chr. Sitzungsberichte der Heidelberger Akademie der Wissenschaften, Philosophisch-historische Klasse, 3 (1983).

Pflaum, H.-G. *Less fastes de la province de Narbonnaise.* 30th supplement to *Gallia.* Paris: Centre National de la Recherche Scientifique, 1978.

Phillips, C. W. (ed.). *The Fenland in Roman Times.* Royal Geographical Society Research Series 5 (1970).

Pilet, C. *La Nécropole de Frenouville: étude d'une population de la fin du IIIe à la fin du VIIe siècle.* British Archaeological Reports International Series 83 (1980).

Pirazzoli-t' Serstevens, M. Iran and China: importation and influences, in Flon, pp. 282ff. The ceramic route, in Flon, pp. 284ff.

Pirenne, H. Mahomet et Charlemagne. *Revue Belge de Philologie et d'Histoire* 1 (1922): 77ff.

Pirling, R. *Das römisch-fränkische Gräberfeld von Krefeld-Gellep 1964–1965.* Germanische Denkmäler der Völkerwanderungszeit, serie B, Die fränkischen Altertümer des Rheinlandes 10 (1979).

Römer und Franken am Niederrhein. Mainz: von Zabern, 1986.

Planson, E. (ed.). *La Nécropole gallo-romaines des Bolards, Nuits-Saints-Georges.* Paris: Centre National de la Recherche Scientifique, 1982.

Plat Taylor, J. du and H. Cleere (eds.). *Roman Shipping and Trade: Britain and the Rhine Provinces.* Council for British Archaeology Research Report 24 (1978).

Pohl, G. Die Ausgrabungen auf dem Lorenzberg bei Epfach. *Ausgrabungen in Deutschland* 2 (1975): 99ff.

Poinsignon, V. Implantation et esquisse d'une typologie des villas gallo-romaines en Alsace et en Lorraine. *Cahiers Alsaciens d'Archéologie d'Art et d'Histoire* 30 (1987): 107ff.

Polanyi, K. The economy as instituted process, in K. Polanyi, C. M. Arensberg, and H. W. Pearson (eds.). *Trade and Market in the Early Empires,* pp. 243ff. Glencoe: Free Press, 1957.

Poly, Z.-P. and E. Bournazel. *La Mutation féodale Xe–XIIe siècles.* Nouvelle Clio 16. Paris: Presses Universitaires de France, 1980.

Popovic, V. Desintegration und Ruralisation der Stadt im Ost-Illyricum vom 5. bis 7. Jahrhundert n.Chr., in Prückner, pp. 545ff.

Potter, T. W. Valleys and settlement: some new evidence. *World Archaeology* 8, no. 2 (October 1976): 287ff.

The Changing Landscape of South Etruria. London: Elek, 1979.

Poulík, J. Mikulčice: capital of the lords of Great Moravia, in Bruce-Mitford, pp. 1ff.

Pounds, N. I. G. *An Historical Geography of Europe 450 B.C.–A.D. 1330.* Cambridge: Cambridge University Press, 1973.

Price, S. R. F. *Rituals and Power: The Roman Imperial Cult in Asia Minor.* Cambridge: Cambridge University Press, 1984.

Prückner, H. (ed.). *Palast und Hütte: Beiträgen zum Bauen und Wohnen im Altertum von Archäologen, Vor- und Frühgeschichtlern.* Mainz: von Zabern, 1982.

Pryor, F., C. French, (D. Crowther, D. Gurney, G. Simpson, and M. Taylor) (eds.). *Archaeology and Environment in the Lower Welland Valley.* 2 vols. The Fenland Project 1 / East Anglian Archaeology Report 27, 1–2 (1985).

Pyrgala, J. The reconstruction of agricultural and breeding economy in Plock Mazovia at the decline of Antiquity. *Archaeologia Polona* 16 (1975): 71ff.

Raev, B. A. *Roman Imports in the Lower Don Basin.* British Archaeological Reports International Series 278 (1986).

Rahtz, P. *The Saxon and Medieval Palaces at Cheddar: Excavations 1960–62.* British Archaeological Reports 65 (1979).

Rahtz, P., T. Dickinson, and L. Watts. *Anglo-Saxon Cemeteries 1979.* British Archaeological Reports 82 (1980).

Rainey. A. *Mosaics in Roman Britain.* Newton Abbot: David and Charles, 1973.

Ramqvist, P. H. *Gene*. Archaeology and Environment 1 (1983).

Randsborg, K. *The Viking Age in Denmark: The Formation of a State*. London: Duckworth;
  New York: St. Martin's, 1980.

  Les Activités internationales des Vikings: raids ou commerce? *Annales: Economies,
  Sociétés, Civilisations* 36, no. 5 (September–October 1981a): 862ff.

  Handel, plyndring eller landbrugsekspansion: Tre centrale aspekter af Vikingetiden.
  Historisk Tidsskrift 81, no. 1 (1981b): 250ff.

  Burial, succession, and early state formation in Denmark, in Chapman, Kinnes, and
  Randsborg 1981c, pp. 105ff.

  Ranks, rights, and resources: an archaeological perspective from Denmark, in C.
  Renfrew and S. Shennan (eds.). *Ranking, Resources and Exchange* pp. 132ff. Cambridge: Cambridge University Press, 1982.

  Theoretical approaches to social change: an archaeological viewpoint, in Renfrew,
  Rowlands, and Segreaves 1982, pp. 423ff.

  Women in prehistory: the Danish example. *Acta Archaeologica* 55 (1984a): 143ff.

  The study of slavery in Northern Europe: an archaeological approach. *Acta
  Archaeologica* 55 (1984b): 155ff.

  Subsistence and settlement in northern temperate Europe in the first millennium A.D.
  in Barker and Gamble, pp. 233ff.

  Römische Gläser und Bronzegefässe im Norden: Ein Kommentar. *Acta Archaeologica* 57
  (1986): 211ff.

  The town, the power, and the land: Denmark and Europe during the first millennium
  A.D., in T. C. Champion (ed.), *Comparative Studies in the Development of Complex
  Societies*, pt. 3, *Centre and Periphery* (The World Archaeological Congress, South-
  ampton and London 1986). London: Allen & Unwin, (1988a).

  Denmark and the Mediterranean in the first millennium A.D.: an archaeological
  approach, in Jones et al. 1988b, pp. 37ff.

  (ed.). *The Birth of Europe: Archaeology and Social Development during the First Millennium
  A.D.* Analecta Romana Instituti Danici, supplement. Rome: L'Erma di
  Bretschneider, 1989.

  Golden fields: archaeological discoveries in Gudme on Funen, Denmark. In press.

Randsborg, L. and C. Nybo. The coffin and the sun, demography and ideology in
  Scandinavian prehistory. *Acta Archaeologica* 55 (1984): 161ff.

Rathbone, D. W. The slave mode of production in Italy. *Journal of Roman Studies* 73
  (1982): 160ff.

Rau, G. Körpergräber mit Glasbeigaben des 4. nachchristlichen Jahrhunderts im Oder-
  Weichsel-Raum. *Acta Praehistorica et Archaeologica* 3 (1972): 109ff.

Rav, A. J. History and archaeology of the Northern fur trade. *American Antiquity* 43, no. 1
  (1978): 26ff.

Raynaud, C. L'habitat rural romain tardif en Languedoc oriental (IIIe–Ve s.). Unpublished
  thesis, University of Montpellier, 1984.

Reece, R. (ed.). *Burial in the Roman World*. Council for British Archaeology Research
  Report 22 (1977).

Reece, R. Roman monetary impact on the Celtic world: thoughts and problems, in
  Cunliffe 1981, pp. 24ff.

  Roman coinage in the western Mediterranean: a quantitative approach. *Opus* 2, no. 2
  (1982a): 341ff.

  A collection of coins from the centre of Rome. *Papers of the British School at Rome* 50
  (1982b), pp. 116ff.

  Rome in the Mediterranean world: the evidence of coins, in Malone and Stoddart, vol.
  4, pp. 85ff.

Reese, D. The faunal remains, in Humphrey 1977, pp. 131ff.

  Faunal remains from three cisterns, in Humphrey 1981, pp. 191ff.

Renfrew, C., M. J. Rowlands, and B. A. Segraves (eds.). *Theory and Explanation in Archaeology*. New York: Academic, 1982.

Renfrew, C. and S. Shennan (eds.). *Ranking, Resources, and Exchange*. Cambridge: Cambridge University Press, 1982.

Restle, M. *Studien zur frühbyzantinischen Architektur Kappadokiens*. Veröffentlichungen der Kommission für die Tabula Imperii Byzantini 3 (1979).

Reynolds, J. M. and J. B. Ward-Perkins (eds.). *The Inscriptions of Roman Tripolitania*. Rome: British School at Rome, 1952.

Rice, D. T. *Islamic Art*. Revised edn. London: Thames and Hudson, 1975.

Riedel, A. Ergebnisse von archäozoologischen Untersuchungen im Raum zwischen Adriaküste und Alpenhauptkamm (Spätneolithikum bis zum Mittelalter). *Padusa* 22, nos. 1–4 (1986): 1ff.

Riley, J. A. The pottery from Cisterns 1977. 1, 1977. 2 and 1977. 3, in Humphrey 1981, pp. 85ff.

The coarse pottery from Berenice, in Lloyd, pp. 91ff.

Roberto, C., J. A. Plambeck, and A. M. Small. The chronology of the sites of the Roman period around San Giovanni: methods of analysis and conclusions, in Macready and Thompson 1985, pp. 136ff.

Rodziewicz, M. *La Céramique romaine tardive d'Alexandrie*. Alexandrie 1. Warsaw, 1976. *Les Habitations romaines tardives d'Alexandrie, à la lumière des fouilles polonaises à Kôm el-Dikha*. Alexandrie 3. Warsaw, 1984.

Rollins, A. M. *The Fall of Rome: A Reference Guide*. Jefferson: McFarland, 1983.

Romancuk, A. I. Die byzantinische Provinzstadt vom 7. Jahrhundert bis zur ersten Hälfte des 9. Jahrhunderts (auf Grund Materialien aus Cherson), in Köpstein, pp. 57ff.

Rosen, S. A. Demographic trends in the Negev Highlands: preliminary results from the emergency survey. *Bulletin of the American Schools of Oriental Research* 266 (May 1987): 45ff.

Rothenberg, B. and A. Blanco-Freijeiro. *Studies in Ancient Mining and Metallurgy in South-West Spain: Explorations and Excavations in the Province of Huelva*. London: Institute of Archaeology, 1981.

Röthlisberger, F. *10000 Jahre Gletschergeschichte der Erde*. Aarau: Sauerländer, 1986.

Rouche, M. *L'Aquitaine des Wisigoths aux Arabes (418–781)*. 2 vols. Lille: University of Lille III, 1977.

La crise de l'Europe au cours de la deuxième moitié du VIIe siècle et la naissance de régionalismes. *Annales: Economies, Sociétés, Civilisations* 41, no. 2 (March–April 1986): 347ff.

Rougé, J, *Recherches sur l'organisation du commerce maritime en Méditerranée sous l'empire romain*. Ports, Routes, Trafics 21 (1966).

Rowland, R. J. Jr. Foreigners in Roman Britain. *Acta Archaeologica Hungarica* 28 (1976): 443ff.

Rupp, D. W., L. W. Sørensen, R. H. King, and W. A. Fox. The Canadian Palaipaphos (Cyprus) Survey Project: second preliminary report, 1980–1982. *Journal of Field Archaeology* 11 (1984): 133ff.

Rupp, D. W., L. W. Sørensen, J. Lund, R. H. King, W. A. Fox, T. E. Gregory, and S. T. Stewart. The Canadian Palaipaphos (Cyprus) Survey Projects: third preliminary report, 1983–1985. *Acta Archaeologica* 57 (1986): 27ff.

Russell, J. C. *Late Ancient and Medieval Population*. Transactions of the American Philosophical Society, n.s., 48, no. 3 (1958).

Rutkowski, B. *Terra Sigillata znalezione w Polsce*. Bibliotheca Antiqua 2 (1960).

Sanders, I. F. *Roman Crete: An Archaeological Survey and Gazetteer of Late Hellenistic, Roman, and Early Byzantine Crete*. Warminster: Aris and Phillips, 1982.

Sawyer, P. H. (ed.). *Medieval Supplement: Continuity and Change*. London: Arnold, 1976. (ed.). *Names, Words, and Graves: Early Medieval Settlement*. Leeds: School of History, University of Leeds, 1979.

From Roman Britain to Norman England. London: Methuen, 1987.

Scammell, G. *The World Encompassed: The First European Maritime Empires c. 800–1650.* London: Methuen, 1981.

Schell, G. Die römische Besiedlung von Rheingau und Wetterau. *Nassauische Annalen* 75 (1964): 1ff.

Schietzel, K. *Stand der siedlungsarchäologischen Forschung in Haithabu: Ergebnisse und Probleme.* Ausgrabungen in Haithabu 16 (1981).

Schindler, R. Trier in merowingischer Zeit, in Jankuhn, Schlesinger, and Steuer, vol. 1, pp. 130ff.

Schmid, P. Der Handel der römischen Kaiserzeit im niedersächsischen Nordseeküsten-gebiet aufgrund archäologischer Zeugnisse, in Düwel et al., pp. 451ff.

Schmid, P. and W. H. Zimmermann. Flögeln - zur Struktur einer Siedlung des 1. bis 5. Jhr. n. Chr. im Küstengebiet der südlichen Nordsee. *Probleme der Küstenforschung* 11 (1976): 1ff.

Schneebeli, W. and F. Röthlisberger. *8000 Jahre Walliser Gletschergeschichte: Ein Beitrag zur Erforschung des Klimaverlaufs in der Nacheiszeit.* Die Alpen (Zeitschrift des Schweizer Alpen-Club) 52, nos. 3/4, special issue, 1976.

Schnurbein, S. von. *Die römer in Haltern.* Einführung in die Vor- und Frühgeschichte Westfalens 2 (1979).

Schönberger, H. The Roman frontier in Germany. *Journal of Roman Studies* 59 (1969): 144ff.

Schwartz, J. H. The mammalian fauna, in Hurst and Roscams, pp. 229ff.

Schwärzel, D. *Handel und Verkehr des Merowingerreiches, nach den schriftlichen Quellen.* Kleine Schriften aus dem vorgeschichtlichen Seminar Marburg 14 (1983).

Scrinari, V. S. M. and M. L. M. Matini. *Antivm, Regione prima, Mosaici antichi in Italia.* Rome: Consiglio Nazionale delle Ricerche, 1975.

Sedgley, J. P. *The Roman Milestones of Britain.* British Archaeological Reports 18 (1975).

Seeck, D. (ed.). *Notitia Dignitatum.* Berlin: Weidmann, 1876.

Selinge, K.-G. (ed.). *Fornlämninger och bebyggelsehistoria.* Bebyggelse-historisk Tidskrift 11 (1986).

Sellevold, B. J., U. L. Hansen and J. B. Jørgensen. *Iron Age Man in Denmark.* Prehistoric Man in Denmark 3 / Nordiske Fortidsminder, serie B, 8 (1984).

Settia, A. A. *Castelli e villagi nell'Italia padana: popolamento, potere e sicurezza fra IX e XIII secolo.* Nuovo Medioevo 23. Naples: Liguori, 1984.

Shaw, B. D. Bandits in the Roman Empire. *Past and Present* 105 (1984): 3ff.

Sitwell, N. H. H. *The World the Romans Knew.* London: Hamish Hamilton, 1984.

Slane, D. A. The History of the Anchorage at Serçe Liman, Turkey. Unpublished thesis, Texas A & M University, 1982.

Slicher van Bath, B. H. *The Agrarian History of Western Europe A.D. 500–1850.* London: Arnold, 1963.

Small, A. M. The early villa at San Giovanni, in Malone and Stoddart, vol. 4, pp. 165ff.

Smith, C. A. Exchange systems and the spatial distribution of elites: the organization of stratification in agrarian societies, in Smith, vol. 2, pp. 309ff.

   (ed.). *Regional Analysis.* 2 vols. New York: Academic, 1976.

Smith, R. R. R. Roman portraits: honours, empresses, and late emperors. *Journal of Roman Studies* 75 (1985): 209ff.

Sodini, J.-P. Mosaïques paléochrétiennes de Grèce. *Bulletin de Correspondence Hellénique* 94 (1970): 699ff.

Sodini, J.-P., G. Tate, B. Bavant, S. Bavant, J.-L. Biscop, and D. Orssaud. Déhès (Syrie du Nord): Campagnes I–III (1976–78). *Syria* 57 (1980): 1ff

Solier, Y. (ed.). *Les épaves de Gruissan.* Archaeonautica 3 (1981).

Soproni. S. *Der spätrömische Limes zwischen Esztergom und Szentendre.* Budapest: Akadémiai, 1978.

Die letzen Jahrzehnte des pannonischen Limes. Müchner Beitrage zur Vor- und Frühgeschichte 38 (1985).

Spahiu, H. Monnaies byzantines des Ve–XIIIe siècles découvertes sur le territoire de l'Albanie. *Iliria* 9–10 (1979–80): 357ff.

Sperber, D. *Roman Palestine 200–400, the Land: Crises and Change in Agrarian Society as Reflected in Rabbinic Sources.* Ramat-Gan: Bar-Ilan University, 1978.

Spiro, M. *Critical Corpus of the Mosaic Pavements on the Greek Mainland. Fourth/Sixth Centuries.* 2 vols. New York: Garland, 1978.

Stančev, S. Pliska und Preslav: Ihre archäologischen Denkmaler und deren Erforschung, in Boševliev and Irmscher, pp. 219ff.

Steady, I. M. *Excavations at Winterton Roman villa and other Roman sites in North Lincoln-shire.* Department of the Environment Archaeological Reports 9 (1976).

Stein, F. *Adelsgräber des achten Jahrhunderts in Deutschland.* Germanische Denkmäler der Völkerwanderungszeit, serie A, 9 (1967).

Stern, H. *Province de Belgique*, pt.1, *Partie ouest.* Recueil général des mosaïques de la Gaule, 10th supplement to *Gallia*, 1 no. 1 (1957).

Belgique, pt. 2, *Partie est.* Recueil général des mosaïques de la Gaule, 10th supplement to *Gallia*, 1, no. 2 (1960).

Province de Lyonnaise, pt. 1, *Lyon.* Recueil général des mosaïques de la Gaule, 10th supplement to *Gallia*, 2, no. 1. (1967).

Stern, H. and M. Blanchard-Lemée. *Province de Lyonnaise*, pt. 2, *Partie sud-est.* Recueil général des mosaïques de la Gaule, 10th supplement to *Gallia*, 2, no. (1975).

Steuer, H. *Frühgeschichtliche Sozialstrukturen in Mitteleurope: Eine Analyse der Auswertungsmethoden des archäologischen Quellenmaterials.* Abhandlungen der Akademie der Wissenschaften in Göttingen, Philologisch-historische Klasse, Series 3, no. 128 (1982).

Der Handel der Wikingerseit zwischen Nord- und Westeuropa aufgrund archäologischer Zeugnisse, in Düwel et al. 1987, pp. 113ff.

Gewichtsgeldwirtschaften im frühgeschichtlichen Europa, in Düwel et al. 1987, pp. 405ff.

Swan, V. G. *Pottery in Roman Britain.* 3rd edn. Shire Archaeology 3. Aylesbury: Shire, 1980.

Sørensen, L. W., P. Guldager, M. Korsholm, J. Lund, and T. E. Gregory. The Canadian Palaipaphos Survey Project: second preliminary report of the ceramic finds 1982–1983. *Report of the Department of Antiquities, Cyprus* (1987). In press.

Tamaro, B. F., L. Bertacchi, L. Beschi, M. C. Calvi, L. Bosio, G. Rosada, G. Cuscito, and G. Gorini. *Da Aquileia a Venezia: una mediazione tra l'Europa a l'Oriente dal II secolo a.C. al VI secolo d.C.* Milan: Scheiwiller, 1980.

Tchalenko, G. *Villages antiques de la Syrie du nord: le massif du Bélus à l'époque romaine.* 3 vols. Institut Français d'Archéologie de Beyrouth, Bibliothèque Archéologique et Historique 50. Paris: Geuthner, 1953–58.

Tchernia, A. *Le vin d'Italie romaine: essai d'histoire économique d'après les amphores.* Bibliothèque des Ecoles Françaises d'Athènes et de Rome 261 (1986).

Tejiral, J. Markomanské války a stazka rímského dovozu na Moravu v období po. *Archeologické Rozhledy* 22 (1970): 389ff.

Mähren im 5. Jahrhundert. Studie Archaeologickeho Ústavu Československé Akademie Ved v Brne 3 (1973).

Tempelmann-Maczyńska, M. *Die Perlen der römischen Kaiserzeit und der frühen Phase der Völkerwanderungszeit im mitteleuropäischen Barbaricum.* Römisch-germanische Forschungen 43 (1985).

Theodor, D. G. *The East Carpathian Area of Roumania in the V–XI Centuries A.D.* British Archaeological Reports International Series 81 (1980).

Thirion, M. *Les Trésors monétaires gaulois et romaines trouvés en Belgique.* Cercle d'Etudes Numismatiques 3 (1967).

Thomas, C. *Britain and Ireland in Early Christian Times AD 400–800*. London: Thames and Hudson, 1971.

Thomas, E. B. *Römische Villen in Pannonien*. Budapest: Akadémiai, 1964.

Thompson, E. A. *The Early Germans*. Oxford: Clarendon, 1965.

    Romans and Barbarians: The Decline of the Western Empire. Madison: University of Wisconsin Press, 1982.

Thompson, E. H. *Archaeology and Coastal Change*. Society of Antiquaries Occasional Papers, n.s., 1 (1980).

Thompson, J. D. A. *Inventory of British Coin Hoards*. Royal Numismatic Society Special Publications 1 (1956).

Thomsen, P. O. Lundeborg I: Havn og handelsplads fra 3. og 4. århundrede efter Kr. *Årbog for Svendborg & Omegns Museum* 1986, pp. 12ff.

    Lundeborg. *Årbog for Svendborg og Omegns Museum* 1987, pp. 17ff.

Thrane, H. (ed.). *Kontinuitet og bebyggelse: Beretning fra et symposium d. 12.-14. maj 1977 afholdt af Odense universitet*. Skrifter fra Institut for Historie og Samfundsvidenskab 22 (1977).

    (ed.). *Gudme problemer: Beretning fra et bebyggelsesarkæologisk symposium på Hollufgård afholdt den 25.–25. oktober 1984*. Skrifter fra Historisk Institut, Odense Universitet 33 (1985).

Todd, M. *The Northern Barbarians 100 B.C.–A.D. 300*. London: Hutchinson, 1975.

Toubert, P. *Les structures du Latium médiéval: le Latium méridional et la Sabine du IXe siècle à la fin du XIIe siècle*. Bibliothèque des Ecoles Françaises d'Athènes et de Rome 221 (1973).

[Toubert, P. (ed.)]. *Structures féodales et féodalisme dans l'occident méditerranéen (Xe–XIIIe siècles): Bilan et perspectives de recherches*. Collection de l'Ecole Française de Rome 44 (1980).

Tushingham, A. D. *Excavations in Jerusalem 1961–1967*, vol. 1. Toronto: Royal Ontario Museum, 1985.

Udal'cova, Z. V. Die Besonderheiten der Feudalismus in Byzanz, in Köpstein, pp. 11ff.

Udovitch, A. (ed.). *The Islamic Middle East 700–1900*. Princeton: Princeton University Press, 1981.

Ulbert, T. Zur Siedlungskontinuität im südöstlichen Alpenraum (vom 2. bis 6.Jahrhundert n.Chr.), in Werner and Ewig, pp. 141ff.

    Ad Pirvm (Hrusica): Spätrömische Passbefestigung in den Julischen Alpen. Münchner Beiträge zur Vor- und Frühgeschichte 31 (1981).

Uslar, R. von. *Studien zur frühgeschichtlichen Befestigungen*. Beiheft der Bonner Jahrbücher 11 (1984).

Vallet, J. P. La cité des Séguisiaves à l'époque romaine, in Walker, pp. 167ff.

Vasiliev, A. A. *History of the Byzantine Empire 324–1453*, vol. 1. 2nd English edn. Madison: University of Wisconsin Press, 1952.

Vierck, H. Imitatio imperii und interpretatio Germanica vor der Wikingerzeit, in Zeitler 1981, pp. 64ff.

    Ein Schmiedeplatz aus Alt-Ladoga und der präurbane Handel zur Ostsee vor der Wikingerzeit: Zur frühmittelalterlichen Betriebseinheit von Produktion und Absatz im Metallhandwerk. *Münstersche Beiträge zur Antiken Handelsgeschichte* 2, no. 2 (1983): 3ff.

    Mittel- und westeuropäische Einwirkungen auf die Sachkultur von Haithabu/Schleswig, in *Archäologische und naturwissenschaftliche Untersuchungen an Siedlungen im deutschen Küstengebiet*, vol. 2, *Handelspalätze des frühen und hohen Mittelalters*, pp. 366ff. Weinheim: Chemie, 1984.

Vila, A. *La prospection archéologique de la vallée du Nil, au sud de la cataracte de Dal (Nubie Soudanaise)*, vol. 2. Paris: Centre National de la Recherche Scientifique, 1979.

Vilas, F. A., P. le Roux, and A. Tranoy. *Inscriptions romaines de la province de Lugo*. Publication du Centre Pierre Paris (E.R.A. 522). Paris: Boccard, 1979.

Villedieu, F. *Turris Libisonis: Fouille d'un site romain tardiff à Porto Torres, Sardaigne*. British Archaeological Reports International Series 224 (1984).

Vita-Finzi, C. *The Mediterranean Valleys: Geological Changes in Historical Times*. Cambridge: Cambridge University Press, 1969.

Vitelli, G. Grain storage and urban growth in imperial Ostia: a quantitative study. *World Archaeology* 12, no. 1 (June 1980): 54ff.

Vives, D. J. *Inscriptiones cristianas de la España Romana y Visigoda*. 2nd edn. Monumenta Hispaniae Sacra, Serie Patrística 2, Biblioteca Historica de la Biblioteca Balmes, serie 2, 18 (1969).

Vorbeck, E. *Militärinschriften aus Carnuntum*. Wien: Niederösterreichische Landesregierung, 1980a

Zivilinschriften aus Carnuntum. Wien: Niederösterreichische Landesregierung, 1980b.

Waas, M. *Germanen im römischen Dienst im 4. jh. n. Chr.* Bonn: Universität Bonn, 1965.

Wacher, J. *Roman Britain*. London: Dent, 1978.

Waines, D. The third-century internal crisis of the Abbasids. *Journal of the Economic and Social History of the Orient* 20, no. 3 (1977): 282ff.

Walke, N. *Das römische Donaukastell Straubing-Sorviodurum*. Limesforschungen 3 (1965).

Walker, S. (ed.). *Récentes recherches en archéologie gallo-romaine et paléochrétienne sur Lyon et sa région*. British Archaeological Reports International Series 108 (1981).

Wallerstein, I. *The Modern World-System: Capitalist Agriculture and the Origins of the European World-Economy in the Sixteenth Century*. New York: Academic, 1974.

Walser, G. *Die Meilensteine: Die römische Strassen in der Schweiz*, vol. 1. Itinera Romana 1 (1967).

Ward-Perkins, B. *From Classical Antiquity to the Middle Ages: Urban Public Building in Northern and Central Italy AD 300–850*. Oxford: Oxford University Press, 1984.

Ward-Perkins, B., H. Blake, S. Nepoti, L. Castelletti, G. Barker, A. Wheeler, and T. Mannoni. Scavi nella Torre Civica di Pavia. *Archeologia Medievale* 5 (1978): 77ff.

Warry, J. *Warfare in the Classical World*. London: Salamander, 1980.

Watson, A. M. *Agricultural Innovation in the Early Islamic World: The Diffusion of Crops and Farming Techniques, 700–1100*. Cambridge: Cambridge University Press, 1983.

Waywell, S. F. Roman mosaics in Greece. *American Journal of Archaeology* 83 (1979): 293ff.

Webster, G. *The Roman Army*. Rev. edn. Chester: Grosvenor Museum, 1973.

Weidemann, K. Die Topographie von Mainz in der Römerzeit und dem frühen Mittelalter. *Jahrbuch des römisch-germanischen Zentralmuseums Mainz* 15 (1968): 146ff.

Zur Topographie von Metz in der Römerzeit und im frühen Mittelalter. *Jahrbuch des römisch-germanischen Zentralmuseums Mainz* 17 (1970): 147ff.

Untersuchungen zur Siedlungsgeschichte des Landes zwischen Limes und Rhein vom Ende der Römerherrschaft bis zum Frühmittelalter. *Jahrbuch des römisch-germanischen Zentralmuseums Mainz* 19 (1974): 99ff.

Ausgrabungen in der karolingischen Pfalz Ingelheim. *Ausgrabungen in Deutschland* 1 (1975): 437ff.

Wendel, M. et al. *Iatrus-Krivina: Spätantike Befestigung und frühmittelalterliche Siedlung an der unteren Donau*, vol. 3, *Die Mittelalterliche Siedlung*. Schriften zur Geschichte und Kultur der Antike 17 (1986).

Wenke, R. I. Imperial investments and agricultural developments in Parthian and Sasanian Khuzestan: 150 B.C. to A.D. 640. *Mesopotamia* 10–11 (1975–76): 31ff.

Werner, J. *Münzdatierte austrasische Grabfunde*. Germanische Denkmäler der Völkerwanderungszeit, serie A, 3 (1935).

Byzantinische Gürtelschnallen des 6. und 7. Jahrhunderts aus der Sammlung Diergardt. *Kölner Jahrbuch für Vor- und Frühgeschichte* 1 (1955): 36ff.

Beiträge zur Archäologie des Attila-Reiches. Abhandlungen der bayerischen Akademie der Wissenschaften. Philologisch-historische Klasse, n.s., 38 A-B (1956).

Fernhandel und Naturalwirtschaft im östlichen Merowingerreich nach archäologischen und numismatischen Zeugnissen. *Bericht der römisch-germanischen Kommission* 42 (1961): 307ff.

Studien zu Abodiacum-Epfach. Münchner Beiträge zur Vor- und Frühgeschichte 7 (1964).

Zur Verbreitung frühgeschichtlicher Metallarbeiten (Werkstatt – Wanderhandwerk – Handel – Familienverbindung). *Early Medieval Studies* 1 / *Antikvarisk Arkiv* 38 (1970): 65ff.

Bemerkungen zur mitteldeutschen Skelettgräbergruppe Hassleben-Leuna: Zur Herkunft der 'ingentia auxilia germanorum' des gallischen Sonderreiches in den Jahren 259–274 n.Chr. *Mitteldeutsche Forschungen* 74 no. 1 (1973): 1ff.

Werner, J. and E. Ewig (eds.). *Von der Spätantike zum frühen Mittelalter: Aktuelle Probleme in historischer und archäologischer Sicht*. Vorträge und Forschungen 25 (1979).

Wheeler, R. E. M., A. Gosh, and Krishna Deva. Arikamedu: an Indo-Roman trading-station on the east coast of India. *Ancient India: Bulletin of the Archaeological Survey of India* 2 (July 1946): 17ff.

Whitcomb, D. S. and J. H. Johnson. *Quseir al-Qadim 1980: Preliminary Report*. American Research Center in Egypt Reports 7 (1982).

Whitehouse, D. The Schola Praeconum and the food supply of Rome in the fifth century A.D., in Barker and Hodges, pp. 191ff.

Whitehouse, D., G. Barker, R. Reece, and D. Reese. The Schola Praeconum, pt. 1: The coins, pottery, lamps, and fauna. *Papers of the British School at Rome* 50 (1982): 53ff.

Whitelock, D. (ed.). *English Historical Documents*, vol. 1. London: Eyre and Spottiswoode, 1955.

Whittaker, C. R. Trade and the aristocracy in the Roman Empire. *Opus* 4 (1985): 49ff.

Wickham, C. *Early Medieval Italy: Central Power and Local Society 400–100* London: Macmillan, 1981.

The other transition: from the ancient world to feudalism. *Past and Present* 103 (May 1984): 3ff.

Il problema dell'incastellamento nell'Italia centrale: l'esempio di San Vincenzo al Volturno. Quaderni dell'Insegnamento di Archeologia Medievale della Facoltà di Lettere e Filosofia dell'Università di Siena 5 (1985).

Widgren, M. *Settlement and Farming Systems in the Early Iron Age: A Study of Fossil Agrarian Landscapes in Östergötland, Sweden*. Stockholm Studies in Human Geography 3 (1983).

Wielowiejski, J. *Kontakty Noricum i Pannonii z ludami pólnocnymi*. Wrocław-Warsaw-Kraków, 1970.

Funde von römischen Medaillons zu beiden Seiten des Rhein-Donau-Limes, in Hanson and Keppie, pp. 1077ff.

Wightman, E. M. *Roman Trier, and the Treveri*. New York: Praeger, 1971.

The Lower Liri valley: problems, trends, and peculiarities, in Barker and Hodges, pp. 275ff.

Wigley, T. M. L., P. D. Jones, and P. M. Kelly. Scenario for a warm, high-CO^2 world. *Nature* 283, no. 5742 (3 January, 1980): 17ff.

Wilhelmi, K. et al. (eds.). *Ausgrabungen in Niedersachsen: Archäologische Denkmalpflege 1979–1984*. Stuttgart: Theiss, 1985.

Wilkes, J. J. and C. R. Eldrington (eds.). *Roman Cambridgeshire*. A History of the Country of Cambridge and the Isle of Ely 7. Oxford: Oxford University Press, 1978.

Willems, W. J. H. *Romans and Batavians: A Regional Study in the Dutch Eastern River Area*. Amersfoort: ROB, 1986.

Willems, W. J. H. and R. W. Brandt (eds.). *Het Project Wijster*. Instituut voor Prae- en Protohistorie Working Paper 3 (1977).

Williams, L. D. and T. M. L. Wigley. A comparison of evidence for late Holocene summer temperature variations in the Northern Hemisphere. *Quaternary Research* 20 (1983): 286ff.

Willroth, K.-H. Siedlungsarchäologische Untersuchungen in Angeln und Schwansen. *Bericht der römisch-germanischen Kommission* 67 (1986): 397ff.

Wilson, P. R., R. F. J. Jones, and D. M. Evans (eds.). *Settlement and Society in the Roman North.* Bradford/Leeds: Archaeological Sciences, University/Yorkshire Archaeological Society, 1984.

Wilson, R. J. A. Changes in the pattern of urban settlement in Roman, Byzantine, and Arab Sicily, in Malone and Stoddart, vol. 1, pp. 313ff.

Woltering, P. J. Occupation history of Texel, pt. 2: The archaeological survey, preliminary report. *Berichen van de Rijksdienst voor het Oudheidkundig Bodemonderzoek* 29 (1979): 7ff.

Zeiss, H. Die Grabfunde aus dem spanischen Westgotenreich. *Germanische Denkmaler der Völkerwanderungszeit* 2 (1934): 93ff.

Zeist, W. van and S. Bottema. Palaeobotanical studies of Carthage: a comparison of microscopic plant remains. *Centre d'Etudes et de Documentation Archéologique de la Conservation de Carthage (CEDAC Carthage). Bulletin* 5 (June 1983): 18ff.

Zeitler, R. (ed.). *Les pays du nord et Byzance (Scandinavie et Byzance).* Acta Universitatis Upsaliensis, Figura, n.s., 19 (1981).

Zervos, D. H. Coins excavated at Corinth, 1978–1980. *Hesperia* 55, no. 2 (April–June 1986): 183ff.

Zimmer, G. *Römische Berufsdarstellungen.* Archäologische Forschungen 12 (1982).

Önen, Ü. *Ephesus: Ruins and Museum.* Izmir: Akademia, 1983.

[Ørsted, P. (ed.)]. *Rapport vedrørende projekt Africa Proconsularis; Segermes recognoscering.* Copenhagen, (1984).

Roman Imperial Economy and Romanization. Copenhagen: Museum Tusculanum, 1985.

INDEX